YOURS CRUELLY,
ELVIRA

YOURS CRUELLY,

Elvira

MEMOIRS
OF THE
MISTRESS
OF THE DARK

CASSANDRA PETERSON

hachette
BOOKS

New York

Hachette Books

Hachette Book Group
1290 Avenue of the Americas
New York, NY 10104

HachetteBooks.com

Twitter.com/HachetteBooks

Instagram.com/HachetteBooks

First Edition: September 2021

Published by Hachette Books, an imprint of Perseus Books, LLC, a subsidiary of Hachette Book Group, Inc. The Hachette Books name and logo is a trademark of the Hachette Book Group.

The Hachette Speakers Bureau provides a wide range of authors for speaking events. To find out more, go to www.hachettespeakersbureau.com or call (866) 376-6591.

The publisher is not responsible for websites (or their content) that are not owned by the publisher.

Library of Congress Cataloging-in-Publication Data
Names: Elvira, 1951– author.
Title: Yours cruelly, Elvira : memoirs of the mistress of the
dark / Cassandra Peterson.
Description: First edition. | New York: Hachette Books, 2021.
Identifiers: LCCN 2021006083 | ISBN 9780306874352 (hardcover) |
ISBN 9780306874369 (ebook)
Subjects: LCSH: Elvira, 1951– | Actors—United States—Biography. |
Television personalities—United States—Biography.
Classification: LCC PN2287.E522 A3 2021 | DDC 791.4502/8092 [B]—dc23
LC record available at https://lccn.loc.gov/2021006083

ISBNs: 9780306874352 (hardcover), 9780306874369 (ebook), 9780306828010 (signed edition), 9780306828003 (B&N.com signed edition), 9780306827853 (B&N Black Friday signed edition)

Printed in the United States of America

LSC-C

Printing 1, 2021

To T & M

Magic is believing in yourself; if you can do that, you can make anything happen.

—Johann Wolfgang von Goethe

"Begin at the beginning," the King said, very gravely, "and go on till you come to the end: then stop."

—Lewis Carroll

CONTENTS

PROLOGUE

I nearly died when I was a baby. According to a palm reader I met when I was seventeen, I did. The lifeline on my right hand is severed by a short, deep crease that cuts across it at an angle, just after it begins. Then the line starts up again, ending in a star on each palm.

The fortune-teller held my right hand, bringing my palm closer to his face in the dim light. Silence. He lifted my left hand, which was resting on the table, to within inches of his eyes and squinted. "You, my dear," he murmured in a deep, almost hypnotic voice, "are destined for stardom."

If only he'd foreseen what a long, strange trip it would be.

It was the summer of 1981. A B-list movie actor had just become the new president of the United States; *Raiders of the Lost Ark* debuted in theaters across the country; and my favorite record, John Lennon and Yoko Ono's *Double Fantasy*, won the Grammy for album of the year.

I lay in bed on the 5th of July, gazing out the window at the piercing, azure-blue Aspen sky, when an even more piercing sound jolted me from my reverie: the shrill ringing of the phone on my bedside table. Mark, my husband of just twenty-four hours, managed to pry himself off me just long enough for me to answer it.

"Mrs. Pierson?" the hotel receptionist asked. For a split second I thought she was looking for my new mother-in-law, then I realized she meant me. "You've just received a call from a Dawna Kaufmann asking you to call her back right away. She said it's urgent." With great fear and trepidation, not because I was afraid of what my friend Dawna had to say, but because I worried we couldn't afford the long distance call, I had the front desk transfer me to Dawna's apartment in Los Angeles.

"This better be good, Dawna-ski." I sighed.

"Cassandra-ski, you've got to get back to LA right now!" she babbled into the phone. "A friend of mine is holding auditions for a TV horror host and you'd be perfect for it!" I'm not sure why we referred to each other with our version of Russian names, but we'd done it ever since our days working together as assistants on the '70s musical variety TV show *Don Kirshner's Rock Concert*. I imagine the names had something to do with the term "brewskis."

There's an old unspoken showbiz superstition that whenever you leave LA, you're sure to get the call for that audition of a lifetime. I'd dragged my sorry ass back to Los Angeles one too many times, cutting short a multitude of pleasure trips, and had I ever aced the part? What do you think? If I had, Mark and I would be honeymooning at the Four Seasons in Bali instead of near my hometown in the Colorado Rockies.

"Are you out of your mind?" I sputtered into the receiver. My husband rolled off me, groaning like Frankenstein's monster.

"First of all, what's a horror host?" I asked. "You know damn well I just got married yesterday. There's no way I'm coming home for another stupid audition that I won't—"

"Listen! Just listen a minute," Dawna interrupted.

I sighed and leaned back in bed, prepared for a huge long-distance bill.

"This guy I know, Larry Thomas, is a director at a local TV station in LA and he's reviving their late-night horror movie show," she rambled. "They've got tons of scary films they want to air but need someone to host them. The last guy they had was Sinister Seymour, but he died. Larry really likes the idea of replacing him with a sexy Morticia Addams type."

KHJ Channel 9 had a long-standing tradition of showing late-night horror movies book-ended by a ghoulishly gruesome "horror host." It began in the local Los Angeles market in 1954 with *The Vampira Show*, the very first horror host on TV. Her show lasted only a few months on KABC in LA but was later picked up by Channel 9. Again, it was short-lived, but marked the beginning of the horror-movie host, a tradition that would endure for decades. Vampira was followed in 1972 by *Fright*

Night, hosted by Moona Lisa in her tight, black catsuit. The most recent KHJ horror host had been Sinister Seymour, played by Larry Vincent, who entertained the LA market until his demise in 1974. Since then, KHJ had remained horror host–less.

Now they were looking to fill two hours of late-night programming by bringing back their library of B-movie horror films.

"Dawna-ski, I really can't," I protested.

Dawna ignored me and barreled ahead. "I told him all about you and it turns out he's seen you perform at the Groundlings. Small world, huh? He loved that valley-girl thing you do!" Dawna paused to catch her breath. "Anyway, he really wants an actress who can play both sexy and funny and he hasn't been able to find one. You'd be perfect!"

Dawna was right about one thing: finding a woman who was both sexy and funny was a tall order in those days. Women were allowed to be sexy *or* funny, but not both. If you were the least bit attractive it was impossible to have a sense of humor. If you were funny, you needed to look like Phyllis Diller, Totie Fields, or Joan Rivers (with their original faces). I loved old horror movies and I'd been working in LA's top comedy improvisational group, the Groundlings, for a little more than four years, so had the timing been better, horror host actually seemed like a bill I could have filled. Damn.

Dawna began to whine. "Cassandra-ski, please, please, *please*! You've gotta come back and try out!"

But at that time, I was very serious about performing my wifely duties. "I appreciate you thinking of me, Dawna-ski. I really, really do. Thanks soooo much," I said. "But, seriously, no thanks."

A week later, the happy couple returned home to our little one-bedroom love nest in the Hollywood hills. The first ten messages on my answering machine were from Dawna.

"Larry's been posting audition ads in the papers and running commercials on TV and they still haven't found anyone. Call him now!"

Beginning my new married life with both of us unemployed was a little daunting, so we were excited and hopeful about the possibility of me landing the gig.

"Hi Larry. I'm Dawna's friend, Cassandra Peterson," I said, trying to sound cool and vaguely uninterested.

"Oh hey, thanks for calling me! I don't know if Dawna told you, but we've seen literally hundreds of girls for this part and still haven't found anyone," he explained. "We're holding the final auditions here at KHJ tomorrow. I'd love it if you'd come in and read."

When I hung up the phone, I threw my arms around Mark's neck and squealed, "I can't believe they still haven't found anyone!"

"It's a sign," he beamed. "This part is meant for you."

The next afternoon when I arrived at KHJ-TV, a brusque reception-ist signed me in, shoved a page of copy into my hands, and escorted me to the morning-news team's makeup area. The tiny room contained only a long countertop and a large chair in the center that looked like something you'd see in a dentist's office. Fluorescent lights glared over-head and a large makeup mirror reflected a few metal folding chairs lined up against the wall. Until that moment, I thought I looked pretty hot in my summery turquoise minidress and white high-heeled san-dals. But when I got a look at the girls crammed into that claustrophobic cubbyhole, my confidence took a nosedive. All six of the finalists were dressed in their full-on fiendish finery: pasty white makeup, skin-tight black leotards, and Bride of Frankenstein silver-streaked hair. A gaunt-looking girl wearing a Cher wig glared back at me like *I* was the freak. With my strawberry-blonde 1979 Farrah Fawcett do, I felt like one.

"Are *you* auditioning?" she asked, squinting her black-rimmed eyes and looking me up and down.

"Uh, I think so," I mumbled.

"You were supposed to come in costume." Oops. The room suddenly smelled like a funeral home. A combination of face powder and cheap perfume made me want to sneeze. "No shit," I thought, but instead chirped a perky, "Oh right, thanks!"

A black leather–clad woman gazed up at me and attempted a sym-pathetic smile, but because she was wearing permanently affixed fangs on her incisor teeth, it came off more like a vicious snarl.

I wanted to melt into the woodwork, and because of the heat coming from the dozens of lightbulbs surrounding the makeup mirror, I almost did. Flop-sweat trickling from my armpits down the sides of my rib cage, I squeezed into a seat next to a busty vixen and buried my face in the copy.

Oh, did I mention the script they gave me sucked? It was full of tired, old, hackneyed horror-host-of-days-gone-by lines like, "Come in, darling, drink a glass of bloooood." Considering myself a comedian—granted, an out-of-work comedian, but still—I couldn't imagine delivering those lines and trying to sell them to an audience. One by one, the other girls left the room and took their turns reading for the station bigwigs. I thanked God that I was last to be seen, because it gave me time to fool around with the script, adding a few improvised lines in an attempt to make it my own, or at least, to get a laugh.

"I'm your hostess with the mostest, the toast of Tinseltown! Y'know why they call me the toast of Tinseltown? 'Cause I'm always workin' for crumbs!"

"What's this movie about, you ask? It's about an hour and a half too long. This flick's so bad, I'd walk out on it even if it was playing on a plane!"

"I may not be the sharpest tool in the shed, but hey, some of us got brains, and some of us just got a couple of nice consolation prizes."

My ad-libs must have worked because I'd barely made it off the stage floor and out to the lobby before Larry Thomas ran up behind me and clapped a hand on my shoulder. I turned around to see him grinning from ear to ear. "Congratulations, you've got the job!"

Okay. Let me just get this out of the way. I'm seventy years old. There's no hiding it from Wikipedia. My age is always announced in the first sentence of any interview I do. I'm going to do my absolute best to remember as much of my life as humanly possible even though nowadays I can barely remember what I did last night. I'll try to recall every gory detail and be as factual as possible because I sure as hell don't want to end up like that James Frey dude who got reamed by Oprah after she found out his autobiography was bogus. The bottom line is, this story is the truth. My truth.

My life has taken a lot of unusual twists and turns, to say the least. If I had a dime for every time someone told me I should write my life story, I'd be able to support my ex-husband in the style to which he's become accustomed.

I've never come anywhere close to being what you'd call an A-lister. I'm more of a B- or even C-lister, not an actress as much as an underground-pop-culture thingy. Mine is a story of the tortoise and the hare. I eluded the short, hot burst of fame and fortune that many stars enjoy, in exchange for a long, slow, productive career that's stretched for forty years and counting. And in the business of "show," that's a damn long time. I once read that the average successful Screen Actors Guild performer's career is five years, so I'm pleased that I've made a pretty good living for myself and my family, doing what I love, for four decades. And I've got to admit, it still gives me goose pimples to hear Elvira referred to as an icon or a legend. Love her or hate her, if you've heard of Halloween, you've probably heard of Elvira.

As an actor, landing any job in Hollywood other than a temporary secretary gig sounded really good to me, so that day I walked out of KHJ happy as the proverbial clam. Sure, they were paying me only $350 a week, before taxes, but at that point in my career it felt like a fortune. It meant I would finally be able to cut down on the number of brain-numbing, data-entering temp jobs I'd been forced to suffer through between acting gigs, which was the majority of my time. Also, just by the hair of my chinny-chin-chin (Ew. Remind me to pluck that!) I'd managed to avoid the dreaded, self-imposed, arbitrarily set date of my thirtieth birthday, when—dun-dun-DUNNNN—I'd give up my showbiz aspirations for good. Yes, in a few short weeks I would hit the big three-O, stop this crazy showbiz shit, and get a "real" job for the first time in my life.

It was harder to come to this conclusion than you might imagine. I was throwing away a lifetime of working toward my goal—endless interviews, dance classes, voice lessons, and acting workshops—and felt like I'd be flushing all that time and money down the toilet. The thought of starting over at the age of thirty terrified me. I had no experience in *anything* except some form of show business. Now I'd go back to square one with no one to blame but myself.

I'd made a meager living going from one brief TV or movie appearance to the next while living in a run-down apartment and driving a cruddy, orange '69 Volkswagen Beetle. In between auditions, I worked part-time as a secretary, a hatcheck girl, a restaurant hostess, and a model for Hugh Hefner's agency, Playboy Models. I also sold a little weed on the side and used my ex-boyfriend's old Nikon to take topless photos of my girlfriends, which I sold to Japanese men's magazines. All this was going on while I performed two to four nights a week with the Groundlings. I was nothing if not enterprising.

But as you may have already guessed—because after all, you're reading this book—it turned out I was one of the lucky ones. I happened to be in the right place at the right time and ready when the chance presented itself. As Elvira always says, "Opportunity only gives you knockers once!"

The decision to call it a day, as far as continuing to bang my head against the showbiz wall was concerned, had come just a few months earlier, when I lost my dream job (cue dreamy, trance-inducing flashback music). . . .

Yes, I'd miraculously landed the role of Ginger in the remake of one of my all-time favorite childhood TV shows, *Gilligan's Island.* Every day after school, I'd rush my prepubescent self home to wade through another episode, just to see my favorite character, the sultry, sexy Ginger Grant. Then I'd spend hours in front of the mirror practicing everything she did and said—from her poor-man's Marilyn Monroe breathy whisper to her slinky walk. I wanted to be the redheaded bombshell so bad that—okay, I know you won't believe this, but I swear to God—I somehow grew the very same beauty mark that she had in exactly the same spot, next to the same eye!

Incredibly, I was one of two finalists for the new Ginger—my childhood dream was coming true! The one-hour special that would serve as the season opener for the revamped sitcom was called *The Harlem Globetrotters on Gilligan's Island.* Catchy, right? In addition to playing one of my favorite characters, I was thrilled out of my mind at the possibility of being in a made-for-TV movie and then, if the show was a success, on an actual, honest-to-God weekly network TV series! After three separate, anxiety-inducing auditions—one for acting, one for singing, and one for dancing—the number of Ginger wannabes dwindled down to me and one other actress: coincidentally, my next-door neighbor, Judy Baldwin. Judy had played Ginger in a previous incarnation of the role, in a TV movie called *The Castaways on Gilligan's Island,* but I'd privately been assured that the producers were looking for someone "fresh." I was going to be the new Ginger Grant! The days that followed were a flurry of activity. I went to CBS Studios for wardrobe fittings, received my script to study, and made plans to pack up my apartment because— icing on the cake—we were shooting in Hawaii! As far as I was concerned, my days of pounding the pavement, poring through *Variety*, and attending humiliating cattle calls were over. I was going to star on a network television show—almost too good to be true!

Guess what? It *was* too good to be true. Days before I was to leave for Hawaii, I got a call from the producer and creator himself, Sherwood Schwartz, telling me that despite his wishes, the network had indeed decided to go with a fresh face. Judy was out—but for some unexplained reason, so was I. The part of Ginger was going to be played by newcomer Constance Forslund. I was beyond devastated. I couldn't believe my dream job had slipped through my fingers. Many years later, I ran into Sherwood at a party. When I asked him why I didn't get the part, he confided that one of the network heads had seen me in the comedy improv troupe, the Groundlings, doing a sketch in which I played a patient in a gynecologist's office. It wasn't that unusual because, during an improv, audience members are often asked to supply the character that each of the actors play. Other than hooker or stripper, gynecology patient was my number-one request. The network veep reported back to the producers that they didn't need "that kind of element" in their programming. *I*, on the other hand, believe the job went south because, years before, I'd lost my shit when I walked in on the same network exec in bed with my boyfriend, Matt. Guess we'll never know for sure.

Not only had I lost my dream job, but I'd just dropped my agent because he had a problem with his hands. He couldn't keep 'em off me! I'd spent the previous month going from agent to agent without so much as a return call. The last agent I was unlucky enough to interview with was the appropriately named Edgar Small.

This one-man operation was comprised of a weathered, silver-haired Jewish agent who'd been around for an eternity but came highly recommended as someone who could open Hollywood doors. The walls of his musty office in a posh, older building on the "good" end of Sunset were lined with photos of his clients: the used-to-be-famous and hopefully-soon-to-be-famous. Sitting across from him, his cluttered, gray metal desk between us, I did my best to exude confidence while rattling off my credits. He grunted intermittently, which I took as a sign that he was impressed or at least interested. When I'd said all I could say about how fabulous I was, he sat for a silent moment, seeming to take it all in.

"How old did you say you were?" he asked in his raspy smoker's voice.

"I didn't. But I'm, uhhhh…twenty-nine," I replied, slurring my words so he might miss the "nine" part.

But his hearing was still sharp. "Twenty-*nine*!?" he spat, before launching into a coughing fit. When he finally stopped hacking, I gave a tentative nod of my head. I'd been in town long enough to know that, by Hollywood standards, I might as well be dead.

"Well, I hate to be the one to break it to you, kiddo, but your days as an actress are over." He wheezed. "No one, and I mean *no one* in this town is looking for a thirty-year-old actress. You might as well pack your bags and head back to wherever it is you came from because, and you'll excuse me for being blunt here, you're all washed up." I managed to keep the tears that had welled along my lower lids from spilling over and ruining my mascara before standing up and leaving with what little dignity I still had intact. I think the door actually *did* hit me in the ass on the way out.

A gratifying postscript, for *me* anyway: *The Harlem Globetrotters on Gilligan's Island* bombed and the series never materialized. In the forty years since, I've never hired an agent for acting roles again. I'll always take solace in the fact that an agent would forever miss out on a sweet chunk of change from the luckiest over-the-hill actress in Hollywood.

CHAPTER 1

KANSAS

I was born on September 17, 1951. *This* is how long ago that was: Harry Truman was president, Patti Page was kicking record-chart butt with "Tennessee Waltz," and *All About Eve* took home the Oscar for best picture. Oh, and the wheel had already been invented.

I was born at a very early age, an age that was too young to have a sense of good judgment, which I understand doesn't kick in until around thirty. Unfortunately for me, it still hasn't.

If I'd had better judgment, I wouldn't have chosen to be born in Manhattan, Kansas. The Little Apple. The city that *always* sleeps. Not that Manhattan is a bad place; it's actually a very pleasant small city. It's just a bad place to be from if you're destined for a life in show business.

My father, Dale Warren August Peterson, had barely finished high school before he left to join the Merchant Marines toward the end of World War II. Upon returning to his hometown of Randolph, Kansas, he encountered a beautiful eighteen-year-old redhead, Phyllis Schmidt, at the local swimming pool. A senior in high school, Phyllis aspired to become a nurse, and after graduating, she wasted no time in moving to Manhattan to sign up for nurse's training. Dale followed her, and they married on Groundhog Day, 1951, shortly after Phyllis discovered she was pregnant.

After a quick courthouse wedding, they returned to Randolph. The town was too small to support a hospital, so I was born in the nearest "big city," Manhattan. My parents chose the name Cassandra after one of my mother's teachers whom my dad had dated. I know, right?

Cassandra (pronounced Ka-SAWN-dra, not Ka-SAND-ra) was such a bizarre name for 1951 rural Kansas that I might as well have been called Zor-El. It was one of the things that would later contribute to my feelings of freakishness. For expediency's sake, my name was shortened to Soni (Sawn-ee), a name everyone in my family could pronounce. Daddy enjoyed telling the story that upon hearing the name Cassandra, my German great grandmother exclaimed, "Accch! Zuch an uk-lee name ver zuch a bee-*u*-tee-ful baby!"

Broke, newly married, and with their first child, my parents were given the enticing offer of a free place to live. All they had to do was take over the farm Grandma and Grandpa had vacated because, as oldsters, it was becoming too much work. Mother and Daddy packed up their few belongings and their new, bee-*u*-tee-ful baby and headed to the farm, twenty-five miles away. They tried their hand growing milo, a type of corn used for cattle feed, and when that didn't pan out, they used what little money they had to buy several calves. Despite being kept in the barn and fed with baby bottles, the poor little things died during the first winter, which was unusually cold. My mother hated every *second* of living on the farm. She told Daddy in no uncertain terms that if he didn't find a normal job and get them the hell out of there, she was taking me and leaving.

Miraculously, Daddy found a job as a salesman in the Singer sewing-machine store in Manhattan. On the first day, he showed up for work in his overalls with no shirt and was given the job of vacuuming the store. He vacuumed all day, eight straight hours, which not only made the Singer store's carpet the cleanest in town but earned Daddy enough to buy a secondhand suit (even though he was afraid it would "make him look like a queer").

Although he had no experience as a salesman, he took to it as if selling had been in his blood his whole life. It was a perfect fit. He had a fierce competitive streak and had always been able to cajole, beg, or threaten people into doing whatever he wanted.

The drama began only a year and a half into my life.

Good Friday, 1953, seemed no different than any other day on the farm. Daddy took the Singer truck to work in Manhattan and left my mother alone to care for me and Jeannie, my eleven-year-old cousin who was visiting. It was the first warm April afternoon of the year. Crocuses popped their purple heads up through gray patches of snow and the first pink blossoms burst from the crab-apple tree in the yard. Jeannie helped my mother, who was eight and a half months pregnant, spread a blanket on the grass in the sun to color eggs for our Easter Sunday get-together at Grandma and Grandpa Peterson's.

Meanwhile, I was left alone in the house to explore on my own, which always struck me as a little odd. According to my mother's account of what happened next, at only eighteen months old, I apparently had the strength and ingenuity to drag a kitchen chair across the linoleum floor to our worn-out O'Keefe and Merritt stove. I climbed up on the chair to check out the sound the eggs made knocking against the sides of the kettle as it bubbled.

Sometimes I have to wonder about what happened next. I must have lost my balance and grabbed on to the closest thing to me, the enormous cast-iron pot of boiling water. When Mother heard my cries, she ran into the house to find me lying on the kitchen floor, bathed in scalding water, going into shock. She slathered me in lard (so much for nurse's training), trying her best to ignore the skin that kept slipping off in her hands. Wrapping me in a clean sheet, she and Jeannie got me into her old Pontiac station wagon and hauled ass over the deep-rutted dirt roads to the hospital in Manhattan, twenty-five miles away.

Third-degree burns covered a third of my small body, so the prognosis wasn't good. Back then, if more than twenty-five percent of your body was burned, you were pretty much history. Along with a good amount of skin, all the hair on my head had melted off and my eyelids were fused shut. When I was still alive after a night and a day, the doctor told Daddy he needed to get me to the University of Kansas Medical Center as fast as possible or there was no hope.

Once I was there, with no other option, the doctors suggested treating the raging infection that resulted from the burns with a new experimental derivative of penicillin, only recently mass-produced. They couldn't make any promises, but what did my parents have to lose? My father gave the go-ahead and I was pumped full of the stuff. Several touch-and-go days went by and, miraculously, I was still alive. When the doctors finally declared me stable, skin was peeled from my stomach and thighs and grafted onto my back, shoulders, neck, and ankles. I stayed in the hospital for several weeks and over the next year would return to the burn center in Kansas City again and again.

While I was recovering, my mother was admitted to the hospital across the street from the burn center, where she gave birth to my baby sister, Melody. Once home, while Mother cared for my newborn sister, Daddy spent every night of the following year lying on the cool, bare floor of my parent's bedroom rubbing my back, while I cried and squirmed from the relentless pain and itching.

Just take a look at the lucky things that happened. Penicillin had just come into widespread use. The nearest burn center was one of the best in the country. Okay, pulling a pot of boiling water on top of myself—not so lucky, but ironically, I'd eventually come to think of the accident as one of the best things to ever happen to me.

During my recovery, my parents gave up on farming and moved into town. Randolph was a sleepy little burg of 350 of the most whitebread residents ever assembled in one place, and it seemed the majority of them were my relatives. Before

CASSANDRA GAY PETERSON

Cassandra Is Better

(Special to The Daily Tribune)
RANDOLPH—Cassandra Gay Peterson, badly burned by hot water Apr. 3, is improved, her aunt, Mrs. Carl Bergman, reported this morning on her return from Kansas City, where the 18-months old girl is in University Medical Center.

Although Cassandra Gay's general condition is reported as "good," it will be a week or 10 days before skin-grafting can be begun.

Mrs. Dale Peterson, who live on a farm north of Randolph, are both in Kansas City with her.

Cassandra, who is an only child, was born Sept. 18, 1951. She was seriously burned when she grabbed for a sauce-pan in which water was being heated for Easter Egg dyes.

Her aunt, Mrs. Bergman, was called to Kansas City from her home in Colorado Springs, after the child was taken to the med-

My first press!

I left Kansas, I wasn't aware there were Blacks, Asians, Latinos, Jews, or gays, only people who looked and acted like me.

My grandma, Ivah Singer, was a tall, big-boned gal with short, curly, apricot-colored hair. She was from strong German stock. Think Kaiser Wilhelm in a dress. My grandpa, who was a diminutive five foot one, exaggerated Grandma's five-ten frame whenever he stood next to her. I still have old valentines she gave him calling him her "little man."

Grandma had come west to Kansas with her family as a baby. She married my grandpa, August Peterson, when she was only fifteen and he was sixteen. He'd come from Sweden and had such a heavy accent that most of the time I had no idea what he was saying. His best English erupted when he got mad. Several times a day, we could hear him yell, "Yumpin' Yiminy!" or "Ye-sus Christ!" which always cracked us kids up. Whenever I walked next door to Grandpa and Grandma's house, past the lilac bushes with their intoxicating aroma, past Grandma's huge bed of purple irises, and up the porch steps of their two-story, whitewashed house, Grandpa always opened the door and called out a cheery "Gudag!" I was almost nine before I realized he wasn't mistaking me for the family pet.

Randolph was mainly populated by northern European immigrants— Petersons, Bergstoms, and Schmidts, oh my! It was a real-life version of *The Andy Griffith Show* nestled in a valley carved by the Snake River, a town full of people with nicknames like "Wuzzy," "Hooney," and "Dudd," where every few feet of pavement was studded with bricks that commanded "DON'T SPIT ON THE SIDEWALK."

In the center of town was a square dotted with enormous shade trees, surrounding a white wooden gazebo where, on Sunday afternoons, my grandpa led a band. On the streets bordering the square were a post office, a church, a beauty salon/barber shop, a grocery store, and my favorite place, Peterson's Drugstore, which happened to be owned by my Uncle Lyle and Aunt Vergie.

I lived for the afternoons when one of my older cousins, usually Jeannie, would take me along with her to the drugstore, where we got to sit up on the high metal stools at the soda fountain. Jeannie, who was a teenager, hadn't yet bleached her natural dishwater-blonde hair, but she made up for it by wearing short shorts to show some leg.

Peterson's Drugstore looked like a place you might see in an old movie starring Lana Turner. The floor was made up of tiny, white mosaic tiles with a decorative black pattern running through it. The few small, round tables that dotted the room were flanked by twisted wire "ice cream parlor" chairs. Ornate tin ceiling tiles gleamed overhead and a long, polished-wood soda fountain ran the length of the store.

"What'll it be, girls?" Uncle Lyle always asked, even though he already knew what we wanted.

"Chocolate phosphates, please!" we shouted back.

Uncle Lyle squirted a shot of chocolate syrup into each of two tall Coke glasses he took from the icebox, added the acid phosphate, and stirred in the fizzy seltzer water while we watched with anticipation. Finally, he set the drinks on the counter and slid them toward us.

"That'll be twenty cents!" he bellowed. We both laughed because we knew he wouldn't really make us pay. While the noisy ceiling fan hummed overhead, giving us a temporary break from the sticky Kansas-afternoon heat, we sipped our frosty drinks through paper straws and were allowed to peruse the comic books on a rickety, rotating wire rack. Superman was my favorite. I couldn't get enough of him and his amazing adventures. He reminded me of Daddy, with his bulging, muscular arms and shiny blue-black hair slicked back over his perfect skull. I sometimes daydreamed that Daddy could fly. Then he would scoop me up, just like Lois Lane, and carry me away, zooming across the sky to Metropolis, far away from Randolph, away from Kansas, away from my mother.

CHAPTER 2

COLORADO BOUND

July 13 of the year I was born came to be known as Black Friday. That's the day the rivers overflowed and caused a devastating flood in Manhattan and the surrounding towns.

Randolph was situated in the Blue Valley, a beautiful, serene place comprised of some of the richest farmland in Kansas. To prevent future disasters, the Army Corps of Engineers, in their wisdom, devised a plan: they would create a dam and flood the valley. A billboard reading "Stop the Big Dam Business" was erected in Randolph's town square, and the 3,000 residents of the Blue Valley fought the federal government valiantly, protesting the flooding by petitioning the state. But by the time I was five, my family—including my grandparents, aunts, uncles, and cousins—was forced to pack up their belongings, sell their property to the government for a pittance, and evacuate. Randolph was where the Petersons had lived for decades, been born and raised, and owned homes, farms, and businesses that they'd built from scratch. Tuttle Creek Lake was created in the Blue River Valley, and Randolph disappeared forever.

When I took my last trip with my mother back to Kansas for her sixtieth Randolph High School reunion in 2013, we drove by Tuttle Creek Reservoir. It had been an unusually dry winter and the water level was low. To our surprise, there in the middle of the lake, we could see the steeple of the old Presbyterian Church rising from the murky, snuff-colored water like a derelict ghost.

The entire Peterson and Schmidt clan moved to Manhattan. My

7

parents rented a small house not far from the Singer store, I finished first grade, and my mother gave birth to my youngest sister, her third and last child, Robin Dawn. A year later, we packed up again and moved to Colorado Springs to join my beloved Aunt Lorrayne, who had broken with family tradition and moved away with Uncle Carl a few years earlier.

Because my parents' car was crammed full of my sisters and grandparents, I got to ride with one of my dad's best friends, Alan Wagner, in his snazzy baby-blue and white Chevy. We traveled across miles of cornfields and endless flat prairie with the windows down all the way and the radio blasting the Everly Brothers' hit "Wake Up Little Susie," while we sang along at the top of our lungs.

Colorado Springs turned out to be cool, dry, and mountainous— a welcome break from the hot, humid scenery of Kansas. Somehow, I suspect with a little help from Grandma and Grandpa, my parents were able to buy a small house near them. Daddy *had* to be close to Grandma because he was the baby of the family and was tied tightly to her apron strings. Living just down the street from Grandma and Grandpa came in handy when my parents needed to get away. I was often left alone with Grandma Peterson. This gave her the opportunity to hoist me up onto her ample lap and lay her crazy Jehovah's Witness shit on me.

"Your daddy's going to die, Soni," she'd say, looking me straight in the eye. "And if he doesn't stop drinkin' and cussin' he's going to hell where he'll burn in eternal damnation." Being the gullible five-year-old that I was, it terrified me beyond words. According to Grandma, he was (1) taking off to hell and abandoning me; and (2) going to burn, which I knew from experience was no fun. Daddy was my savior, my hero, my protector. He was Superman! If he wasn't with me, I couldn't exist.

Grandma's gnarled, arthritic hands gripped my skinny arms and held me in place. Her face was so close to mine that all I could see were the dozens of tiny red lines radiating from her mouth into which her lipstick bled. She wore one of her usual flowery housedresses with a matching cap-sleeved bolero my Aunt Lorrayne had sewn for her. Her wrinkled skin smelled of roses, the cologne she always wore that made me so carsick on Sunday drives through the mountains with my family.

"Pray with me, Soni," she commanded, bowing her head and squeezing her eyes shut.

I closed my eyes but couldn't help peeking through the slits while pretending to pray. Sunlight slanted through the picture window in the dining room, making the leaves of her houseplants cast scary, jungle-like shadows across the faded Oriental rug. A crumpled, white Kleenex had fallen out of her flowered pocket and lay on the floor at her feet.

Years before, back in Randolph, Grandma had fallen through the ceiling of the garage, hitting the concrete floor below, breaking an arm, a leg, and her jaw while trying to escape from Grandpa, who had just discovered she'd been bestowing sexual favors on the town pharmacist in exchange for pain pills. For years, Daddy drove her back and forth to Kansas City for electroshock-therapy treatments, but they did little to help. Her addiction ran in the family and would be passed down to her children and grandchildren. After the infamous incident, she repented, and with Jesus's help and a zealot's fury, found God.

As I listened to the antique clock on the buffet ticking off the seconds to the "end of days," I imagine I was thinking that I liked her a lot better as the happy, pill-popping Granny from before.

Our house at 1713 Arbor Way was my parents' pride and joy. It was only a small two-bedroom, one-bath, faux ranch–style tract home, but it seemed like a palace to us. My dad soon landed a job at Sears selling Kenmore appliances, for which he received a twenty-percent employee discount, so every stick of furniture in our house and every shred of clothing on our backs came from Sears from then on. (Which explains why, to this day, I have no fashion sense.)

We were definitely in the lower income class, just slightly more sophisticated than "white trash." Think about it: small-town farmers suddenly transported to the big city. We were like the Beverly Hillbillies, only without the mansion or the "cee-ment pond." Money was scarce. Almost every day I was reminded that it didn't grow on trees. When my mother overheard me asking Daddy for money to buy lunch at school, she made sure I felt guilty about taking my dad's last dime, literally. "Thanks to you, Miss Selfish, he'll have to go all day without a cup of coffee!"

When Daddy first started selling kitchen appliances at Sears, he liked to impress friends and relatives who stopped by with his famous garbage-disposal routine. While everyone stood around the kitchen sink, he would put a Coke bottle down the drain, turn on the disposal with the cold water running, and after a minute or so of ear-splitting noise and looks of horror from the guests, open the cupboard under the sink, remove the bottom of the disposal, and produce a fine ground powder that had once been a Coke bottle. But the show didn't end there. He'd then scoop up a handful of the powder, rub it hard between his hands, and smooth it all over his face, spreading it on with gusto. The guests oohed and ahhed and stared in disbelief, probably because they couldn't imagine anyone being crazy enough to do such a stupid thing. I absolutely loved seeing their reaction and couldn't get enough of this crazy stunt that was performed every time we had company. Along with his hot pepper–eating contests, it became the highlight of that summer.

My family had this odd tradition of giving the oldest child of each of my dad's brothers or sisters a rhyming middle name, thus, we were Jeannie Kay, Geraldine Fay, Danny Jay, Verne Ray, and me, Cassandra Gay (which would someday be good for lots of laughs when I was carded at gay discos).

I lived a chaotic life within a big group of grandparents, aunts, uncles, and cousins. Danny and Jeannie were the cousins I saw most because they lived with their single mom, "Boxer," and my Grandma and Grandpa, right down the street. Danny and I played with marbles, Pick-Up Sticks, Lincoln Logs, Tonka trucks, and all the usual boy stuff together. Jeannie, ten years my senior, was my childhood idol. By this time, she had a bleached-blonde beehive, wore tight sweaters over pointy bras, and was "stacked." She attended beauty school and often needed a willing model, and I was it. Even though I was only in grade school, she taught me all her tricks. She painted my nails, did my hair up in French twists, piled makeup on me, and paraded me down the street like a tiny hooker. She showed me how to use baby oil and iodine to get a tan (I only burned) and taught me how to "wiggle when I walked" by swinging my hips from side to side. She said it would attract boys. She had lots of guys after her, so she obviously knew whereof she spoke.

I started second grade at Ivywild Elementary, just a few blocks from our new house. My childhood might have seemed idyllic to the outside observer, but at home with my mother, it was anything but. She was a tough one, man. She didn't take crap from anyone, least of all her kids. Mother came from the do-it-because-I-say-so-or-I'll-give-you-something-to-*really*-cry-about school of parenting. She wasn't the kind of person who should have had kids to begin with. She was a nervous, anxious woman of the '50s who did what you were supposed to do in those days: get married and start a family.

At home, I walked on eggshells. There seemed to be no correlation between how I behaved and how I was treated. My mother was unpredictable, with no rhyme or reason for her moods. I could get kicked, pinched, hit, or even bitten for walking in the door just as easy as I could for talking back. She would haul off and hit me with whatever happened to be closest—a hairbrush, yardstick, you name it. All that was missing was the wire hanger. Oh, wait, that wasn't missing.

What hurt more were the constant demeaning insults, the name-calling and humiliation. *That* shit would last a lifetime. It was uncanny how she could find the softest, most vulnerable spot in my psyche, then plunge an ice pick into it. Calling me "stupid" or "idiot" was the norm. When I was little, she called me "Dumbo" because she knew I was embarrassed that my ears stuck out. I was especially touchy about my receding chin line, so she added "Chinless" to her repertoire. When I went through puberty and was self-conscious about my weight, she enjoyed poking me in the stomach and calling me "Fatso," which infuriated me. But Mother had her favorite way to hurt me. If I was moping around and she sensed I was sad or upset, she'd ask, "What's *your* problem?" and when I made the mistake of replying, she'd attack the most sensitive part of me. "Of course boys don't like you," she'd hiss through clenched teeth. "Look at you! You think any man would want to be with someone with all those scars?"

I couldn't fight back when I was a child. At least I didn't want to because she was a lot bigger than me and could knock my block off. I held all the anger and rage inside where it became one big, burning ball of impotent rage that ate away at my stomach lining and eventually got released on others. I woke up each morning like any child of a narcissistic parent—with no idea what the crazy would be that day. I learned at an early age that avoiding my mother was the safest thing to do, and I stayed away from home as much as a little kid could.

On the other hand, I worshipped my dad, and he worshipped me.

"When they told me at the hospital you might not make it," he'd tell me time and time again, "I swore that if you didn't die, I'd give you everything in my power to give." He made good on that promise, even going so far as buying me the expensive white French provincial canopied bedroom suite (or "suit" as Daddy called it) that I'd seen in the Sears catalog.

Daddy was my knight in shining armor. Unlike Mother, he was never angry with me. He didn't hit me or yell at me, and he never called me names or made fun of me. Every night I counted the minutes until I heard his car pull in the driveway. After stopping off for a beer or two with the guys, he'd waltz through the front door and the first thing he'd do was grab me around the waist and swing me up over his head.

"How much do you love me?" he'd always ask. I'd sing-song back, "A bushel and a peck and a hug around the neck!" I threw my arms around him, kissed his stubbly cheek, and breathed in the faint, calming scent of Old Spice aftershave. After a tense dinner where Mother berated him for coming home late, not making enough money, or drinking too much, the dishes were done and Mother and my younger sisters were off to bed. That was my cue to grab Daddy a cold Coors from the fridge, while he stripped down to his "wife-beater" and Jockey shorts. Then he and I would stretch out on our thick shag carpeting to watch *Gunsmoke*, *The Untouchables*, or wrestling until I fell asleep, my head on his strong, tattooed bicep.

When I was a little girl, Daddy was magic. Daddy was my superhero. He was kind, funny, generous, and charming. He had a sweet tenor singing voice and played the trumpet like Louis Armstrong. He was a master storyteller, and listening to him recall times he'd had as a kid was magical. If you were a friend, there was nothing he wouldn't do for you. He'd go out of his way to help anyone who was down on their luck.

But he could be rough and tough when he needed to be, like when he'd go hand-fishing in our pond on the farm or beat the crap out of someone who looked at him sideways. Once when we were tooling down the road in Daddy's used, mist-green Cadillac, he started cussing to beat the band at the car behind us, which was tailgating, a *major* pet peeve of his. He pulled off the highway and motioned the other driver to the side of the road. Wondering what the problem was, the other driver pulled over and stopped. "Stay here," my dad commanded, "I'll be right back." Daddy got out, calmly strolled up to the stranger's car, and made a "roll-down-your-window" motion with his hand. Then he popped the guy straight in the kisser with all his might. Lucky for my dad, no one carried guns in those days.

Every other word out of his mouth was "damn," "goddamn," "son of a bitch," "bastard," or "hell." And that wasn't when he was angry; it was just his normal, everyday speech.

"I was just downtown," he'd say. "Of course, it was hotter than hell, and there was that crazy bastard Garner, and goddammit if he wasn't with that son of a bitch, Ted."

If someone called Dale Peterson a dirty name, lied to him, or disrespected him or any member of his family, they were asking for serious trouble. I can't count all the times he came home with a black eye or bloody nose. One Thanksgiving morning I woke up to find him sprawled on the living-room couch, his lips swollen and a raw steak over his eye. The night before, he'd gone to a nightclub on "the wrong side of the tracks" to repossess a sewing machine, a job he did for a little extra spending money. Apparently, the bar owner's wife wasn't quite ready to part with her new modern convenience, so Daddy was jumped by several drunken bar patrons who came to her defense. He was on crutches for the next several weeks and, to top it off, he didn't get "the goddamned sewing machine back!"

Once, on one of our many family vacations to visit my Uncle Dorton and Aunt Arlene in Chino, California, my parents managed to cram Grandma and Grandpa and their suitcases into the back seat along with us three girls. Because there were no seat belts to bother with back then, my sisters and I spent the entire trip bouncing around the car, fighting like banshees, and getting slapped by my mother every few miles. We pulled over at every truck stop from Colorado to California so Grandma could pee. My grandparents didn't believe in eating at restaurants, so my mom brought along a loaf of Wonder Bread, French's mustard, bologna, and cans of Underwood deviled ham to make sandwiches. We ate them for breakfast, lunch, and dinner while my dad zipped down Route 66, whiskey and Coke propped between his legs. My mother was making sandwiches on the front seat when the open jar of mustard flew off the dashboard, splattering all over the turquoise upholstered seats of my dad's precious Olympic white Cadillac El Dorado.

"Goddamn it to hell!" my dad yelled, jerking the steering wheel hard to the right and screeching to a halt on the side of the road. Using the only thing available, some Kleenex Grandma had floating around the bottom of her purse, Daddy and Mother mopped up what they could of the electric-yellow mustard while the rest of us watched in silence, trying not to breathe for fear of being sucked into the front-seat drama. We pulled off at the next town, Needles, to stay the night, so my parents could look for a dry cleaner that might be able to steam-clean the mustard stains. My sisters and I got to splash around in the motel pool, which was the highlight of our trip.

The supposed reason my grandparents came along was to visit my uncle and his family, but they were *really* in it to see Lawrence Welk, their favorite performer of all time. His show was broadcast from the Hollywood Palladium on Sunset Boulevard. Every week after our usual big Sunday dinner at Grandma and Grandpa Petersons, me, my sisters, and cousins were forced to watch him play his "champagne bubble music" on TV. If we didn't sit patiently in front of the television for the entire show, we weren't allowed to watch *The Wonderful World of Disney* afterward. Grandma had aspirations that we would one day become singers like the Lennon Sisters, or dancers like the dancing duo of Bobby and Sissy. They even forced me to take much-hated accordion lessons so I might one day follow in the footsteps of Myron Floren.

Back to the action. Once we finally made it to Chino, the grown-ups made a big to-do about taking Grandma and Grandpa into Hollywood to see their idol. It was an exciting night out for all of them. They dressed in their "Sunday best" and left me and my sisters at home with my older cousin, Rex. After many, many cocktails were imbibed and the show came to an end, they all piled back into my dad's Caddy for the long drive back to Chino. As they cruised down Sunset Boulevard, just blocks away from the Palladium, Grandpa and Uncle Dorton got into it.

"I beleef dat Lawrence Velk is da best bandleader in da whole vorlt," Grandpa sing-songed in his Swedish lilt. And he should have known. After all, Grandpa had been a bandleader most of his life.

Uncle Dorton was riding shotgun next to my dad. He'd drunk more than his share, as usual. He whipped his head around to confront his father.

"Best bandleader in the *vorlt*?" he mocked, his face growing red and his eyes swimming around in their sockets, trying to focus. "Better than Benny Goodman? Better than Tommy Dorsey? You're outta your goddamn mind, old man. Those guys could run circles around your precious Lawrence Welk."

This was too much for Grandma, who up to this moment had managed to keep her mouth shut. Her bony body quivering, she leaned forward and boxed her oldest son hard on the side of his head.

"Dorton, what in heaven's name is the matter with you?" she blubbered. "How could you say something like that about Lawrence Welk?" The bright lights and snazzy clubs of Sunset whizzed past outside the windows as the tension in the car mounted.

Dorton pressed his palm against his ear where Grandma's punch had landed.

"I'll talk about him any goddamn way I want," he slurred. He turned around and fixed his eyes on Grandma. "And as far as I'm concerned, Lawrence Welk is nothing but a little *pissant*!"

That was the final straw for my dad. No one called Lawrence Welk a pissant and got away with it. Daddy slammed on the brakes, got out, walked around to the passenger's side door, and jerked his older brother out of the car. Dorton was an ex-Navy man, the biggest and toughest of my dad's brothers, but a little detail like that would never stop my dad.

He and Dorton proceeded to beat the living crap out of each other right there on the hood of the Caddy in the middle of Sunset Boulevard. The sound of knuckles meeting flesh and bone rang out in the hot summer night as the brothers exchanged blows. From the safety of the car, Mother and Aunt Arlene screamed, begging them to stop. But they knew better than to get in the middle of this rumble. Passing cars honked their annoyance or approval. Drivers rolled down their windows and hooted, egging them on while Grandma and Grandpa cowered in the back seat, their Lawrence Welk "high" evaporating before their eyes.

Still wearing my baby-doll jammies, I was rousted from a sound sleep in the wee hours of the morning, and along with the luggage, my sisters, and my grandparents, tossed into the back seat of the car. I had no idea what was happening. Daddy's face was bloody, which wasn't all that unusual, and his indestructible Timex watch was smashed. I noticed the hood of the car was seriously scratched and dented, too. As the first rays of sun broke from behind the Chino hills, Daddy peeled out of the driveway and sped away from my Uncle's house, headed for Colorado.

CHAPTER 3

HORROR, HOLIDAYS, AND HORMONES

Toward the end of the '50s, when a little more money started coming in, Daddy embraced the latest craze and built a fallout shelter under our house. When the threat of the Cold War eased, he expanded it to a "rec" room, decorated with a fake leather couch and matching chairs featuring bucking broncs stitched on the seat backs and wooden wagon-wheel arms. The new wallpaper had a lovely cowboys-massacring-Indians motif. The floor was an array of multicolored individual linoleum tiles, and of course there was the all-important bar that my parents had adorned with bathroom-style pink mosaic tiles and lined with shelves stocked with every imaginable type of booze.

Liquor was a big deal in my family. Many of my relatives were alcoholics, but nobody called them that back then. They just liked to drink. When we went with my parents for family drives in the mountains on weekends, which we were frequently forced to do, it was normal for Daddy to have me drink the top third out of his Coca-Cola so he could fill it with Jim Beam while careening down the mountainside on cruise control. I couldn't wait for him to fling the empty bottle from the window, because I knew what was coming—more Coke! I love those cute emails that used to circulate on the Internet about how great it was to grow up in the '50s, before there were rules about drinking and driving or wearing seat belts. It's a miracle anyone survived.

Beginning in junior high, because my room was in the basement right next to the rec room, which gave me easy access to the bar, I took a cue from my dad and uncles and used the contents to regularly top off my orange juice or soda pop.

My parents were very big on entertaining and threw lots of parties, inviting relatives and my dad's coworkers. My mom rarely drank alcohol, but at these parties, she let her hair down. I wish she had drunk more because she was always so much nicer after she'd had a Tom Collins or two. They laughed, danced, smoked, and drank long after we kids were sent to bed. I can still hear the sounds of Nat King Cole's "Stardust" wafting up from the rec room through the heater vents as I drifted off to sleep.

The holidays were almost always a good time for me and my family. At Christmastime, my mom wore her "outside face" because there was always company around. As far as I could tell, she had two completely different and separate faces: her mean "inside face," reserved for us kids and Daddy; and her nice outside face that she presented to most relatives and all strangers. People were always telling me how much fun she was to be around and how lucky I was to have her for a mom, which confused the hell out of me. Were they were talking about the same person I lived with?

Christmas Eve festivities were usually held at our house and relatives would come from all over the Midwest. Because Grandpa Peterson was Swedish, we always celebrated Christmas with spicy sausages called *potatiskorv* (or "potato carve" as we called it), a long, coiled sausage that we cut into bite-size pieces and speared with toothpicks. The main course was *lutfisk,* creamed dry cod served over boiled potatoes. I was the only kid in the family who would eat the stuff.

My sisters and I loved Christmas Eve and Christmas Day. We were allowed to eat whatever we wanted and didn't have to clean up afterward because there were so many aunts there to do the job, and my mother was distracted cooking, serving, and gossiping, so she paid no attention to us at all.

I remember only one bad Christmas, and that was when I was five and we still lived in Randolph. Mother and Daddy had been running around the house all day, cleaning like maniacs and making last-minute preparations before the onslaught of relatives began. The highlight of Christmas Eve was always Santa showing up with his big pillowcase full of toys for me, my sister, and my cousins. Santa always knew our names and exactly what was on our Christmas lists. He always seemed vaguely familiar, but it took me a few years to realize he was really just one of my uncles dressed in a cheap Santa suit and fake beard.

I'd been waiting weeks and weeks for this night and had been as good as I could stand to be, just so Santa didn't pass us by. I'd made my list and asked him for a Terri Lee doll. My parents had gone to great lengths to get a Christmas tree. I stood before it, gazing up at the star on the top, and I remember thinking it was the biggest, most beautiful tree I'd ever seen—and it was in our living room! My mother had spent much of the day hanging the brand-new, shiny ornaments on the tree and stringing the multicolored bulbs. Melody and I weren't allowed to do that part because the balls were so fragile, but we did get to toss sparkling silver tinsel on the branches after the ornaments were hung.

As my mother put the finishing touches on the tree, I heard a plaintive "meow" outside the front door and looked out the window to see my poor kitty-cat standing on the stoop in the snow, looking pathetic. I opened the door a crack, just enough to let him in and keep the cold air out, and he slipped into our tiny living room. "Don't let that filthy cat in!" Mother snapped.

The fat, gray-striped tomcat skittered across the newly waxed wood floor and made straight for the Christmas tree. He batted a paw at a sparkly red ornament. Mother hollered, "Get away from that tree, you damned cat!" She rushed forward and just missed grabbing hold of his tail. He darted under the branches and before I could register what was happening, he shot up the trunk of the tree to the very tippy top and clung there for an endless second. Mother stood stock still, her hands covering her mouth. Her hair was still up in rollers and wrapped in a scarf that had little pictures of red and blue sailboats scattered across it. She wore her handmade turquoise apron, the one with the rows of rickrack, tied over her red, short-sleeved "Christmas dress." Time seemed to stand still as the late afternoon light reflected off the snow and bathed the living room in an eerie, bluish glow.

The presents Melody and I bought with our allowance at the Woolworths dime store in Manhattan for aunts, uncles, and cousins were tucked under the tree on the candy cane–striped tree skirt my mother had made. A lone strand of silver tinsel draped itself along the edge of our big, oval rag rug. For a moment, the room was dead silent, except for the hum of the furnace droning in the background.

Crash! Down came the cat, the tree, the ornaments, the lightbulbs, and the tinsel. I held my breath as I looked from my mother's face to the mess of tangled branches and broken glass on the floor. "That's it!" Mother shrieked. "Christmas is cancelled!" She stormed down the hall and a moment later the bedroom door slammed so hard the floor reverberated under my feet.

I have absolutely no recollection of what happened after that, whether Christmas went on that year or not, just the vivid memory of that moment and the aching feeling in the pit of my stomach as I pictured Santa Claus flying over our house without stopping. And it was all my fault.

My parents were hard workers and extremely upwardly mobile, so they were always able to come up with new resources for making money. Daddy went to people's houses at night after work to repair, or sometimes repossess, sewing machines, washers, dryers, and vacuum cleaners, and my mom opened a day-care center in our home. During my grade-school years, in addition to my baby sister, we had anywhere from three to five screaming infants at our house every weekday. This led to me putting off having a child until I was forty-three.

With not only my mom, but several crying babies at home, I stayed away as much as possible. I usually went to my best friend Marilyn's house, right across the back alley. She was the first "latchkey" kid I'd ever encountered, and I thought it was really neat that *both* her parents worked out of the house, because that meant we had free rein until they got home at night. It was like living an exciting scene from one of our favorite books, *Lord of the Flies*.

We could pretty much do whatever we wanted without getting yelled at, like create science experiments using chemicals from under the kitchen sink, take off all our clothes and play nudist colony just like in the magazines we'd found under her dad's bed, or just peel off our unlimited scabs and add them to the extensive collection we kept hidden in a milk bottle in the pantry. With the money Marilyn "borrowed" from her mom's savings jar, we bought our favorite snacks: various flavors of Gerber baby food. Our favorite toys were thermometers, which we bought and broke open so we could play with those fascinating little silver balls that ran every which way—*mercury*—hellooooo?!

At my house you ate whatever my mother put on your plate, whether you wanted it or not, and stayed in your chair until you finished every last bite. (I once refused to eat something—I think it was liver and onions—and woke up the next morning still sitting at the table when it was time to go to school.) When I got the lucky opportunity to have dinner at Marilyn's, I couldn't believe that each person was asked whether they'd like a particular dish and how much!

On Halloween, we were allowed to create a haunted house in her basement and invite all the trick-or-treaters in to roam through the darkened hallways and sit in an "electric chair" (a vibrating massage cot), dig their hands into the guts of a recently departed convict (a bowl of spaghetti), and hold his eyeballs in their hands (peeled grapes).

I yearned for adventure and spent a lot of time in my head creating elaborate fantasies. Marilyn and I referred to each other as Nyliram and Ardnassac (our names spelled backward, in case you hadn't figured that out) and spent our summers with the other neighborhood kids in the alleys, streets, and creeks that were the perfect setting for bringing these fantasies to life. For months, we played "flying horses," inspired by the movie *Fantasia*, building large nests out of sticks and leaves down by the creek. We staged elaborate circuses for the neighborhood kids and charged admission, of course, and with her mom's eight-millimeter camera, we made movies that we played backward, so we appeared to be superheroes, able to leap up into trees or magically produce food from our mouths.

Nyliram and I also collected Breyer scale model horses. She had many more than I did because her older sister, Corliss, was already off at college, so she was treated like a spoiled only child. Later on, our obsession with horses paid off. We said to hell with the toy horses and made up our minds that we wanted the real thing. Marilyn's parents got her a big, gray Appaloosa she named Blue, and, after much begging and expressly against my mother's wishes, Daddy bought me a beautiful buckskin Indian pony I named Apache. From then on, no matter what the weather, the two of us spent our afternoons and weekends on Blue and Apache exploring the nearby mountain trails. We joined an equestrian drill team, got to ride in a Pikes Peak or Bust parade, and participated in gymkhanas, practicing relay and barrel racing. My passion for horses kept me sane through my preteen years. Whenever things got too intense at home, I could always jump on Apache and take off for the hills.

Thanks to Nyliram's influence, my favorite pastime became reading. I loved books—all kinds of books, but especially ones about animals. We spent as much time as we could at the city library, checking out the maximum number of books allowed and carting them home. *Charlotte's Web* and *Stuart Little* were favorites, and we were both especially obsessed with books about horses: *Black Beauty, Misty of Chincoteague, National Velvet*. When I wasn't riding, books were my salvation, my soother, my escape from reality.

My pink cat-eye glasses with the rhinestones on the corners helped make me an exceptionally homely kid. Throughout grade school, my mom sewed all my clothes using Butterick and McCall's patterns, keeping me in "jumpers" and pinafores with crinoline petticoats that stuck straight out from my skinny body. It didn't help that she forced me to have regular Toni home permanents so that my hair looked like a tight, frizzy ball of yarn. All that, combined with my scars, made me lovable to no one but Daddy.

Girls weren't allowed to wear pants to school in those days, making for a frigid hike through the snow in winter with bare legs. By the time

I reached school, my legs were red and chapped from the cold and I had to dig the icy slush out of the tops of my shoes and "anklets." I was sent home one particularly snowy day because I'd worn ski pants under my dress. It's the one time in my childhood I remember Mother standing up for me. She stormed into Ivywild and went crazy on the principal's ass. From then on I was allowed to wear pants to school under my dress, as long as I took them off when I arrived. Stretchy ski pants in bright primary colors with little stirrups to hold them down were all the rage at the time, so I felt not only warm, but fashionable.

Other than Nyliram, I didn't have many friends in grade school. I was actually put in the "smart" class along with her and Kathy Mitten, the school's genius nerd, which made me even more of a pariah. The two most popular girls, Jinda Norris and Alice Spencer, invited me to their "pajama parties" a few times, where I felt strange and out of place. But when they'd put on a record like *Leader of the Pack* or *Sugar Shack* and I danced the way I'd learned from watching *American Bandstand* with Jeannie, I could tell the girls were impressed.

I spent a lot of time during the summer break from grade school hanging out alone. Because my mother considered reading a waste of time, I had to find a hiding place to do it. I spent endless hours up in the big elm tree in our front yard, reading the Superman comics and *Mad* magazines I'd bought with my allowance. Sitting on my butt reading or drawing was grounds for a slap in the face or a yank of my hair. As far as Mother was concerned, if I wasn't cleaning something, I was a lazy bum.

On Saturday mornings my older cousin Danny took me to the movies. I'm not sure if he wanted company, or just felt sorry for me, but in any case, I couldn't wait to go!

I loved the British humor in *Carry On Sergeant, Carry On Nurse,* and *Carry On Teacher* from the film series that played at the more "artsy" Peak Theater downtown. I also adored any film starring Jerry Lewis, like *Cinderfella* and *The Nutty Professor*—the big blockbusters that the historic Chief Theater showed on weekends. But what I *really* craved were the scary movies.

I saw my first horror movie at the age of eight—William Castle's *House on Haunted Hill*. I was simultaneously fascinated and repelled by it. My favorite part was when a rat was dropped into a hole full of murky liquid and, moments later, floated to the top, nothing but a skeleton! I had horrible nightmares for weeks and woke up time after time in the middle of the night, screaming. I'm sure Danny's ass was royally kicked for exposing me to "that kind of trash." In any case, I couldn't wait to see more of the same: *House of Usher* followed, then *The Pit and the Pendulum*, and finally *The Tomb of Ligeia* in 1965—the last of the American International Pictures films directed by Roger Corman that were loosely based, and I mean *loosely*, on Edgar Allan Poe stories. They always starred the dark and sinister Vincent Price, who became my favorite antihero.

Suddenly, I couldn't get enough horror! I somehow got ahold of a copy of *Famous Monsters of Filmland* magazine—a publication edited by Forrest J. Ackerman (who coined the term "sci-fi" and would later become a pal). Late-night horror movies abounded on TV back then, conveniently timed to air after my parents had gone to bed. *The Twilight Zone* and, later, *The Outer Limits* became my TV-watching staples. I soon learned from the back pages of *Famous Monsters* that real, lifelike plastic model kits of my favorite Universal monsters were available from Aurora. I put Frankenstein, Dracula, and the Wolfman at the top of my Christmas wish list, and that ghoul-lovin' Santa delivered! While my sisters played with Barbie, Midge, and Ken, I spent hours lovingly assembling and painting my little monsters. Actually, I have no idea how much time I spent on them, probably because I was high from the glue and enamel-paint fumes.

Later on, TV series that combined monsters and witchcraft with humor, like *The Munsters*, *Bewitched*, and my favorite, *The Addams Family*, became my must-see TV. They obviously had a big impact on my developing personality.

As I mentioned, my parents were very industrious, and soon my mother ditched the babies and began working for Evelyn, the neighbor lady across the street, who ran a costume-rental shop out of her garage.

Evelyn was a mom, but she was nice, and her son Kree was one of the neighborhood kids I often played with. Once, they invited me over for dinner and Evelyn served artichokes, which were the weirdest things I'd ever seen! It might have been the first time I'd actually seen a vegetable that didn't come from a can. My mother was really big into convenience food.

Mother took a liking to the costume-rental business. With the money she'd made, she and Aunt Lorrayne, who was an exceptional seamstress, opened a costume shop in the little one-room "patio house" my dad had built in our backyard. After business picked up, they were able to afford bigger digs, renting an old house a few blocks away and opening Colorado Springs' largest costume shop, Peterson's Party Land.

Summer break seemed to drag into endless, lazy days until just like that, an electric charge filled the air and the weather changed overnight. Red and gold leaves drifted from the trees and the smell of logs burning in fireplaces wafted on the crisp breeze. Autumn had arrived—my favorite time of year. With it came the return to school, my birthday, and my family's busiest, most exciting time: Halloween. After school, Melody and I rushed to the costume shop, a block away from school, to help stuff chunks of foam rubber into tiger tails, tack fringe onto Roaring '20s "flappers," and hang freshly washed and ironed bats and devils back on the racks.

During the Halloween season I felt like the luckiest kid on Earth. My mom and aunt made costumes for me that were heads and tails above all the other kids' cheap polyester suits and cheesy dime-store masks. My obsession with dressing up in costumes began when my mother still worked with Evelyn at her shop across the street. When her son Kree and I were eight years old, our moms entered us in a costume contest in Manitou Park. He dressed as the gunslinger Maverick, from the popular TV show of the same name, and I dressed in heels, fishnet stockings, and a feather boa as Miss Kitty, the saloon girl from the show *Gunsmoke*. Inappropriate? Maybe. But we took first place and each won a one-hundred-dollar bond, which was the equivalent of about a million dollars back then. Best of all, I got my picture in the paper again. I was becoming a regular media whore!

AND IN THIS CORNER—Dude cowboys and a well dressed couple get together for a little formal posing before the party breaks up. The youngsters who won the Dude Cowboy division and the couple who won the Pairs division at the Kiddies Rodeo Dress Up Revue held Saturday at Acacia Park shone in all their glory as they faced the camera. The winners were (left to right) Christi Cook and John Moss, first place dude cowboy and cowgirl; Kree Saunders and Cassandra, best dressed pairs.
(Gazette Telegraph Photo)

Halloween took over as my new favorite holiday. As our ex–first lady so eloquently put it, "Who gives a fuck about Christmas?" And was there any reason I couldn't wear costumes all year round? I didn't think so. I wore them to stage elaborate shows for the neighborhood kids, to hang out around the house, and even to go to school. Unfortunately, wearing costumes at a Gestapo-run place like Ivywild, which didn't even allow girls to wear pants, didn't go over so well.

As I got older, my mother and aunt used me as a guinea pig to model their creations, making me costumes from whatever TV show was popular at the time: Jeannie from *I Dream of Jeannie,* Ellie from *The Beverly Hillbillies,* and, my favorite, Ginger from *Gilligan's Island.* I knew when I put on that skin-tight sequined gown and red bouffant wig, I was home!

Despite my scars, I'd never been shy about performing in front of people, which was odd considering I was especially shy and withdrawn in my everyday life. At just three or four years old, my mom and dad had me dancing on tables in restaurants, singing "Que Será, Será" or the big Patti Page hit, "(How Much Is That) Doggie in the Window." They scraped together the money to give me tap, ballet, and modern-jazz dance lessons from the time I was five.

At twelve years old, I saw Ann-Margret for the first time in the film *Bye Bye Birdie* and instantly identified with her in ways I was still too young to articulate.

Then, one warm spring afternoon...

I was sitting in the back seat of Mother's old baby-blue Ford Fairlane while she ran into Safeway to grab something for dinner. I lolled against the ultramarine cloth upholstery, listening to the car radio, the sun streaming through the windows and spilling across my bare legs. Barbara Mason's top-ten hit "Yes, I'm Ready" played on the radio. "Are you ready? Yes, I'm ready...for loooooove..."

I was feeling warm and drowsy. Every word she crooned sank deep into the recesses of my mind. Note by note, lyric by lyric, the whole sex-and-love thing clicked in my head like tumblers being dialed into place on my school locker. I got a tingly feeling all over my body, but especially "down there," and in that instant, I got it. I'm telling you it was a goddamn epiphany! The focus of my life changed in the three short minutes that song took to play. Suddenly, my life was all about boys. I was about to become a temptress.

At thirteen, I saw Ann-Margret for the second time, costarring in the movie *Viva Las Vegas* with Elvis Presley. As I sat in the dark theater staring at the screen and munching my popcorn, I suddenly stopped and drew in a breath. My eyes glazed over and time stood still. That was it. I wanted to be like Ann-Margret. I wanted to look like Ann-Margret. I wanted to *be* Ann-Margret. In the film, she plays a swim instructor (something that would have been a terrible job for me because I never learned to swim), but near the end of the film, she competes with Elvis in a talent show, and her hip-shaking, hair-whipping performance mesmerized me. I sat through that movie over and over until I'd memorized every line, every lyric to every song, and every move she made. There were also several glitzy musical numbers in the film, featuring glamorous Las Vegas showgirls, something that until that moment, I never knew existed. I dreamed about the movie at night. I daydreamed about the movie all day. My fantasies starred me in the Ann-Margret role and Elvis as my love interest.

Since my fifth birthday, when I'd gotten a portable record player and a forty-five single of "Hound Dog" from my dad, I'd been in love with Elvis and his music, even the less-than-stellar soundtracks to his schlocky movies, which I swooned over. I performed in the rec room for anyone I could force to watch. I played cuts from classic Elvis fare like "Little Egypt" from the film *Roustabout,* "Do the Clam" from *Girl Happy,* and best of all, the soundtrack from *Viva Las Vegas,* which would eventually play into my life in a big way. I wore my little black leotard and lip-synched for my life, long before RuPaul made it a thing. Later on, I'd sometimes wear a red turtleneck with three-quarter-length sleeves over black tights, just like Ann-Margret wore in the movie, and during school events inexplicably leap to my feet at a moment's notice to perform a sexy, improvisational dance, much to the delight of my male classmates.

The Beatles burst on the scene when I was in seventh grade, and their influence on me, and an entire generation, was staggering. They literally changed the way I saw the world, and I cannot overstate the profound impact they had on my life. I was exactly the right age to be hit by Beatlemania head on. I collected every picture of John, Paul, George, and Ringo I could find, saved every penny of my allowance for their singles and LPs, and caught them on every TV appearance they made. Each new Beatles album was a revelation!

Being the fickle girl I was, I threw Elvis over like an old, used dish-rag. When I heard the Beatles sing "I Want to Hold Your Hand" on *The Ed Sullivan Show*, it was like I'd been struck by lightning. Overnight my world became mod, gear, *fab!*

From that moment on, I ate, slept, and breathed the Beatles. The downside was that this spelled the end of my long friendship with Nyliram, because she *hated* them and said they looked like girls. That was it. I was forced to drop her like a hot potato and search out other like-minded Beatlemaniacs. I found them in the form of my new BFFs, Molly, Kathy, and Eileen. We talked in British accents like the Beatles, dressed in Beatle boots and hats, and screamed our heads off whenever one of their songs came on the radio. We went to the Chief Theater to see *A Hard Day's Night* at least a half dozen times and shrieked and sobbed our way through it until we lost our voices. When one of the Beatles' birthdays rolled around, we held a party, complete with candles and a Jiffy cake we whipped up ourselves. We put a lot of energy into hating the guts of Cynthia Lennon, John's wife, and Jane Asher, Paul's girlfriend, because we were so jealous. Although I loved *all* the Beatles, in the beginning my favorite was Ringo, but I quickly moved on to George, then to Paul for a while, and eventually settled on John, which never changed. I spent hours lying on my bed listening to him sing "I'm a Loser" and bawling my eyes out because I loved him so much and he wasn't mine. My room was papered floor to ceiling in Beatles posters, trading cards, and pictures cut from teen magazines. My cousin Jeannie, who was working as a hair stylist by this time, chopped off my long red locks at my insistence and gave me a Beatles haircut (something I immediately regretted).

Kathy, Molly, Eileen, and I were the only mods in South Junior High. We went to a school dance together and I spent weeks planning what to wear, finally deciding on a sheer, empire-waist, baby-doll minidress—white with black polka dots—along with a pair of black tights with *white* polka dots. Kathy painstakingly painted black dots on my white fingernails and I did a fab job of adding black and white patent leather Twiggy eyelashes to my lower lids. We all looked unbelievably gear! Boys still didn't ask us to dance, but we didn't care. The music they played there sucked anyway.

Suddenly one day I sprouted boobs. Not *just* boobs. Enormous boobs. When puberty finally struck, I developed faster than a Polaroid. In my mind at least, I remember going to bed flat as a board one night and waking up with ginormous breasts the next morning. It was like, whoa, dude—this is better than the tooth fairy!

To emphasize my newly sprouted bosom—which wasn't really necessary, but why not—I borrowed a Frederick's of Hollywood catalog from a neighbor girl's older sister and ordered a major push-up bra. The cleavage this little miracle invention created was insane. Each cup contained more foam rubber than a Tempur-Pedic mattress. It really made the boys in school, and more than a male teacher or two, sit up and take notice. This bra was one of the best things that ever happened to me and I ordered a couple more as backups. The only time it betrayed me came years later, on a trip to Las Vegas when I wore it under my bikini top in a swimming pool and it absorbed so much water I nearly drowned.

Almost overnight I'd gone from pariah to princess, at least in my mind. I lost the glasses, refused the Toni perms, and began picking out my own clothes from seventh grade on. For my thirteenth birthday, Grandma and Grandpa Schmidt took me shopping at The Fashion Bar, Colorado Springs' ritziest store, and bought me a wardrobe of clothes that made me look like I'd just come from Carnaby Street—lots of burgundies with pink trim and brown velvet with tiny English flowers and lace. I still can't imagine how my grandparents came up with that kind of money! They lived in a house the size of a train car and their only income was their Social Security checks. But it was one of the best, most game-changing gifts I'd ever received, and I was so thankful to them. For the first time in my life, I could finally look the way I felt.

I now ironed my hair to make it stick straight and wore the shortest miniskirts and tightest, lowest-cut tops I could lay my hands on. I'd gone from being overly sensitive about my body because of the scars to showing off as much of my "good" skin as possible. It was a lucky thing that I'd grown as tall as I had, and that such an accomplished surgeon had done my skin grafting. No longer the angry red and purple raised scars from my childhood; the color had faded and the skin had smoothed out. I globbed on makeup (yay Pan Stik!) and wore my hair long to cover the worst of it, developing a lifelong habit of pulling my red locks forward to make sure the scars on my neck were covered. Hosiery did the job of hiding the scars on my thighs where the skin had been removed.

At one point, a modified "Ginger" became one of my signature looks and went over very big at South Junior High. With the boys, any-way. I wasn't allowed to wear the sparkly gown, but I did get away with the flaming-red bouffant wig (flipped up on one side and rolled under on the other). I was sent home on quite a few occasions when the girls' counselor, Mrs. Dean, deemed my skirt too short or my neckline too low.

Around this time the mutual lovefest between Daddy and me came to a screeching halt. One day I ran over to him and jumped into his lap, and much to my surprise, he gave me a rough shove and growled, "Get off me." I was shocked and surprised. "You're too old for that kind of thing now," was his only explanation. I had no idea what he meant, and was left crushed and confused. I'd always been Daddy's little girl, his fishing buddy, his dance partner, his best friend. What had changed?

CHAPTER 4

THE VIRGIN GROUPIE

My teenage years were upon me. When I turned thirteen and the hormones kicked in, my horror collection went into deep storage, replaced by photos, records, and memorabilia of musicians. My monster friends were gone for now, but not forgotten.

The white French provincial canopy bed with the pink dotted Swiss bedspread was replaced by a mattress tucked into a corner on my bedroom floor and covered with a shiny, black, fake panther fur bedspread. Despite my parents' protests, I painted the cinder-block walls of my basement bedroom pitch black (only to discover that black walls attract every spider and salamander within a ten-mile radius). I was now steeped in black to match my mood.

Kathy, Molly, Eileen, and I were boy crazy, music crazy, and band crazy. We dressed in leather fringe jackets, fur vests, army jackets, and navy peacoats and went to see every band that came to the City Auditorium. Surprisingly, some pretty great musicians came through town. The first real "name act" that I got to see was Brian Hyland of "Itsy Bitsy Teenie Weenie Yellow Polka-dot Bikini" fame. I got his autograph after the show and thought I was going to faint. I also got to see the singing duo of Peter and Gordon. They were the first real English people I'd ever seen, and even more amazing, Peter's sister was model Jane Asher, Paul McCartney's girlfriend, which was beyond fab even though I still hated her. That night I clung onto the front of the stage, so close I could almost touch the pointed toe of Gordon's Beatle boot. One of my most memorable moments was when Peter inadvertently spit on me while he was singing. I refused to ever wash my face again until my mother threatened to beat the crap out of me if I didn't. I went to see Wilson Pickett, Strawberry Alarm Clock, Mitch Ryder and the Detroit Wheels, Shirley Ellis of "The Name Game" fame, Buffalo Springfield, The Yardbirds, The Young Rascals, Stevie "Guitar" Miller, Love, and The Crazy World of Arthur Brown, to name just a few. I collected their autographs, drumsticks, guitar picks, and sometimes their kisses. My mother tossed most of my treasures in the trash when my parents sold my childhood home, but I'll always have the memories safely tucked away in my mind.

I quickly went from stalking bands in the backstage area of the "City Aud" to tracking them down in their hotel rooms after the show. One of my first experiences at being a junior groupie was with one of my all-time favorite bands, the Yardbirds. Keith Relf, Jim McCarty, Chris Deja, and Jimmy Page, who had recently replaced their former guitarist Jeff Beck (and before that, Eric Clapton), were known as one of the most impressive guitar bands in rock music. Jimmy Page would later go on to form the group Led Zeppelin. (Perhaps you've heard of them?)

On the day the Yardbirds were scheduled to play the City Aud, my best friend, Kathy Hall, and I did a little reconnaissance work after school. We went downtown and walked from hotel to hotel—literally, that was it, two hotels—to see if we could find out where the band was staying. We hit pay dirt when we happened to see a couple of roadies moving equipment through the lobby of the newly renovated Antlers Hotel. Kathy and I sprang into action. I called my Aunt Luci, who had often been an ally of mine in the ongoing battle against my mother, and pleaded with her to help us meet the band. Unfortunately, that day we were wearing dorky-looking school clothes but didn't dare stop at home to change for fear of running into one of our moms, so we convinced my aunt to pick us up and take us to her house where she loaned us each something to wear. Her clothes weren't exactly "happening," but we figured out a way to make them work. I wore her tightest and lowest-cut sweater, naturally, and a straight skirt that I rolled up around my waist about a thousand times to create a mini. We piled on as much makeup as we could scavenge from my aunt's limited Avon collection, then she drove us back to the Antlers. While Aunt Luci waited in the lobby, we methodically combed the hotel corridors, floor by floor, looking and listening for signs of famousness and finally detecting the faint sound of rock music coming from one of the rooms. We put our ears to the door and listened. It was definitely them. Jubilant but scared shitless, we knocked on the door. After a moment, it swung open and there was the incredibly gorgeous, shaggy blond-headed lead singer himself, Keith Relf! Behind him on the bed sat Jim McCarty, the drummer, and rhythm guitarist Chris Deja. I was thunderstruck! "Uhhhh, could we get your autograph?" I managed to squeak out. Clearly pleased, Keith turned to the other guys and said, "Look! A couple of birds! Come on in, girls." Keith returned to the table where he'd been in the midst of creating a psychedelic picture with colored markers. I looked on as Keith continued to draw, while Kathy somehow ended up in the bathroom shampooing the drummer's hair in the sink. Keith later signed the drawing for me, which I stuffed into my purse and still have to this day. Suddenly, the door flew open and in stalked lead guitarist Jimmy Page. Without saying a word, he grabbed me by the hand and whisked me out the door and down the hall to his room. No sooner had his door slammed shut than he was on top of me, kissing and tugging at my aunt's sweater while simultaneously unzipping his fly. Strangely, my main concern was that Luci's sweater would get stretched out. It was my first experience touching a penis and all I remember thinking is that it felt like a long, skinny worm. (Sorry, Jimmy.) To think I was actually there, lying on the bed making out with *the* Jimmy Page from the Yardbirds was thrilling for about two minutes, but then reality struck. I was still a virgin and my aunt was waiting in the lobby right downstairs. What a buzzkill! I suddenly panicked. I snatched my hand off his wang and flew off the bed, grabbing Aunt Luci's sweater from the floor in the process. I ran to the door and threw it open. "I'm a fucking virgin!" I screamed at Jimmy, which didn't make a lot of sense, but I must have thought it sounded good at the time. Whipping around with a dramatic flourish, I ran into the hallway—straight into a group of surprised businessmen waiting for the elevator. Wearing only my skirt and bra, I tried to act as nonchalant as possible, while I scurried down the hallway, pull-ing my Aunt's stretched-out pink and green sweater over my head. Once I got to the room where I'd left Kathy, I discovered she'd been left alone with Jim McCarty and was almost as disheveled as I was. I was franticly worrying that we'd been gone too long, and terrified my aunt was down-stairs freaking out.

Even though Kathy and I were a mess, with red, razor-burned faces and ratty, tangled hair, my aunt didn't lose it. I don't know whether she'd had a couple of cocktails while she was waiting or was just unaccus-tomed to dealing with teenaged girls, but other than a gentle scolding because we'd been gone so long, she was cool. In the end, Kathy and I escaped being raped and/or murdered by strange rock gods, and had a really good time.

This was the beginning of my junior groupie escapades. Oh *God* how I loved bands! Any time a band would come to town, I was there. When I heard music playing live, right before my eyes, I went into an altered state of consciousness. My favorite band's lyrics spoke to me more powerfully than any parent or teacher ever could. They helped me figure out who I was, what I was feeling, and, possibly, where I was headed.

Another close call came when, at fifteen, I went to see the band Eric Burdon and the New Animals. The original band, the Animals, whose bluesy English beat I'd worshipped, had evolved into a more psyche-delic version, with songs like "San Francisco Nights" and "Monterey." I managed to talk my way backstage, as usual. The dressing room was strangely quiet for after a gig, and I could feel the tension in the air. The roadies and the slightly sullen band members packed up their stuff while a very stoned or drunk Eric Burdon sat in a corner alone. Without bothering to say hello, he asked if I'd give him a lift back to the Holiday Inn. I had a learner's permit and the keys to my mother's yellow Impala, so how'm I s'posed to say no to that? He's Eric Burdon for Chrissake! All the way back to the hotel he ranted and raved about what a horrible gig it had been and wondered aloud why the fuck he was playing such a shithole. All the while he brandished an open bottle of Wild Turkey, intermittently taking swigs. I smiled and nodded my head, doing my best to keep my eyes on the road, but he was really starting to freak me out. Once parked in front of his room, he grabbed hold of me and we had a brief, rough make-out session before he commanded, "Come up to my room." Despite my excuses, he was adamant, physically pulling me by the hand, until, against what little good judgment I possessed, I followed him up the stairs. The door slammed shut behind us, and he was on me like a fly on caca-doodoo! When the opportunity presented itself, I turned and bolted for the door with the crazed little hobbit on my tail. But before he could grab me, I was out the door and down the stairs. Heaving a sigh of relief, I dug frantically through the junk pile I called my purse when a sudden realization hit me. I'd left my car keys in his room! Scared and embarrassed, I trudged back up the stairs to his door. "Hello?" I called, giving a timid knock. "Would my keys happen to be in there?" He threw open the door, and there he stood in the door-frame, shirtless and smirking, dangling my car keys from his stubby lit-tle finger. Before I could snatch them, he tugged on his waistband, and down went the keys, disappearing into the dark recesses of his jeans. He glared at me with bloodshot eyes. "Come 'n' get 'em," he growled. At this point, I was much more worried about what might befall me if I didn't get my mother's car back to her on time than what he would do to me. "Give me my keys or I'll, I'll..." I thrust my open palm toward him. "You'll *what?*" he sneered. Beads of sweat popped out on my upper lip and my mind raced. "I'll...call the police!" He didn't budge an inch. "Go right ahead," he slurred. I took a deep breath and, with every ounce of bravado I could muster, screamed at the top of my lungs, "Help! Police! Hellllppp!" In a flash, doors along the balcony flew open and heads popped out. "He stole my car!" I shrieked, jabbing a finger in his direction. No sooner had the words left my mouth when the keys flew over my head, skidded off the balcony railing, and landed on the asphalt below. I still get the creeps whenever I hear "House of the Rising Sun."

Together with my sister or another cohort, I climbed in the second-story window of Buffalo Springfield's dressing room, ambushed Steve Miller on his way to a hotel, made out with Dino Danelli from the Young

Rascals in a dark stairwell, had a romantic but sexless sleepover with the drummer of Mitch Ryder and the Detroit Wheels, squeezed myself into an empty trunk in the back of Paul Revere and the Raiders' tour bus, and generally practiced for the big-time world of becoming a *real* groupie. Come to think of it, I'm not sure the term "groupie" had even been invented yet. I just knew I loved music and the guys who played it, and if I couldn't *be* a rock star (which almost no girls were in those days), I'd be the next best thing: *with* a rock star.

CHAPTER 5

LIFE-A-GO-GO

By the time I was fourteen, I was frequenting a nightclub for under-twenty-ones called Hullabaloo. Whether it actually had anything to do with the popular TV show of the same name, as its sign proclaimed, was doubtful, but in any case, it gave it a little credibility. When I heard they were staging a go-go-girl contest, I was all over it. I *loved* to dance. Always have. Still do. When the music's playing, I'm in my element.

Coincidentally I just happened to have a Roaring '20s flapper costume, a short, sleeveless, shocking-pink and black fringy dress that my mom and Aunt Lorrayne made me one Halloween. All I needed was a pair of shiny, white vinyl go-go boots, which I coerced my parents into buying, and I was the spitting image of the girls on TV. Or at least, *I* thought so. The contest dragged on over three long weekends of elimination trials, much like *American Idol* only much lower-rent. When I made it through to the finals, I was in heaven!

I ended up coming in second to an older girl named Betty who smiled all the time and wore a white, fringed, *two*-piece outfit that showed her bare midriff. Unfair competition. She got a whole new wardrobe from JCPenney and I got to ride with her in the back of a convertible in a parade down the main street of town. You can tell I'm still bitter because I remember the details like it was yesterday.

Oh, did I mention that one of the perks from winning second place in the Hullabaloo Go-Go Girl contest was that I got a gig dancing at a local nightclub in downtown Colorado Springs called Club A-Go-Go? That's right, by day I was a mild-mannered junior high school student

38

and by night I was shaking my ass in a glass cage. After a little begging and pleading, my mom and aunt whipped me up a few outfits. Because Betty won first place wearing her miniskirt and midriff top, it didn't take a genius to figure out that less equaled more, so my new costumes were basically bikinis covered in fringe. My favorite was my old standby, a Frederick's push-up bra adorned with alternating rows of short, lime green and hot pink fringe that glowed fluorescent under black light. My white-fringe bikini trimmed in marabou was pretty sassy, too. The nightly showstopper was the song "Wipe Out" by the Surfaris because the audience loved to see my fluorescent bra seemingly take on a life of its own, gyrating wildly under black lights to a three-minute drum solo.

The other girls working there were quite a bit older. Of course, *Betty*, who was nineteen, also got a gig there. Ugh. But there was another nineteen-year-old dancer, Cindy, who I immediately anointed my new best friend. I have no idea how all these underage girls were allowed to work at a twenty-one-and-older bar, but hey, it was the '60s and strange shit happened. Older dancers worked there, too, of course. One girl was pushing thirty—practically my mom's age! Each girl alternated sets of five or six songs, and when I wasn't up, I retired to our closet-size dressing room to do my homework. While the other girls came and went, stepping over me to change out of their sweaty costumes, I spread my school books and papers out on the sticky carpet and enjoyed a cigarette and my beverage of choice, a White Russian, which I figured was pretty healthy as drinks go because other than Kahlúa and vodka, it contained mostly milk.

While working there, I was fortunate to catch the act of a traveling burlesque dancer named Tracy Summers, who did a short stint at the club. She was a petite, bleached-blonde bombshell in her twenties and she could do something that made her the new star of Club A-Go-Go: twirl tassels. I'd never seen or even imagined anything like it before! Over her nipples, she wore glittery pasties with long, fringed tassels attached, which she could spin to the right, to the left, inward, outward, and even while doing a backbend. I was absolutely stunned! From the positive feedback she received from the club's owner, Tony Paris, and the patrons, I instantly knew it was something I had to learn. Believe it or not, I talked Mother and Aunt Lorrayne into making my first tassel-twirling bra from an old maroon swimsuit top of mine that they dyed black and trimmed with rhinestones. (Just in case you're thinking they were too lenient, they drew the line at letting me wear pasties.) Our bra design formed a star over each breast with little areas of nude mesh fabric in between that allowed tiny triangles of flesh to peek through. Rhinestone pasties were glued to the center of each star, from which silver beaded tassels dangled. These weren't just any old tassels. Tracy taught me all the basics: each one had to be just the right length and thickness. Fishing swivels were used to attach the tassels to the pasties and then were weighted with lead fishing weights, all of which I conveniently found in my dad's tackle box. I practiced in front of a mirror every day after school, and in no time, I was ready to show off my new skills at the club. It was a hit!

Going to school was hard enough as it was, but staying up till 2:00 a.m. every morning and then having to leave for school by 7:30 a.m. was damn near impossible. At this point, I didn't have a driver's license, so my dad had to pick me up after work every night at 1:45 a.m. and take me to school in the morning—a lot of work on Daddy's part for which I'm sure I wasn't grateful. I spent the next three years sleep-walking through school. My grades, which had actually been pretty good up until eighth grade, took a nosedive. With the exception of music and art, I lost all interest in school. I'd previously tried out a few short-lived after-school jobs—delivering papers, cleaning motel rooms, and bussing tables—all of which *sucked*, so compared to those jobs, go-go dancing was a dream!

Cindy was the first person I'd ever met from the East Coast and, to me, she was cosmopolitan and exotic, with her New York accent, big Jew-fro, and slight resemblance to Barbra Streisand. She'd driven out to Colorado on her own in her beat-up old Plymouth (which we would later spray-paint Day-Glo orange and cover with psychedelic daisy decals) and was headed to California in search of the hippie lifestyle. When her money ran out halfway across the country in Colorado Springs, she was forced to stop and get a job. Soon, I was spending more time at her apartment than at my family's home.

How could my parents allow me to do this when I was only fourteen, you ask? I know. It's hard to believe. But they really didn't have a say in the matter. By this time, I was out of control. I didn't listen to a thing they said or do a thing they asked. I was a hormonally charged, know-it-all, rebellious teenager—every parent's worst nightmare. They were both working feverishly toward their goal of having the American dream and really didn't have much time to deal with me and my sisters anyway.

Not long before my fifteenth birthday, I'd finally had enough of my mother's shit. During one of our ferocious daily arguments, she called me a whore and slapped me across the face. For the first time, I backhanded her right back, knocking her to the floor and breaking her glasses. That was the last time she ever laid a hand on me. It didn't stop the verbal and emotional abuse, but it was a start.

On and off I crashed at either Cindy's apartment or other friends' places, but sooner or later they'd get fed up with my overly dramatic, emotional teenage highs and lows, decide they were too young to raise a child, and send me packing back to my parents' house. Eventually, however, I was making good money and could afford a one-bedroom apartment in one of the newest and most modern buildings in Colorado Springs, the Satellite Towers. I shared it with fellow go-go dancer Sue Ousley, who was eighteen—old enough to sign the rental agreement, but young enough to put up with my bullshit. She told everyone she was related to underground LSD chemist Stanley Owsley, but I had a sneaking suspicion she was making that up, especially because their names were spelled differently. Psychedelic posters of Big Brother and the Holding Company, The Doors, and Jefferson Airplane glowed from the walls under a black light, and their music blasted from our hi-fi speakers day and night.

Over the years, my parents lured me back home for short periods, but it always ended in a screaming fight and me slamming the door on my way out. Using threats, punishment, and the occasional monetary reward, they somehow managed to keep me in school until I graduated. There was never any talk of college in my house, however. No mention of what I might do with my life. With the exception of Aunt Lorrayne and my cousin Vern Ray, no one in our family had ever gone further than high school. It just wasn't something they deemed necessary. For a while, my art teacher, Mr. Samuelson, encouraged me to attend college to study art, but those aspirations lasted about five minutes. When I mentioned it to my parents, my mother just laughed. "Are you kidding? Where would we get the money to send you to some fancy school? You're not that good at drawing, anyway."

After our stint at Club A-Go-Go, Cindy and I landed jobs dancing at the Fort Carson Army base. This was back in the day when the Army supplied go-go girls to the EM (enlisted men) and officers' clubs. Your tax dollars at work. It was a lot farther to drive because it was outside of town, but our gigs started at 5:00 p.m. and ended at 10:00 p.m., which made it much easier to get to school the next day, and the pay was better—nothing like working for the Federal government!

I vividly remember my first night dancing at the base at an NCO club (noncommissioned officer). The room looked like a small school gymnasium with a raised, inset stage designed more for military speeches than go-go girls. Bookended by the American flag and the Colorado state flag, I danced my little heart out to Sam and Dave's "Soul Man." The audience of young soldiers went wild, whistling, cheering, and actually throwing money on stage. Now *this* was something I could get used to!

It was fun performing for the GIs, or "doggies," as we referred to them. (I have no idea where *that* came from—maybe "dog tags"?) They were mostly around eighteen or nineteen years old, which was a nice switch from the old geezers at Club A-Go-Go, and they were generally sweet and respectful. It was 1966 and most of them were soon to be deployed to Vietnam. Confined to the base and under strict supervision before they were shipped out, probably because the Army worried they'd bolt, coming to these clubs was one of their only forms of entertainment. They dubbed me "Big Red" and, boy, did they love me! I mean, what's not to love about a fifteen-year-old girl with long, red hair and big boobs wearing a skimpy outfit?

I was never interested in any of them as boyfriend material, partly because I'd be fired for any hanky-panky, but also because I only liked guys with long hair, and these poor suckers were practically bald. Between sets I had lots of heavy conversations with the guys. Away from home for the first time, they were usually feeling sad and lonely and were scared to death of going to Vietnam. Who could blame them? It was heartbreaking to hear their stories, even though they were the enemy of peaceniks like me. There was always one GI in the crowd with too much testosterone, who was gung ho about "fighting the gooks," but being antiwar and antiracism, I stayed as far away from them as I could get. For others, I became a teenage "therapist," listening while they poured out their hopes and fears. But no sooner would I strike up a friendship with a GI then he'd be shipped out and I'd never see him again. I can't remember their names, but I remember lots of faces, and to this day, still wonder sometimes whether they ever made it home.

I considered myself a hippie and was very much against the war in Vietnam, so working at the base and talking to GIs was pretty hypocritical. I attended "love-ins" and "pic-IN-iks" in Acacia Park across the street from my school, Palmer High. Local bands played and we all smoked pot (that's "weed" for you younger readers) until the cops showed up, then we scattered like cockroaches when the lights came on. But we believed we were somehow making a difference.

Even though I wasn't staying at my family's home much of the time, I couldn't turn down my mom and dad's invitation to go to California for summer vacation. This time, we went to San Francisco. Once there, Melody and I were allowed to wander around the Haight-Ashbury district in its heyday, probably not the best idea, while my dad went looking for my druggie cousin Gerry so he could slap some sense into her. I came back to the Springs two weeks later with some amazing brown velvet hip-hugger bell-bottoms, tan wide-wale cords, a psychedelic paisley print glow-in-the dark micro-mini dress, and a lid of wicked pot. That was when I became popular with the other local hippies. No one in my group had ever ventured as far away as the exotic fantasyland known as The Golden State, and they were all jealous. I was a *real* hippie now.

You couldn't live the hippie lifestyle without drugs. I began cutting class to smoke pot in the park with my friends, who were either dropouts or long past high school age. At night we hung out at Kelker Junction, a hot new club on the outskirts of town that became our one-stop shop for live bands, light shows, head shop, and psychedelic body painting. It wasn't long before I was wearing a Day-Glo minidress and matching body paint, and rockin' out on a tall pedestal next to the stage. Lots of regional bands came through there, including my favorite, The Frantics, whose lead singer I had a massive crush on. I remember dancing one night on my little platform alongside an English band I'd never heard of. I wasn't all *that* wild about their music, except for a couple of tunes, but they *were* English, so that made up for it. During their closing song, the lead guitarist suddenly went berserk, picked up his electric guitar, and smashed the shit out of it on the stage, causing sparks and debris to fly everywhere. To avoid being set on fire, I took a flying leap from my lofty perch and twisted my ankle when I hit the floor. It pissed me off so much that I didn't even want to meet them afterward. It turned out to be The Who on their first US tour. The cover charge for the evening was a whopping three dollars. Man, they must have *really* been desperate!

I smoked a lot of pot, mainly to fit in, because it only made me sleepy, hungry, and paranoid. My older friends coerced me into trying various new drugs we'd heard about: magic mushrooms, opium, and, of course, LSD. In general, I had less than mind-blowing experiences each time. All I remember about eating mushrooms and taking mescaline was getting sick and barfing my head off in the parking lot of Kelker Junction. The one time I smoked opium, I spent four hours straight staring at the aquarium in my parents' kitchen as the fish acted out various roles in a dramatic soap-opera-style production. When my mother and father got home and saw I was still sitting in the same spot at the kitchen table as when they'd left, and no homework was done, Mother grabbed me by the hair and shoved me down the basement stairs, which was extra unpleasant when you're high on opium.

I'd previously tried teensy amounts of LSD, or "acid," as we called it—licking a little blotter paper—and experienced a slight magnification of lights and music at concerts. But this time, Cindy and another friend, Sheri, decided we should all drop acid together at Kelker Junction. We pooled our money and bought some from a guy we trusted. I got a small, flat, black piece called "windowpane," about the size of a postage stamp, with little indentations dividing it into six pieces. No one mentioned that I was supposed to break off and swallow just *one* of the sections. I popped the whole thing in my mouth and, before Cindy and Sheri could stop me, swallowed it. They were pissed, and I was scared shitless. I wandered around the club alone for a while, watching the light show and listening to the band play. The music became louder and the drumbeat seemed to be coming from inside my chest. The light show got more and more intense, with psychedelic colors taking on a life of their own.

The next thing I remember was Sheri's voice screeching, "Soni! Soni! Get up, you dumbass!" I'd apparently gone out the back of the club, which was in an industrial park, and stretched out on the railroad tracks to watch the light show, which had moved from the stage to the inside of my eyelids.

Sheri, who had gotten ahold of more acid, was also tripping, but managed to load me into her car. She definitely wasn't as stoned as I was or she would have realized the car was no longer solid—just a huge, gelatinous glob of multicolored goo. Miraculously, the goo-mobile got us safely to my parents' house, which was the *last* place on Earth I wanted to be in my state. I literally didn't know which way was up much less how I was going to get through the house and downstairs to my room undetected. But Sheri didn't give me time to panic. Ignoring my pleas to let me come home with her, she reached across and shoved open the passenger door. "Get the hell out, Soni!" she shrieked." You're bumming me out!"

I suddenly found myself standing on the lawn in front of my family's house, lights and colors swirling around me. It didn't seem to make any difference whether my eyes were open or shut; the vibrant, pulsating colors wouldn't stop. I tried curling up and sleeping on the lawn, but the limbs of our big elm tree kept trying to grab me, so I made the risky decision to go inside. I'll never know how I got past my dad, who always unlocked the door and let me in at night. Maybe he'd had a few more beers than usual? In any case, I made it to my bedroom in the basement unscathed. Once there, I curled up on my bed, shivering and shaking while weird shit happened all around me. I just wanted someone, *anyone*, to be there with me and make it stop! All of a sudden, my little black poodle, Gigi, appeared, happy to see I was home. I was so relieved that I picked her up and hugged her to me like a drowning man clings to a life preserver. In the midst of crying tears of joy, I glanced down and noticed that Gigi had no head—just a butt on both ends! I threw the grotesque creature off and crouched in a corner to hide from it.

Next, it dawned on me that I was in a basement, underground. But not just a basement, *a crypt*! I ran to look in the mirror of my black vanity table from Sears and confirmed my worst suspicions. *I was dead!* Clumps of hair fell from my scalp, maggots wriggled in and out of my nose and empty eye sockets, rotting patches of skin slid from my face. Despite the risk of being discovered by my parents, I found myself half running, half crawling up the undulating stairway toward Melody and Robin's room. Once there, I grabbed onto Mel and shook her awake. "Melody, please, please help me!" I begged in a frantic whisper. "I dropped acid and I'm freaking out!" She rolled over and looked at me like I was crazy. "Shut the fuck up or I'll tell Mommy and Daddy!" I lay next to her, afraid to even breathe, *praying* it would end. Time passed—slowly, slowly, slooooowly. At last, I saw a glimmer of light peek through the window. "Oh, thank you Jesus, thank you! It's over!" I sobbed under my breath. Colors had lost some of their intensity and the noise they made sounded less like a freight train roaring through the center of the house. Just as I was breathing a big sigh of relief, I noticed the little surfer dudes and tiny beach bunnies on Melody's turquoise and purple beach-themed wallpaper were fucking the shit out of each other, wriggling and writhing and moaning like crazed miniature heathens. Being a virgin and all, it was terrifying to me. It felt like I was a child who'd accidentally walked in on my parents "doing it." The hundreds of tiny fornicating figures continued to go at it until I was forced to flee and, reluctantly, head back to my basement mausoleum. Once there, I pulled my fake-fur bedspread over my head, and for what seemed like days later, finally drifted into a deep, exhausted sleep. I woke up in the late afternoon to the familiar sound of my mother screaming at me to get my lazy butt out of bed, and for the first time, her voice sounded like heaven.

But my long, strange trip didn't end there. A week or so later, in the middle of a school volleyball game, it began to snow. I came to a dead halt, standing there in my little blue gym suit with arms outstretched, catching fluffy white snowflakes on the tip of my tongue. "It's snowing! It's snowing!" I shouted with glee. The only problem was that we were inside the gym and the roof was still intact. That not only completely freaked me out but landed me in the principal's office for disruptive behavior. Of course, she called my parents, who threatened to put me in a mental institution, but later dropped the idea after finding out it would cost too much money.

I've often wondered how much that trip changed my personal perspective on life. Despite being a horrible experience, had it "expanded my consciousness"? Contributed to my worldview? I'd like to try LSD again someday, only under better, safer circumstances. Maybe for my next birthday, like John Waters did for his seventieth.

One night, on my way home from Fort Carson, I stopped off at a club called The Purple Cow that I'd passed a million times. I was shocked and amazed by what I found. There, dressed in sparkling rhinestones and miles of gold lamé, were the most glamorous creatures I'd ever seen outside of the movies. And they were so...*big*! It took some time, but I finally realized they were *men* dressed in sexy women's clothing. I'd never heard about, let alone seen, anything like it before. Of course, I became a regular, stopping in after work at the base every night to watch them impersonate stars like Diana Ross, Judy Garland, and Barbra

Streisand. They didn't actually sing, but mouthed the words to songs, just like I was so fond of doing as a youngster. I wondered, could you really make a living doing that?

Soon, I struck up a conversation with the person who seemed to be the star of the show, a very tall, thin Black man named Tawny Tann. He introduced me to the other performers, Stephan and Mr. Bobbie (who sometimes played the role of "the man," if they happened to be lip-synching to, say, Peaches and Herb). For some reason, maybe so there would be some entertainment for the occasional straight GI who accidentally wandered in, they decided I would make a great addition to the lineup, and invited me to go-go-dance there on weekends. Mr. Bobbie rigged up a three-foot-by-three-foot cube, which was strategically placed in the middle of the room and surrounded by cocktail tables. After my gigs at Fort Carson, I finished up the night at the Purple Cow to make a few extra bucks. Not long after I started working there, Stephan went MIA one night and I was pressed into service. In a last-minute frenzy, Tawny pinned me into a glitzy gown, smeared some white lipstick on my mouth, and stuck an Afro wig on my head. Under the glow of a black light, I was transformed into Flo from the Supremes, while we lip-synched our hearts out to "Stop! In the Name of Love." Yes, dear gay reader—I was a teenage drag queen!

The fabulous Tawny Tann took me under her sequined wing and gave me tips on how to do my hair and makeup, and how to choose fashion accessories that would make the most of what I had. In turn, I introduced her to Peterson's Partyland. My mother and aunt, who were at first dumbfounded when I brought a six-foot-two, bald, Black man to their shop to try on dresses, eventually fell in love with him just like I had. He was funny, kind, and sassy and had them both wrapped around his bejeweled pinky in no time. Before I knew what was happening, they were sewing Tawny, Bobbie, and Stephan new ensembles. As a thank you, Tawny gave me one of her old gowns—a sexy, skin-tight, floor-length, leopard-print dress with gobs of black nylon netting jutting out of the back to form a train—and Aunt Lorrayne overhauled the enormous dress to fit me.

That leopard gown gave me the jolt of confidence I needed, and I soon took it, and my newly acquired beauty tips, to the hottest club in town, a strip joint called The Body Shoppe. (The extra "pe" apparently set it apart from the place you got the dents in your car fixed.) A tough gangster type named Andy DeJesus (pronounced with a hard "J" just like Our Lord and Savior) owned the club, and I gave him my best pitch, pleading with him to let me do a "new" kind of act, since I was too young to strip. I promised it would be something he'd never seen before, and I delivered. I figured if a fabulous drag performance worked at the Purple Cow, why not at The Body Shoppe? For the audience's listening plea-sure, I chose various cuts from the soundtrack of the film *Sweet Char-ity*, which I'd recently seen and fallen in love with. As the music blared, I swirled and whirled around the stage, whipping my nylon-net train into a frenzy and lip-synching to my tracks, just like I'd seen the "big girls" do. I performed such strip-club show-tune favorites as "Hey Big Spender," "If My Friends Could See Me Now," and a song I really took to heart, "There's Got to Be Something Better Than This," in which the "dime a dance" girls in the film bemoaned the "groping, grabbing" jok-ers they were forced to put up with nightly.

But alas, the all-male audience watching my act was so busy yelling "Take it off!" that I doubt they even heard the lyrics. What can I say? I did my best to bring some culture to that straight, trench-coat-wearing crowd, but obviously failed. After the first week, I was canned.

In 1968, with money I'd saved from dancing, I shocked my friends, family, and teachers by signing up for a school-sponsored, three-week art-history course that would take place in Europe. Frankly, I didn't care if we were studying astrobiology; I just saw it as my ticket to merry olde England! For years, I'd schemed, planned, and saved for some way to get over to the Beatles' country of origin. Now the opportunity I'd been wait-ing for was here! The other students on the trip were all "soshes" (short for "socials")—kids I wouldn't have looked at twice if they'd passed me in the halls at school, and vice versa—but that didn't deter me. At least I liked Miss Sullivan, the student art teacher who was accompanying the group. Although she could be a bit of a prude, she was in her twenties and I felt more in tune with her than any of the kids on the trip. Under the guise of helpful advice, she once pointed out that my boobs were too high. She demonstrated where they were supposed to be by bending her arm at a right angle, and laying her forearm across her diaphragm. Who knew that all this time my boobs had been up around my neck? Miss Sullivan would be happy to know that some fifty years later, they've finally arrived at the place where she thought they should be.

We took a whirlwind bus, boat, and train tour of five countries in three weeks: Greece, Yugoslavia, France, and Italy, ending in the United Kingdom. We visited what seemed like every church, cathedral, and museum in Europe and ate food that didn't come from a can or an aluminum tray. The spaghetti alone would have made Chef Boyardee die of shame. We ate silky, icy gelato (*gelato!*) while basking in the afternoon sun at the Trevi Fountain in Rome; rode donkeys up the craggy, cobbled footpaths of Mykonos; and chatted with teens with strange-sounding accents from Scotland, Ireland, and Sweden, while lazing on the steps of Trafalgar Square in London. Touring through Europe turned out to be the second-most eye-opening, mind-expanding trip of my life after dropping acid. To quote St. Augustine (whoever *he* is), "The world is a book, and those who do not travel read only one page."

Upon returning home, I'm a little ashamed to say that I didn't remember a thing about art history. But I did remember the sounds, sights, smells, tastes, and, most of all, the men of Europe. I felt like I'd been sleepwalking my whole life and had just woken up. I vowed then and there to return at my first opportunity.

CHAPTER 6

ARE YOU EXPERIENCED?

My groupie days peaked with the advent of the Denver Pop Festival in June of 1969, right after my high school graduation. The precursor to Woodstock was held in Denver's Mile High Stadium. The three-day-long festival's lineup included Joe Cocker, Iron Butterfly, Three Dog Night, Frank Zappa and the Mothers of Invention, Creedence Clearwater Revival, Johnny Winter, and Tim Buckley, to name a few. But most importantly, Jimi Hendrix.

Cindy and I bought tickets for all three days the minute they went on sale. The tickets were six dollars a day or fifteen dollars for the whole festival. Can you imagine that? You can't even get a *beer* for six dollars at a concert today.

We had our strategy planned far in advance, and our wardrobe, too. I remember exactly what I wore: a sheer, red midriff top with long, puffy sleeves over one of my famous Frederick's bras, of course, and rainbow-striped hip-hugger elephant bells. I looked hot! (Or at least *I* thought so.) I believe I stuck with that outfit all three days. At least I don't remember ever changing clothes. We didn't bother to get a motel because we figured we'd be up all night in the room of some band or other. All we brought along were our toothbrushes, a change of underwear, makeup and false eyelashes, a few joints, and a lot of eau de cologne. When necessary, we slept in Cindy's car and took "French baths" in gas-station restrooms. I'd been to France—I knew how they rolled.

The festival was a blur. We wandered through hotel room after hotel room, mainly the Holiday Inn, which was closest to the venue, searching out bands. And we found them. We hung out with Iron Butterfly (of "In-A-Gadda-Da-Vida" fame), and Cindy, who'd long been sexually active, slept with one of them (later crediting him with giving her syphilis). I spent my first night of the festival in bed with the drummer from Three Dog Night, but was unceremoniously kicked out sometime in the wee hours of Saturday morning when I refused to put out. After that I drifted into another room at the Holiday Inn, and there, among a motley crew of stoners, encountered The Mothers of Invention. I was a huge fan of their album *Freak Out!* which I'd played until it was too scratchy to listen to. I sat on the floor with my mouth hanging open in awe, thrilled to be in the presence of such greatness. Frank Zappa, the only person in the room who didn't seem high, told me in a fatherly way that I was too young to be wandering around the hotel on my own. I paid no attention to him, of course, but I thought it was very sweet of him to be concerned. Many years later, we'd meet again and I'd get to know him; his wonderful wife, Gail; and their kids, Moon, Dweezil, Ahmet, and Diva. Frank was not only a creative genius but struck me as a loving dad, husband, and family man.

The second day of the festival was the big day—the day Jimi Hendrix was to appear. Cindy and I got to the stadium early and elbowed our way through the crowd to grab the best seats available. The wait for Hendrix took forever, and the tension in the crowd was palpable. The night before, things had gotten out of hand when the crowd outside the stadium, who believed that having to *pay* for tickets was a travesty, knocked down the chain-link fence that surrounded the venue and stormed the field. Luckily, it happened before most of the festival-goers had arrived, because the stampede could have injured or killed someone. The "pigs," as we hippies referred to law enforcement, were everywhere, trying to prevent a repeat of the night before, and people began booing, jeering, and throwing things at them. Shortly after Joe Cocker performed "With a Little Help from My Friends," and during the break before Hendrix, everyone suddenly leapt from their stadium seats and rushed the stage, Cindy and me included. No sooner had we made it onto the field when the cops began lobbing canisters of tear gas into the crowd. Pandemonium ensued. When the hundreds of concertgoers began to run every which way trying to escape the gas, Cindy and I were separated. A voice over the PA system kept yelling, "Cover your face! Cover your face!" Suddenly, I felt a sharp whack on the side of my head, and everything went black. When I woke up, dazed and confused, I was in a trailer behind the stadium with a medic leaning over me. My head was throbbing and the side of my face felt like it was on fire.

"Where am I?" I whimpered. "What happened?"

"Looks like you got hit with a tear-gas canister," the medic replied, matter-of-factly. "You've got a little cut on your scalp and some chemical burns on the side of your face, but don't worry, you'll be fine." Easy for you to say, Mister. I might be missing Jimi Hendrix! He finished rinsing my skin with some kind of solution, and still a little disoriented, I managed to get on my feet and wobble my way back toward my seat.

Just a few yards away, I passed another small motor home where a very large man with a gigantic Afro stood guarding the door. Arms folded, looking a lot like the genie from Aladdin's lamp, he called, "Wanna meet Jimi Hendrix?" I couldn't believe my ears. "If you wanna meet him, c'mon." It was like offering crack to a whore. Being the gullible girl I was, I went with it and hopped right into the trailer. Lo and behold, right before my eyes, was Jimi Hendrix! Half sitting, half lying on a convertible bed in the back of the trailer, Jimi quietly strummed his guitar. He stopped playing, looked up at me, and asked, "What is goin' on out there?" As soon as I regained the ability to speak, I was happy to fill him in. I told him about the crowds, the police, and what had just happened to me, showing off my battle scars. He laid his guitar aside, jumped up, and grabbed a towel from a rack. Wetting it in the sink, he gently dabbed at the burns. After a few moments, he lit up a doobie and offered it to me. We lounged on the bed and smoked it while he launched into an angry diatribe about the pigs, America, Vietnam, and "the system." I listened and nodded enthusiastically in agreement. Even though he was as pissed off as could be, I was struck by the fact that his voice still remained soft, deep, and even. No shouting or yelling. Just as he was telling me he'd had it with the US and was going to leave the country for good, the genie popped his head in the door and hollered, "You're up, man! Time to go!" Jimi scribbled a phone number on a scrap of paper and stuffed it into my hand. "Call me after the show," he said. As he made his way to the door, he stopped, wrapped his arms around me and kissed me so sweet and slow that I thought I'd pass out. He beamed a sexy, heart-melting smile and was gone.

I walked back to my seat in a daze, half wondering whether I was hallucinating from the bang on my head, but the scrap of paper I clutched in my hand confirmed it had really happened. By the time I reached my seat in the stands next to Cindy, The Jimi Hendrix Experience was onstage and Jimi was blasting his psychedelic version of "The Star-Spangled Banner." The packed stadium full of frenzied fans was going apeshit! I tugged frantically at the sleeve of Cindy's hand-embroidered gypsy blouse and tried my best to shout over the wailing guitar distortion, desperate to tell her what had just happened. Mesmerized by the music, she just waved me off. The crowd grew more and more raucous as the band continued their set, and soon, despite the line of policemen that stood between the grandstand and the band, the rabid hordes rushed the stage again. Bottles and cans flew as even more crazed fans crashed the gates, knocked down the chain-link fence, and streamed onto the field. Cindy and I did our best to avoid being crushed by the crowd, hit by flying debris (again), or suffocated by tear gas. The show ended abruptly when Jimi, Noel Redding, and Mitch Mitchell were hustled off stage as the riot continued.

After a harrowing escape from the melee, I was finally able to tell Cindy about my backstage adventures. Even though she was initially pissed at me for disappearing, when she heard I had Jimi's phone number, she immediately changed her tune. Shoving our way through the throngs of concertgoers, we ran toward her car, which we'd parked blocks away, as fast as our legs would carry us. We hopped into the daisy-mobile and sped up and down the unfamiliar Denver streets, frantically searching for a pay phone. When we finally spotted a phone booth, we pulled over, squeezed into it, and dropped a dime in the slot. Hands shaking, I breathlessly dialed the number Jimi had given me. The phone rang. And rang. And rang. Finally, someone answered! It was a girl. My heart sank. This was definitely not in the plans. I could hear loud music and what sounded like a party going on in the background.

"Is Jimi there?" I asked, trying not to sound as disappointed as I was.

"Whosis?" she slurred.

"Tell him it's Cassandra."

I heard her yell Jimi's name a couple of times, then I waited for what seemed like an eternity.

"Whooottrrrrrr shugumm uh huh rrrgggh." It was Jimi's voice.

"Jimi, Jimi! Hi! It's me, Cassandra! Remember? The girl you met backstage?"

Indecipherable grunting, growling, and mutterings came from the other end of the line.

"Remember? I got hit by the tear gas?"

More nonsensical, slurred words.

"Where are you?"

"Shuggg slarmuhhhh....," his voice trailed off. The next thing I heard was the clunk of the receiver hitting the floor. I stayed on the line for a minute listening to the sounds of partying, tears welling up in my eyes. Finally, I put the receiver back on its cradle. As if I wasn't already bummed enough, Cindy was so angry that I hadn't asked him where he was staying that she refused to speak to me. All this made for a long, silent drive back to Colorado Springs.

The Denver Pop Festival turned out to be the last time the Jimi Hendrix Experience would play together. Two years later, Jimi left the US and died in London on September 18, the day after I turned nineteen.

For all my crazy prick-teasing behavior, I never found myself in any serious trouble while chasing bands. I got thrown out of a room or two when I wouldn't put out, but I was lucky. It was definitely a more innocent time. Hippies were preaching "peace not war," love-ins and flower power abounded, and young people were sure they were going to save the world. Life in the '60s, for the counterculture—of which music was a centerpiece—was all about beauty, honesty, and fun, but most of all, love.

I continued to drag my tired ass to school most days, but only so I could go to art, choir, or drama. I had a lot of male friends in my drama class who seemed to like me for me and never tried jumping my bones, a welcome change from the guys I met at the clubs. In retrospect I'm sure they were all gay. Duh. Unfortunately, the teacher wasn't. He cornered me backstage one day during a rehearsal and attempted to stick his tongue down my throat while squeezing my boobs. My reward for rebuffing him was a big, fat F on my report card. I ended up being the only person I know who ever flunked drama—a bad way to begin an acting career.

I loved drawing and painting almost as much as I loved dancing and singing. My art teacher, Mr. Samuelson, or Mr. Sam, as he was affectionately known by generations of students, was a gruff, straight-talking sixty-something who didn't mince words. He'd spent time with me during my high school years, sometimes sharing a joint in the school boiler room and other times coming to see me dance at various clubs around town, but always and only as a grandfatherly friend and mentor.

One day in my senior year, Mr. Sam approached me after class and said, "This is your last year of school, Cassandra. What are you going to do with your life?" Hmm, good question. I'd never been asked that before, so it came as a surprise. What *was* I going to do with my life? He looked at me with his piercing blue eyes, not a hint of humor on his face. "In your wildest dreams, if you could be *anything*, what would it be?" he asked. I avoided his intense gaze and dug the pointed toe of my shoe into one of the millions of multicolored paint droplets that adorned the linoleum floor of his classroom. I wondered whether I should admit it, out loud, to another person, for the first time. I took a deep breath and let it out: "I want to be a Las Vegas showgirl!" I looked at him intently, at his wrinkled, tanned, unsmiling face under his familiar white military-style flat-top, waiting for him to roll his eyes or laugh. But he didn't. He looked me straight in the eye and said, matter-of-factly, "Then *just do it."* He was way ahead of Nike. "If that's what you *really* want to do, then do it!" A lightbulb went on inside my head and I realized he was right. It had been my dream for years. What was stopping me besides the fact that I wasn't pretty enough, talented enough, old enough, or tall enough? That's the moment I decided not to let little things like facts discourage me. One way or another, I was going to become a showgirl!

CHAPTER 7

FEAR AND LACK OF CLOTHING IN LAS VEGAS

During spring break of my senior year of high school, I once again joined my mother, father, and sisters on what was to be our final family vacation. We packed into the "Caddy" and headed for California. Along the way, we made our usual stop in Sin City and got a motel with a pool on the north end of the Las Vegas Strip—quite a treat for my sisters and me. None of us could swim because my mother always said, "You're not going to swim until you learn how!" but it was an unusually blistering desert spring day, so we spent most of our time splashing around in the shallow end of the pool.

From the moment we left Colorado, I'd begged and pleaded with Mother and Daddy to take me to see one of the big Las Vegas "tits and feathers" shows, as I'd heard they were referred to by Vegas insiders. Although I was still seventeen, I looked a lot more mature, at least in my mind. After a lot of whining, pouting, and arguing, I finally convinced them I could dress up to look twenty-one years old and walk right in with no questions asked. And just in case, I had a fake ID that Cindy had helped rig up. It was actually a xeroxed copy of her driver's license with my picture glued over hers and laminated. In those days, bouncers weren't that picky. My parents finally gave in and I was beyond ecstatic! I'd come prepared for just such an event. I wore my favorite outfit: a low-cut, dark-red jersey top pulled tight over my special super-duper, multi-colored, psychedelic print Frederick's pushup bra, along with matching dark-red, flowy bell-bottoms and the highest platform heels I owned. I stuck on two pairs of eyelashes, top and bottom, and threw a red "wiglet" on top of my own hair that made me even taller and gave me a lion's mane of cascading red curls. I thought I looked incredibly glamorous, but I may have just looked like a call girl.

My parents took me to the Arabian Nights–themed Dunes Hotel to see *Casino de Paris*, one of the biggest and most popular shows on the Strip. The Dunes was the classiest place I'd ever seen, deluxe beyond my wildest dreams. As I walked from the hot, dry, desert night through the big, automatic glass doors and into the casino, the refrigerated air and smell of cigarette smoke hit me like a tidal wave. It was exciting, sexy, dangerous.

We made our way toward the showroom, passing what seemed like miles of glittering chandeliers and gaming tables. Music blared from a live lounge band and the exciting "ching, ching, ching" of coins spilling from slot machines was punctuated by the hoots of slightly looped patrons. In those days, women wore floor-length gowns or glitzy cocktail dresses. Men wore suits and ties or even the occasional tux. Nowadays, a torn T-shirt, flip-flops, and your butt crack showing seems to be the dress code.

Upon entering the showroom, my dad, feeling generous, flashed the maître d' a dollar bill, which landed us in the worst seats in the house—against the back wall in the farthest corner of the showroom. My folks were feeling wild that night and ordered us each a "champagne cocktail" that came with a little wooden stick attached to a tinker-toy thingy that you were supposed to twist back and forth in your drink to release the bubbles. Yum—flat champagne! An entire three-course meal was served. As the dessert plates were cleared, the lights dimmed. I was giddy with excitement (and champagne) and could hardly believe I was finally going to see a real, live Vegas spectacle! Then I looked up and saw the handsome, gray-haired maître d' heading straight for us. I shoved my drink under the table and did my best to avoid his gaze. "Do you work in one of the shows?" he asked. Was he talking to me? I mumbled something under my breath and tried to make myself appear smaller. My mother got nervous and started yammering, and I could detect sweat popping out on my dad's upper lip.

"You're a showgirl, right?" the maître d' asked.

Was he actually trying to pick me up right in front of my parents? "Oh! Uh, me? No, ha ha! I'm a...a..."

He ignored my stammering. "Stay there. I'll be right back," he called over his shoulder as he hurried away.

My parents and I glanced around frantically searching for the closest exit. Just as I was considering sliding under the table, a petite, blonde woman approached.

"Allo! My name eez Puff," she said in a perky French accent. "Won't you come weez me?"

My mind was buzzing. "OhGodohGodohGod, what can I do? Should I make a run for it? Confess I'm underage and let them call the police? Will my parents land in the slammer too?"

Puff led me through the crowd and into a brightly lit office backstage. A good-looking, mature Italian man rose from behind a desk and introduced himself as Sandro Dornini, the associate producer of *Casino de Paris*.

"Tomorrow we have-a try-outa for our new-a show. You can-na dance?" I was sweating profusely now, turning white, and feeling slightly nauseated.

"Uh, dance? Oh, uh...yeah. I guess so."

"Goood-a! Let's-a see."

Puff put a record on a portable stereo and a nondescript pop song blared from the speakers. I pulled every Ann-Margret move I'd seen her do in *Viva Las Vegas* out of my ass and danced like my life depended on it. When the music stopped, I stood there, red-faced from exertion and gasping for air. Sandro and Puff looked at each other and nodded.

"Tomorrow you meet-a wit' da producer, Frederic Apcar. Eef he like-a you, you are een-a da new show!" I sucked in a big breath of air, gulped hard, and burst into tears.

"I can't! I can't! I'm only seventeen!" I wailed. "I'm so sorry! Please don't call the police!" Much to my surprise, they didn't seem fazed by my confession. They sat me down and gave me a glass of water, and Puff gently patted my shoulder.

"Tomorrow you will meet-a Frederic Apcar, the producer of-a da show," Sandro said. "*Non ti preoccupare*—don't worry."

Puff led me back to my parents, who were now seated in "King's Row"—the best seats in the house—enjoying a bottle of expensive champagne.

"They want me to be in the show!" I breathed. My parents looked at me like I'd lost my mind, but a dance number was in full swing and their response was drowned out by the live orchestra. I turned my attention to the spectacle and couldn't believe the showgirls! I was in utter awe. They were the most beautiful, spectacular creatures I'd ever seen in my life—so stunning in their feathers and rhinestones! Some girls were wearing sparkly bras and some weren't, but I wasn't fazed by seeing bare boobs. I'd seen plenty of dancers performing half naked at the Body Shoppe. Although it *was* a little creepy having to watch them with my parents sitting next to me.

When the show ended, Sandro appeared at our table oozing European charm. He asked my parents to bring me back to the hotel at 10:00 the next morning to meet the producer of the show. They weren't thrilled, explaining that we were planning on hitting the road when the sun came up, but after some convincing by the gracious Mr. Dornini, they agreed. I was in shock.

The next morning there we were, my mother, father, and I, sitting on the top floor of the Dunes Hotel in the small, opulent outer office of Frederic Apcar. I was so scared I could hardly breathe, let alone speak, and I could tell from my parents' expressions that they didn't know what the hell to think. While Mother and Daddy waited, the secretary escorted me into the inner sanctum, a huge, lush office overlooking the Dunes golf course and mountains beyond. Mr. Apcar, a good-looking older Frenchman, sat behind an enormous glass-and-metal desk. He seemed to be about as old as my grandpa, which was probably fifty-something, and with his heavy French accent I had a hard time understanding him. After the formalities, he asked his secretary to step into the room. She came in with a tape measure.

"All showgirls must be five feet, seven eenches tall, meenimum," he said. "Ow tall are you?" I had no idea because the last time I remembered being measured was during my physical between grade school and junior high. I removed my shoes, held my breath, and pulled myself up as tall as I could muster to add every millimeter of height to my frame while his secretary measured me.

"Five feet…" she paused. "Six and three-quarter inches," she said, frowning.

"*Nooooo!*" I screamed inside my head. Could I be turned away because of a quarter inch?

Mr. Apcar rested his chin on his hand and sighed, "Hmmm."

He then asked me to step into a small room off to the side and remove my top and bra. Trying my best to be cool, I went into the room without hesitating and shut the door, and a moment later reappeared in nothing but my miniskirt. His eyes grew wide and for the first time, he smiled. "Zees ees *nice*…verrrry nice." He looked at my bare breasts from behind his desk as if he was examining a new chrome job on a bumper.

"Sank you," he said abruptly, and motioned toward the door. I raced into the tiny dressing room and pulled my bra and top on as fast as I could. Once I was fully clothed, I came back out and he motioned for me to take a seat. He asked his assistant to invite my parents in to join us. I was sweating bullets while I waited for the verdict.

"I would like to hire your daugh-taire to dance een my new show thees sum-maire." He intoned, "Eet begins re-hairsing zee end of Joo-ly." I sat perfectly motionless, afraid to breathe. I was doing my best to act mature, while inside I felt like a five-year-old on too many Twinkies. I said a silent prayer that I wouldn't fall off my chair or have some kind of psychotic breakdown. A conversation between Mr. Apcar and my parents followed, in which he explained the details that hiring an underage girl would entail. Basically, they would have to sign a waiver saying they agreed to my working at the Dunes. I was sure they'd never spoken to anyone from France before, and they asked him to repeat a lot of things. He had a very well-bred, sophisticated air about him. He might as well have been the king of France. I could tell they were impressed by his worldliness, but also intimidated. Mother and Daddy listened politely but seemed nervous and suspicious. I could read their thoughts. "This just doesn't happen. What's the catch? Is he planning to sell her into white slavery?" They hemmed and hawed, but he assured them that they could take the contract with them, look it over, and let him know later what their decision was. It was only April and the show didn't start rehearsing until July, so there was plenty of time. I don't remember much more. I was in something akin to a state of catalepsy, still unable to believe this was really happening, but as far as I was concerned, I was a showgirl in the new Dunes production of *Vive Les Girls!*

As soon as we left the room and were out of Mr. Apcar's earshot, the shouting, yelling, and crying began. My parents said there was no way in hell I was going to strut around on a stage in Las Vegas half naked, so I set out on a mission to make them miserable, sulking and pouting my way through the remainder of our trip. Once we returned home, Sandro Dornini patiently called my parents every other week. The time was rapidly approaching when he would have to fill my spot if I wasn't going to join the show. Despite my begging, pleading, and threatening all summer long, my parents wouldn't give me a straight answer.

Eventually, my mom and dad scraped up the money to consult a lawyer, probably just an ambulance-chaser type they'd found in the phone book, but he assured them the offer was legit. Then a miracle happened: they signed the contract! By this time, they probably would have signed anything just to get me the hell off their backs.

I began making plans immediately. But first I had some unfinished business to attend to: graduating from high school. I bought a brand-new, orange Pontiac Firebird (go-go dancing had been good to me) and I had lined up a free place to stay. After our meeting at the Dunes on Easter vacation, and before heading out of town, my family had made a quick stop to take a look at the newest hotel in Las Vegas, Circus Circus, which happened to be right next door to our motel. When I slipped into the ladies' room to fix my tear-stained face, I befriended a beautiful Latina cocktail waitress. She was wearing a super-short, saucy ringmaster's outfit and was so captivating that I had to approach her and ask what it was like to work in Vegas. We struck up a conversation and after approximately two seconds, confident I was going to get my way, I told her about my job offer at the Dunes. She immediately asked whether I'd like to stay with her and her little sister, who was my age, if I came to town. We exchanged info and kept in touch throughout the summer. The stars were aligning.

The day of graduation from William J. Palmer High School finally arrived, and although I was deemed the school "slut" by many of my fellow students, I may have been the only girl graduating that day who was still a virgin. Heck, I was possibly the only girl who wasn't pregnant! Many of the girls who were graduating were preggers or had already had a kid. I saw how it had affected their lives and vowed to *never* get pregnant as long as I lived. And just in case I needed a little inspiration to keep my knees together, my parents threatened to kill themselves rather than live with the shame of me getting pregnant out of wedlock. Okay, I didn't get along with my parents that well, but I certainly didn't want to have their murder/suicide on my hands. (Note to parents: I do not recommend this approach as a viable form of birth control. It proved to have serious repercussions as far as my personality development was concerned.)

CHAPTER 8

VIVE LES GIRLS (IT'S SHOWTIME!)

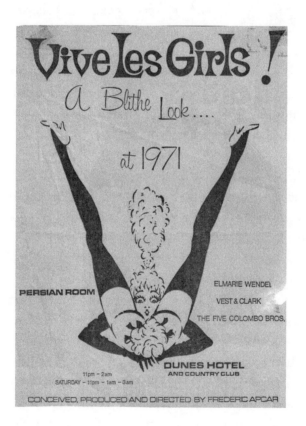

It was 1969. The summer of love was coming to a close. The flower children had come and gone, taking peace and love along with them.

My parents insisted Aunt Lorrayne travel with me to Vegas so I didn't have to make the three-day road trip alone. That was fine by me. My aunt, the oldest of my dad's siblings, was the one person in my family who had always supported me in everything I chose to do, and I adored her. Even though her belief system was that of an old-fashioned schoolmarm, which she'd actually been at one time, she always encouraged me to follow my dreams, no matter how screwy.

When Aunt Lorrayne and I arrived in Las Vegas, she stopped by my new temporary home to meet the Circus Circus cocktail waitress and her kid sister. My Aunt was relieved to find that, although they were complete strangers, they seemed like very nice, normal people. After a tearful goodbye, my favorite aunt flew back to Colorado and my Las Vegas adventures began.

Rehearsals were held in a massive space the size of an airplane hangar, approximately twenty minutes off the Strip, on Spring Mountain Road. In those days it was way the hell out in nowhere land, surrounded by nothing but cacti and lots and lots of sand.

Costume fittings were held there each day, with several busy French ladies taking measurements of every inch of our bodies, from head to toe. The rehearsal hours were long, the heat stifling, and the girls were as bitchy as could be. To top it off, we got only half our regular pay while we rehearsed.

Even though I thought the girls were mean in the beginning, they were angels compared to the choreographer. Ron Lewis's shows were considered the best on the Strip, but he had a reputation for being a beast to work with. His means of getting performers to do what he asked was to be cruel and degrade them. I was feeling way out of my league as the newbie and was nervous, shy, and more than a little scared. Here I was in a strange new place, *really* strange, surrounded by much older people I didn't know who treated me like a child and an outsider.

A big problem for me was that my eyesight was terrible. Obviously, I wouldn't be able to wear my glasses on stage and I was having an awful time with my hard contact lenses because of the dry Vegas air. I wasn't great at following directions in the first place, but not being able to see made everything that much more challenging.

After demonstrating which foot I should stand on for the umpteenth time, Ron stormed to within inches of my face and screeched, *"This* foot!" simultaneously stomping down on my foot with all his might. I don't really think he meant to come down directly *on* it, at least I hope not. Ever the drama queen, I limped through the rest of the day with my foot wrapped in ice packs and let everyone know how unhappy I was.

That night I called my parents. "I hate it here!" I sobbed. "I'm quitting the show and coming back home!" To their credit, instead of saying, "We told you so," which was what I had expected, they gave me their best pep talk ever and convinced me not to give up. After all, they'd just gone through a miserable four months of my whining and spent money on a lawyer, so they weren't about to see it all go down the dumper.

A second choreographer was brought in to stage a couple of numbers. His name was Jerry Jackson, and for every horrible thing Ron said and did, Jerry did something kind and helpful. He had a mild Texas accent and was soft-spoken, funny, and patient. Jerry made up for Ron in spades and became a friend for life.

Four grueling weeks later, our rehearsals came to an end and opening night arrived. I was over-the-moon excited and scared shitless—one big bundle of nerves. More unnerving than the paralyzing fear of forgetting my dance moves or falling on my face were the behind-the-scenes quick changes. At the end of each number, and just like in a NASCAR pit stop, my costumes and headdresses were whipped off and the next one flung on at warp speed by the wardrobe mistress—an older lady we called "Grandma"—and several other dressers. After each change we raced down the stairs and onto the stage for the next number with only seconds to spare.

You'd think the first time I showed up onstage baring my boobies would have been traumatic, but I was totally fine with it. I knew what being a *show*girl entailed, and I was ready to show it! More than once I was approached by tourists who recognized me from the show to ask where I'd had my breasts done. Without their realizing I was only seventeen or eighteen, trying to convince them that my boobs were real usually ended with them stomping away calling me a liar.

Vive Les Girls took place in the Dunes Hotel lounge. It was a hipper, sleeker, sexier version of the mainroom show, *Casino de Paris*, and although it was smaller, "*Vive*," as it was referred to (pronounced "Veev"), was very prestigious. It won the award for Best Las Vegas show ten years running and was packed every night.

I shared a dressing room in the upstairs backstage area with seven other showgirls. The "serious" dancers, or "ponies" as they were called because they were shorter and more compact than the showgirls, had their own room downstairs. They danced "covered" because having your fun-bags flopping all over the place during energetic dance moves isn't that classy.

As showgirls, our goal was to display our elaborate, exaggerated costumes, along with our bare breasts, with dignity and poise. Although the showgirls danced too, what we mainly did was "move." We wore lots of big costume pieces, high heels, and huge headdresses that were heavy and hard as hell to balance, so we performed a lot of smoother, more graceful movements like swiveling our hips and "slow-quick-quicks"—one long gliding step followed by two short ones, repeat as needed, while thrusting our pelvis forward and twisting at the waist to face frontward, giving the tourists their money's worth.

I recently realized that the standing pose I do as Elvira is a throwback to my Vegas days. I generally stand in the iconic showgirl "bevel stance"—achieved when one knee is bent and pulled in toward the body's centerline and the forward toe is pointed and facing out, which apparently makes for a flattering, feminine silhouette. At least it's always worked for me.

Our upstairs dressing room had low ceilings; plush, red carpeting; and a nice, warm, golden glow from the makeup mirror lights. Even though we were in the desert, the hotel air conditioning was always set at a frosty temperature that rivalled the Antarctic. Each girl had her own vanity table. Rows of glittery costumes hung from hangers and hooks that lined the walls.

In her early twenties, Sunny was the showgirl closest to my age. She had long, straight, white-blonde hair, and her athletic body was perennially tanned. A Florida girl who had spent a lot of time on "Muscle Beach," Sunny drove the other girls crazy because whatever dance moves we did, she did *bigger* and with a lot more energy. Her exuberance had the effect of making the rest of us look like we were on Valium, and she received endless notes from the director about toning it down. She and I were the comedians of the group and spent a lot of time entertaining the other girls backstage between shows. Once, during the between-show breaks, Sunny and I reenacted the entire movie *Wizard of Oz* in twenty-minute increments over several nights, playing all the characters, singing all the songs, and doing it all while wearing only our flesh-colored G-strings. It was a hit! (For a while, anyway, until our shenanigans started getting on some of the girls' nerves and we had to cool it.)

Kathleen was the tough one, and rumors of former days as a call girl abounded. She had a major attitude and a bleached-blonde Jean Harlow hairdo with dark roots. She made it plain from the first day that you wouldn't want to cross her. Despite her New Jersey upbringing, Kathleen spoke in an affected foreign accent—English? French? Spanish? I had no idea. She was married to Washington (or "Washing-tone," as she pronounced it), the lead performer of the Argentinian Gauchos, a hugely popular act on the Strip, so she was living *la vida loca*.

Maria was a stunning French-Italian woman from Corsica. Dark-skinned and exotic, she had the sexy, pouty mouth of Brigitte Bardot combined with the striking almond eyes of Sophia Loren. She spoke with a thick French accent and although she could come off as quiet and aloof, she often surprised me with how really wild and zany she could be.

Gabby hailed from London and, in her early thirties, was the oldest of the girls. She wasn't unattractive, just slightly plain, with an average body and bust. Tall and blonde with pale skin and a sprinkling of freckles across her turned-up nose, she came off more like Mary Poppins than a Vegas showgirl. She spoke with a very aristocratic British accent, which, even when she'd say something nice, always made me feel as if I was being talked down to. She could be a doll, and was always polite and pleasant enough; however, she sometimes came off a bit aloof—maybe it was the accent. It sometimes gave me the feeling she was worried about getting cooties from the other girls. Gabby knitted and crocheted on the breaks and God help you if you got trapped alone with her because she loved to regale anyone who'd listen with the dreary details of her home life: what she and her hubby were doing the next day, what she'd baked for him the day before, when and what she was going to buy for her home, blah, blah, blah. They didn't call her Gabby for nothing.

Joan, in her mid-twenties, was the tallest and thinnest of the girls and had the smallest breasts. She looked more like a high-fashion model than a showgirl, stunning in makeup, but gangly and boyish without it. She was engaged to be married, so she led a pretty quiet life, leaving the partying to the rest of us.

Hugette was an attractive "older" redhead from France who barely spoke English. She was friendly, but because of the language barrier, never quite fit into the other showgirls' social circle.

Jennifer, hands down the most beautiful showgirl in Vegas, had pitch-black hair and pale, almost translucent skin. Her perfectly arched eyebrows and aristocratic bone structure gave her a queenly elegance that I envied. People often remarked that she resembled a young Elizabeth Taylor. She had a body to die for and carried herself with a ballet dancer's posture and grace. Jennifer spoke in a soft, husky English accent and had a wide-eyed, almost childlike quality. She was kind and funny and took me under her wing, teaching me the ropes and sometimes defending me. Jennifer is the one who taught me how to glue three pairs of eyelashes together for my top lids and two pairs for the bottom and apply them just above and below my real lashes to make my eyes look bigger from the stage. She's the one who showed me how to create the illusion of cheekbones, which my baby face still lacked, using a combination of dark and light shading powder. She's also the one who explained alternatives to using Nair hair-removal cream on my bikini line, something I'd tried and regretted big time. Despite our ten-year age difference and my hormonal teenage bullshit, which at times must have driven her crazy, she was my friend and ally from the beginning.

In addition to comedienne Elmarie Wendall (who brought the house down with her number, "I'm the Oldest Living Showgirl in Las Vegas") and the Columbo Brothers, five charming Italian acrobats, *Vive Les Girls* starred the singing-dancing duo of Vest and Clark. Buddy Vest and Sterling Clark were former dancers of stage and screen, and ex-lovers who had formed a stage act together. Before coming to *Vive*, they had been the opening act for talented performer Juliet Prowse, who I was especially impressed by since she had played Elvis's love interest in the movie *G.I. Blues*. Coincidentally, Buddy had also been a featured dancer in *Sweet Charity*, the film I adored as a teen. Now, forced to share a dressing room, they fought like bastards. Well, to be honest, Buddy did most of the screaming and yelling. Sterling remained annoyingly calm, which only served to make Buddy even more hysterical. I fell madly in love with both Buddy and Sterling the moment I met them. Not only were they talented and gorgeous as hell, but they were also sweet and fun to be around, and treated me like something special. I had such a crush on them both that I followed them around like a puppy dog the entire run of the show. My 1969 diary was filled with professions of love—one day for Sterling, the next for Buddy.

The costumes, designed in Paris by José Luis Viñas, were *fabulous*! Because the show was comparatively small, the money went into quality as opposed to quantity. Our finale costumes were made of *faux* (I pray to God) leopard skin, trimmed in fox fur, and adorned with row after row of Austrian crystals and exotic plumes. (Unfortunately, PETA [People for the Ethical Treatment of Animals] wasn't around yet.) We entered the stage leading white Russian wolfhounds on glittering rhinestone leashes.

A few weeks after the show opened, my mom and dad came to see it. It was one of the most nerve-wracking nights of my life! Can you imagine dancing around in front of your *dad* half naked? Thank God I couldn't see them because of the lighting or I wouldn't have been able to step onstage. I was told later by the maître d' that my dad cried during my performance. I'm still hoping it was because he was proud of me and not because he was embarrassed.

I only stayed with the Circus Circus cocktail waitress through rehearsals. Once the show opened, Cindy left Colorado and drove out to Vegas to join me and look for a job as a showgirl. I didn't say anything, but I had my doubts that she'd find work in one of the shows. Although she was a great go-go girl, she'd never taken a dance lesson in her life and was a couple of inches shorter than me. And the fact that she was flat-chested didn't help. We found an apartment that was only a stone's throw from my job. I could actually walk to and from the Dunes across the enormous, empty desert lot that Bally's now occupies. One time, in the wee hours of the morning, as I crossed the empty lot, dodging tumbleweeds and keeping an eye out for rattlesnakes, I encountered a snarling coyote, chewing on a large, bloody, dead thing—Jimmy Hoffa? From then on, I drove to work.

Months went by and Cindy still couldn't find a job. I got tired of paying the rent on my own, and we began to argue a lot. We finally went our separate ways. A couple of fellow showgirls and I moved into a duplex that we shared with the Columbo Brothers. It became a big party house, and at any hour of the day you were sure to find a naked showgirl or two dozing by the pool, avoiding tan lines.

My eighteenth birthday came in mid-September, just a month or so after the show opened. I was finally going to be "legal"! The Columbos, Buddy and Sterling, and several other performers from *Vive* planned a big birthday bash for me at one of Vegas's most popular restaurants, Aku Aku, in the Stardust Hotel. Sounds of ukuleles and steel guitars echoed through the tiki-themed rooms, and grass-skirted dancers gyrated on a stage in front of our long table. My friends promptly ordered me a gigantic tropical drink called a scorpion, with a sweet-smelling gardenia floating in it. I chugged it all before the pu pu platter even arrived. The last thing I remember asking was, "Does this drink have alcohol in it?" because it went down like a nice Hawaiian punch. I had to be carried out of the place and poured into someone's car.

Back at home, I got a second wind. Several performers joined us to celebrate, among them the hottest act on the Strip, magicians Siegfried and Roy. Buddy and Sterling had taken me to see their show several times on our breaks between shows, and we had been allowed to watch their act from the wings. The highlight of the show was when a small cage stuffed with a *huge* Siberian tiger was hoisted several feet above the stage. Siegfried tossed a red cloth over the cage, momentarily obscuring the tiger, then, seconds later, whipped it off. In the tiger's place was Siegfried's dark, sexy partner, Roy. I'd watched the trick from the audience before, but seeing it from this angle was doubly impressive because it was easy to tell there were no strings, no trapdoors, nothin'! After the show I asked the chiseled, blond, German magician how it was done and I'll always remember his answer: "Dahling," he whispered, coming within inches of my face and staring me straight in the eye, "If I tolt you, it vouldn't be magic." I had a huge crush on him from that moment on. And as hard as it may be to believe, the night of my eighteenth birthday, Siegfried pulled me into my bedroom, locking the door behind us, laid me across the bed, and after a few minutes of heavy, inebriated kissing, asked to be my "first." Even in my drunken stupor, and as turned on as I was, I managed to once again avoid losing my virginity. Now that's magic!

During the *Vive Les Girls* finale, I was featured along with Vest and Clark in my very first "comedy" performance. Jerry Jackson, our extremely astute choreographer, had the good sense to capitalize on my nearsighted eyes and young age and gave me a short bit to do that turned out to be a high point of the show. While Buddy or Sterling alternately sang an abbreviated version of a song, each showgirl, one by one, danced seductively around them. My song was the 1957 Ray Charles hit "Hallelujah, How I Love Her So." While Buddy sang, I danced onstage wearing my elegant fur-trimmed jumpsuit that covered pretty much everything but my boobs and butt. Sashaying across the stage toward Buddy, I "slow-quick-quicked" right past him, oblivious of his outstretched hand, ostensibly because I couldn't see (which I couldn't!). Buddy ran over to lead me back to where I was supposed to be. I pranced around him momentarily, then wandered off in the wrong direction again, squinting like a semi-naked female Mr. Magoo. At one point I got trapped in the side stage curtains, requiring Buddy to rescue me, and a moment later, I hurtled toward the front of the stage, Buddy snatching me back from the edge in the nick of time, all while he attempted to sing and smile as if nothing out of the ordinary was happening. The audience always roared because they'd never seen a showgirl behave like such a klutz.

We played six nights a week, two shows a night and three on Saturday, with a "swing girl" who took each girl's place on a rotating basis, so we were allowed an extra day off per month plus a week's vacation per year. Child labor laws had obviously not been introduced.

This was my routine: wake up around 8:00 p.m., shower and eat whatever I could find in the fridge that wasn't moldy, get to the Dunes by 9:00 p.m.

During the summer, especially during rehearsals, getting into my car was a whole process. My orange Firebird had a black vinyl top and a black interior. There was only street parking, so my car sat in the sun all day. Being Las Vegas, that sun was *hot*. Hotter than hell. It made the interior of my car hot enough to slow-cook a pork butt. One time, Sunny and I experimented with frying an egg on the hood of my car. Not only did it fry, but the edges turned crisp and burned within moments.

So, I always opened my car door with oven mitts on my hands. I'd wait a few minutes while little waves of scorching desert heat wafted out of the car and hit the cooler air. I then spread a beach towel over the blazing-hot, black vinyl driver's seat. If I was coherent enough the night before, I'd remember to store the towel in the freezer, which helped. Carefully, carefully, I hopped into the car, turned the key, and revved the engine. I then jumped back out and waited in the shade for a couple of minutes more.

I lunged back into the car, this time turning the air conditioning to its fullest capacity before the hot air scorched my eyebrows off. I jumped back out, and finally, after another minute or so, got back in the car still wearing the oven mitts to protect my hands from the blistering hot steering wheel and drove to the Dunes. Ahh, the glamorous life.

I had to arrive an hour before the other girls so Grandma, the wardrobe mistress, could cover the scars on my neck, back, stomach, and shoulders in heavy pancake makeup.

Then I did two or three shows: 11:00 p.m., 1:00 a.m., and, depending on the night, 3:00 a.m. The 45-minute breaks in between flew by on some nights, while on other nights they stretched into endless, boring eternity. To pass the time, Sunny and I would often do things like use the house phones on the casino floor to page fictitious hotel guests with names like "Jack Meehoff" or "Lois Rates," then laugh our asses off when we heard their names announced over the PA system throughout the casino. Good times, good times.

After the second or third show, I'd shower off the body makeup before dressing if I wasn't feeling especially lazy. On the occasions I skipped that step, I'd wake up the next day with "buff beige" sheets. We rarely bothered to take off our makeup after work in our rush to get out of the hotel and hit the bars by 4:00 a.m., so all the showgirls traveled around town looking like circus clowns. Tourists eyed us with a mixture of respect and awe; the dealers and other hotel employees, indifference or downright scorn.

The show had rules. Lots of rules. They had a "three strike" policy just like prison. If you were caught disobeying, your ass was grass.

1. *No* horseback riding, skiing, or any other sport where you could break an arm or a leg and be out of work for an extended time.

2. *Must* wear bright-red lipstick at all times, even though bright lips were *so* not in! The hot lip color of the day was the palest noncolor you could find, the closer to white the better. I hated wearing red lipstick because it made me look like my mother.

3. Must *always* smile while on stage. Not just a friendly, closed-mouth, pleased-with-yourself smile, but a big, wide, open-mouthed, toothy grin.

4. *No* tan lines. (I didn't have to worry about that rule because I only freckled or turned red, so I avoided the sun like poison ivy.)

5. *No* visiting any casino bar, not in the hotel where you worked or any other hotel. Unlike in the '50s and early '60s, when showgirls were encouraged to "mix," we were *never* allowed to fraternize with the customers or drink in a casino bar without a male escort present. This was so you wouldn't be mistaken for a whore.

6. *Must* maintain your current body weight. We were weighed when we signed our contracts and every week thereafter. If you strayed five pounds over your original weight, hotel management issued a "warning slip" letting you know that if you didn't shed the pounds, "immediate action would be taken."

I still had plenty of baby fat, so I was always walking—or dancing—a fine line. That's why most of the girls were forced to resort to diet pills, or "whites" as they were called, just like truck drivers (although I'm pretty sure they don't use them for weight purposes). They had the added bonus of keeping us wide awake all night and buzzed out of our brains. I was already a pretty hyper, high-strung individual, so it wasn't the best drug for me. I drove the other girls crazy with my blabbing and whining nonstop about nothing. I was forced to stop taking the whites when every one of the girls in my dressing room stopped speaking to me. From then on it was pretty much cottage cheese and naked hamburger patties for me.

It turned out that there were unspoken rules as well, like no fraternizing with Black people. I learned this when Sunny was spied out to dinner one night at the Dunes "Dome of the Sea" with basketball legend Wilt Chamberlain. The next day she received a pink slip on her vanity table. Naturally, no reason was given for firing her, but all the older girls knew the truth. After much crying, begging, and pleading, she was given a second chance, but it was understood she'd be watched closely by the management.

Back then, Vegas had a very creepy racist underbelly. Racism was more blatant there in the '50s, but even into the late '60s and early '70s, when I was there, it still permeated the culture, or lack thereof. In the early '60s many of the most popular and highest-paid acts, like Nat King Cole, Lena Horne, and Sammy Davis Jr., were forced to leave the casinos through the back door, then escorted to hotel rooms literally across the tracks that were dumpier *and* more expensive than rooms on the Strip. Of course, their white counterparts enjoyed gambling in the casino and drinking in the bars after their shows. You may have heard the infamous stories about Sammy Davis Jr.'s treatment by the casinos when he was in the "Rat Pack." When he dared marry a white woman, Swedish-born actress May Britt, the only thing that stood between him and a shallow grave in the desert was his pal Frank Sinatra.

I would never have imagined racism existed in Las Vegas. Many of my favorite performers on the Strip were Black: The Fifth Dimension, The Jackson Five, Little Richard, Dionne Warwick, and Ike and Tina Turner. After all, it was the era of "Black is beautiful." As far as I was concerned, nothing was groovier than being "Afro-American." Boy, was I naïve.

In those days, gangsters still ruled Vegas. Every casino head or pit boss I met was either Italian or Jewish and had mob ties. There were lots of rumors about people who hadn't paid their gambling debts mysteriously disappearing in the desert, never to be seen again.

The Dunes owners, Major Riddle and Jake Gottlieb, were two businessmen who had dealings with the infamous crime syndicate "The Outfit," based out of Chicago. In the late '60s, Morris Shenker, a successful defense lawyer, became the chairman of the board of the Dunes. Shenker had made a name for himself representing a slew of underworld figures, including Jimmy Hoffa. There was quite a hubbub at the Dunes when Morris or Major were on the casino floor. I love the film *Casino*, which stars Robert De Niro playing a Jewish gangster, because it perfectly captures the look and feel of Vegas back when I worked there.

I was introduced to Morris only once, but I often saw Major, and he was always very kind to me. Later, when my contract was up, he had one of the casino bosses, "Big Julie" Weintraub, arrange an extremely discounted airfare to Europe for me. As far as I was concerned, they were all good fellas.

The Baccarat pit boss, a short, pockmarked man in his fifties who looked and sounded a lot like the actor Edward G. Robinson, was as old-school mobster as you could get. He had a serious crush on me and when I walked by the Baccarat pit on my way into work each night, he'd always call out in his gravelly Brooklyn accent from the height of his pit boss chair, "How ya doin', Clara Bow?" He often asked me to be his girlfriend, and one late night over drinks he confided that he'd "taken a fall" for one of the Casino bigwigs and had spent twenty years behind bars. For this service, he received a very large cash settlement and one of the top positions in the casino-floor hierarchy. But he was old enough to be my grandpa, so the idea of dating him completely grossed me out.

After the show, I'd often join a group of show kids and go to a bar. Our favorite spot was Le Café, a little dive tucked into a corner mini-mall far from the Strip. It was one of the few places where locals could get away from the tourists to relax and dance for fun, not work. It was a mixed crowd, but largely gay because it was frequented by so many male performers from the Strip. It wasn't uncommon to see Liberace, Rip Taylor, Paul Lynde, or other stars there, letting their hair down.

During my time in Vegas, I met dozens of guys at Le Café who I fell madly in love with and went after with a vengeance, but as one might guess, it didn't always work out.

CHAPTER 9

THROUGH THE LOOKING GLASS

My eighteenth year turned out to be one long Alice in Wonderland trip. Actually, more like Mr. Toad's Wild Ride. There are a million stories in the "naked city." These are a few of mine.

In '69 and '70, showgirls were still treated like Las Vegas royalty, and being in the hottest show in town had its perks. We were invited to all the parties and often "comped" ringside seats to some of the biggest shows on the Strip.

Ike and Tina Turner were one of my favorite acts and I went to see them every chance I got. Tina was wild! I'd never seen a woman who came across so ballsy, powerful, and confident onstage. It came as such a shock to discover years later that she was being abused by her husband and bandleader, Ike. I couldn't believe a little pipsqueak like Ike could tell such a strong woman like Tina what to do. Later in life I would discover firsthand how that could happen.

Another favorite performer was Little Richard, whose shows were just crazy! From the moment he took the stage, he had the crowd on their feet clapping and cheering while he ran back and forth banging on the piano, singing, and hollering. Backstage after his show one night, I lit up a cigarette. Richard sashayed over, snatched it out of my mouth, and gave me some advice I've never forgotten: "Girl, if God would've wanted you to smoke, he would'a put a chimbly on yo' head!"

I got to see the Jackson Five perform when Michael was seven or eight years old. Five-year-old Janet stole the show when she walked out in heels and a floor-length dress, trailing a feather boa behind her.

Growing up, I'd loved Paul Anka's songs, especially "Lonely Boy" and "Put Your Head on My Shoulder," so I was thrilled when he became a regular and a fan of our show—or at least the *girls* in the show. After work one night, he gave me an autographed photo and his phone number and, according to my diary, I called him every other day or so for the month he was performing in town, and we had long, heavy conversations, although I can't remember a thing that was said. One night he took me to a dinner party at Engelbert Humperdinck's house. It was a group of around eight people including me, Paul, and Engelbert. The other guests were singer/pianist Buddy Greco, comedians Totie Fields and Jack E. Leonard, and Paul's friend Andy "Moon River" Williams, who I could tell was very taken with me. He was a handsome man and a big star in those days, but he was waaaay too old for my taste. He invited me out to dinner at a fancy restaurant, and, like the clueless dork I was, I accepted. I had a pleasant enough time with him, even though he insisted I refer to him as "Daddy." Ick ick ick! I somehow managed to fend off his advances the entire evening and was even dumb enough to accept *another* invitation from him to hang out backstage at Caesar's Palace while he performed his mainroom act. The next night, I joined the group of agents, managers, and hangers-on mingling around Andy's plush dressing room, sipping cocktails and chatting. Suddenly, they were gone, and I found myself alone with Andy for the first time. Uh-oh. Right before he went onstage to an adoring crowd, he grabbed me roughly by the back of my head and forced an open-mouthed, tongue-down-your-throat kiss on me. Shocked and pissed, I responded by biting the hell out of his lip. He pulled away wiping a drop of blood from his mouth. "You little bitch!" he snapped as he stalked from the room. The second he was out the door, I took off, never to see "Daddy" again.

I was taken to a family Thanksgiving dinner at the home of Robert Maheu, former FBI agent and chief executive of Nevada operations for reclusive billionaire Howard Hughes, who, at that point, still ruled the city. I was there as his son's date, and although I'm only speculating, I may have also been his "beard," because after all, we'd met at Le Gay

Café. The Maheus had a sprawling, modern, ranch-style house on the edge of a golf course, and dinner was served on their enormous dining table overlooking it. Even though it was announced with pride that his mother was doing the cooking that day, I couldn't wrap my head around the fact that she was wearing dangling diamond earrings, a shiny gold silk-taffeta cocktail dress, and high heels while making frequent trips to the kitchen to check on dinner. This sure as hell wasn't like any Thanksgiving dinner I'd ever experienced! The staff did the serving, of course, but the thing I remember most is that Mom Maheu couldn't stop talking about this newfangled oven they'd just gotten called a Radar Range that cooked the turkey in under an hour. It was the first time I'd heard of a microwave oven and it seemed so space-age that I felt like I was having dinner with the Jetsons! If memory serves, I believe most of the dinner conversation was about that snazzy mod con.

On a day off, I took a trip down to Tijuana with a few of the girls. There, I bought an actual glass eye that I intended to have made into a ring. The eyeball wasn't round, like an actual eyeball, but a concave piece of glass about the size of, uh, an eyeball. When one of the girls announced that Sammy Davis Jr. and his wife, Altovise, were going to be in the audience the next night, I was super excited! Thanks to my parents, I'd grown up well aware of the brilliant singer/actor/dancer/musician and certified member of the Rat Pack, and now, here he was, coming to see my show! Knowing that Sammy wore a glass eye after losing one of his in a car accident, I got the bright idea of gluing my fake eyeball onto one of my nipples for the finale. Actually, the other girls dared me to do it and I've always had a hard time resisting a dare. When "Mister Show Business" came backstage afterward, all I can say is thank God the man had a sense of humor. He doubled over laughing, slapping his knee in that famous Sammy Davis style of his, then gave me a big hug and a compliment that has always stuck with me: "How can you be so beautiful and funny too?"

My friend Sunny, who was very much into the whole health and fitness craze long before it was a thing, was a Joe Weider gym rat. One night at work, she talked me into going on a double date with two guys she'd met there while working out. "They're both really hunky because they're into competitive body building," she explained. "They don't speak the best English, though." Who cares? I'm always up for a free dinner! Arnold Schwarzenegger, Sunny's date, was from Austria, and my date, Franco Columbu, came from Italy. At that time, I discovered, he was considered one of the world's strongest men. They were both in their twenties, shy, sweet, and friendly. I got the serious vibe that they hadn't had much experience when it came to dating. The first evening we went out, we suggested we go to an all-you-can-eat buffet at the Silver Slipper on the Strip. The amount of food these guys loaded onto their plates was *unbelievable.* They carried a plate in each hand, which they piled high with nothing but protein: huge slabs of prime rib, thick slices of ham, a couple of turkey legs. Sunny and I sat in awe while they scarfed it all down within a few minutes, then went back for round two. Arnold and Franco were thrilled with the place because the price, at just $3.99 a person, fit their budget. So, the next night, we decided to return. This time, however, as we were being shown to our table, we caught the host and waiters frantically grabbing the meat and shoving it under the server's station. When Arnold asked, "Vair's duh beev?" they just shrugged their shoulders and gave him a blank stare.

On a night off, Sterling took me to see Liza Minnelli perform. At the time, I didn't know much about her except that she was Judy Garland's daughter, but her energetic Broadway-style act blew me away and I became an instant fan. When Sterl offered to take me backstage after the show, the thought of meeting Liza in the flesh after that performance was beyond exciting! After a little small talk, Sterling introduced me to her, and I'll never forget her immortal words: "Wanna do a line?" I smiled and politely declined. At the time I had no idea what the hell she was talking about, I swear to God, but I thought it was sweet of her to offer.

The next night, I found myself at a star-studded gala for the opening of Nancy Sinatra's show at Caesar's Palace. Strangely, Alan Osmond, the oldest of the seven singing Osmond siblings, was my date. Even though he was only a couple of years older than me and not really my type—the unibrow was a real turnoff—he was respectful and sweet in a folksy kind of way.

The joint was packed with an impressive list of major players from the Strip: Frank Sinatra (of course), along with Dean Martin, Joey Bishop, Johnny Carson, Suzanne Pleshette, Norm Crosby, and more. On the arm of Alan, I joined the entire Osmond clan at their table for dinner. I was wearing my favorite fancy dress: a skin-tight, low-cut, emerald-green gown under a short, matching ruffled jacket. And of course, no bra. (Remember, it was 1970 and, even then, I was all about showing off my best assets.) Straitlaced Mormon Mom Osmond spent much of the dinner glaring at me, and more than once, I caught Dad stealing a glance at my chest. During the appetizer course, the Osmond matriarch leaned toward me with a concerned look. "Would you mind closing your jacket, sweetie?" she said under her breath. "You're upsetting Mr. Osmond." He didn't look all that upset to me.

Ten- and twelve-year-old Donny and Marie couldn't sit still, so they entertained themselves by hopping from table to table and running around like typical kids. Donny, who was obviously already quite the ladies' man, wound up sitting in my lap at one point, much to his parents' chagrin. Years later, when I met him as an adult, I reminded him of that night, and he asked whether we could reenact the scenario. Ha!

The high point, which also turned out to be the low point, came when the Osmond family was introduced to Mr. Sinatra. It was as if we were meeting the freakin' Pope. A "representative" came to our table and escorted us to his highness. The rep rattled off a short spiel to Mr. Sinatra about the Osmonds and then the family introduced themselves one by one, starting with the parents. He shook each of their hands in turn. Steeling myself to meet the big man, I took a deep breath and tried my best to be cool. "Hi, so nice to meet you!" I enthused. "I'm Cassandra Peterson. I work next door at the Dunes." I smiled and extended my hand. But instead of shaking it, Sinatra shoved his hands in his pockets and leaned back to look me up and down. A belittling smirk appeared on his face. The room seemed to grow silent. "Nice tits," he snarled, as the Osmond family looked on in horror. I felt even more embarrassed for them than for myself. They'd probably never even *heard* the word "tits" before! To quote one of Frank's songs, I wanted to "roll myself up in a big ball...aaaand di-i-i-i-e." I think I must have sunk right through the floor because I don't remember another thing that happened that night. Who knows? Maybe I found Liza and took her up on her offer.

As fate would have it, years later, I ran into "Old Blue Eyes" again. I was working as the hostess and coat-check girl at Emilio's Restaurant in Hollywood when he and his entourage came waltzing through the door. He checked his hat with me, and when he wasn't looking, I spit in it. Like Elvira always says, "Revenge is better than Christmas!"

CHAPTER 10

ALL SHOOK UP

One night, Jennifer came into the dressing room and made an announcement that rocked my world and would forever change my life: Elvis Presley was coming to see our show! Squeals and gasps filled the room, with no one squealing or gasping louder than me. I couldn't believe *he* was actually coming to see *me* perform!

His comeback TV special in 1968 had reintroduced him to his fans. Now, after a couple of years in the Army and a decade making movies, Elvis was resurrecting his fading music career at the age of thirty-four. On August 2, 1969, he began his live performances at the biggest showroom in the biggest hotel in Vegas, the International. I'd been lucky enough to catch one of his sold-out shows when Sterling had taken me as his date. There I was, all grown up, watching my favorite childhood star live onstage—his voice, his looks, his charisma—all still as exciting as ever after so many years. His performance was absolutely riveting and all I'd ever imagined it would be!

Over the years Jennifer had been seeing Elvis's former Army buddy and now road manager, Joe Esposito, whenever Elvis and his crew hung out in Vegas, one of their favorite haunts. Now, Elvis was coming to see *Vive Les Girls.* But that wasn't all. Jennifer pulled me aside, out of earshot of the other girls, and whispered, "Want to go to a party in Elvis's suite after the show?" It took everything I had not to jump up and down and screech like a cat in heat. "*DO I?!*" Does a chicken have a pecker?

The rest of the night was a blur. I could hardly breathe, let alone concentrate on my dance moves. The theater was empty except for Elvis and his entourage, fifteen to twenty of them, who jammed into the big, red leather booths in the back of the room, appropriately called King's Row. I thought I could make out the glare of Elvis's sunglasses, which he apparently wore even in the dark, but the stage lights shining in my eyes made it impossible to tell for sure. All the showgirls were nervous and excited, but I was beside myself. I couldn't believe that I was actually performing in front of ELVIS FREAKING PRESLEY!

Somehow I made it through the show without falling off the stage, throwing up, or crashing into a wall, and Jennifer and I got out of our costumes and into our "civilian" clothes at record speed.

When we arrived at the International, Joe escorted us up to a special private penthouse. It wasn't *on* the top floor; it *was* the top floor. I thought that places like this only existed in the movies. It was a sprawling, high-ceilinged series of rooms that went on forever. Miles of white shag carpeting opened to floor-to-ceiling windows with views of the twinkling lights of the Strip stretching out below. A few steps led down into a sunken living room where a U-shaped, white sectional formed an enormous conversation pit. Gold-veined mirror tiles covered entire walls. A spiral staircase led up to a loft. This was the height of '70s glamour!

We gravitated to the bar where Joe introduced me to the "Memphis Mafia"—Sonny and Red West—and "the boys."

"Just what we need around here," Sonny drawled, nodding in his cousin's direction. "Another redhead." Red laughed good-naturedly and reached his hand out to shake mine. Along with Joe and Jennifer and the other twenty or so guests, I sipped my screwdriver while my eyes scanned the room for some sign of the King.

"Here's our boy!" shouted Joe. I turned around and there was Elvis, standing before me like in a dream. Dressed from head to toe in black, the white room against his slim, dark silhouette seemed to create a glowing aura around him. He was *so* tall and his voice was *so* deep— God, that voice! When he spoke, it was the voice I knew so well, the voice on the records, the voice from the movies. Elvis said hello to each person in our circle, Ma'am-ing the ladies and Sir-ing the men. He took my hand and told me how much he'd enjoyed our show. Wait! What!? Elvis Presley was holding my hand and complimenting me? This couldn't be happening!

Eventually the crowd thinned out and Jennifer and Joe slipped away. Elvis invited me to sit with him. He led me over to the conversation pit and that's what we did. For hours. Conversate. We talked and talked and talked. Actually, he did most of the talking and I did most of the listening, which was good because I was so awestruck I could barely move my mouth. For a thirty-four-year-old, he still had a sweet, naïve quality that made him seem closer to my age.

"I gotta ask," he said, leaning toward me. "What the heck are you doin' in Vegas? You're way too young to be alone in a place like this."

"Well," I took a deep breath. "It's a long story, and you'll probably think I'm nuts, but I'm here because of you." I told him about my obsession with his movie *Viva Las Vegas,* and the spring-break trip with my parents when I got picked out of the crowd to be in the show.

"Why didn't you at least get obsessed with…uh, uh…*Blue Hawaii?*" he asked, deadpan. When he saw the befuddled look on my face, his lip suddenly curled into that famous, sexy, crooked smile. That story led to a very heavy, very long conversation about spirituality, religion, numerology, and astrology, which, unknown to me, Elvis had been into for years. He explained that what had happened to me was no coincidence. For emphasis, he grabbed an envelope addressed to his dad, Vernon Presley, and scribbled some numbers and letters on the front and back. The numbers correlated to letters that spelled out words like "love," "light," and "home." That letter is still one of my prized possessions.

He went on to talk about his tour; "the boys"; Ann-Margret; his marriage to Priscilla, which he described as complicated; and his daughter, Lisa Marie, who he clearly adored.

He was just chatty chatty chatty. I was thrilled out of my mind, but couldn't help wondering why he was confiding in a teenage showgirl. At one point he asked whether I'd done drugs. I told him I'd experimented with this and that but mainly just smoked pot. He seemed offended, almost angry, and launched into a very fatherly lecture on the evils of

TWELVE
OMEN
B-RIGHT
HOME
AUM
AMEN
LOVE
L
HISTORY
26 - 8
26 - 8
PRESENT
MAN-KIND
LIGHT
D.EATH

HISTORICAL
TORAH

HIRE THE HANDICAPPED
IT'S GOOD BUSINESS

Vernon Presley
3764 Highway 51 South
Memphis, Tennessee

City of Memphis
Tennessee
Office of the Mayor

IT THE HEART
IT'S ALL THERE SELF
INSIGHT SELVES
UNI·VERSE·AL
ISRAELITES
EVERYONE GOSPEL
EVERYTHING INTERESTING
INSPIRING
GENE·IS·IS
IT DOES NOT MATTER
IF YOU REALIZE
GOD ELEVEN
SEVEN

drugs—even pot smoking—which he explained was not only bad for me, but in case I didn't know, illegal.

"If you ever want to make anything out of yourself, little girl," Elvis said, without a trace of humor on his face, "never do drugs." He seemed one-hundred-percent sincere, which in retrospect, makes it especially sad and ironic.

Later that night Elvis took me into a side room where a huge, black grand piano dominated the decor. He sat down and began to play. I recognized the song; it was Beethoven's "Moonlight Sonata." I was mesmerized by his beautiful piano playing. Even though "Moonlight Sonata" has no lyrics, he began to sing along. He patted the bench next to him, motioning for me to sit down.

After a minute or two, I got the gist of the melody and joined in with a little harmony. When the song was done, he turned to me and said, "Y'know, you've got a pretty voice. Have you sung much before?"

"Just in my high school choir," I said, feeling stupid.

This launched him into another lecture. "I've known a lot of show-girls here and once they get older, they end up being waitresses or deal-ers or…" he cleared his throat and gave me a funny look, "…worse."

"You mean, like, hookers?" I responded.

"Yeah. I mean, like, hookers," he chuckled. "Now, if I was you, I'd take some vocal lessons, get into singing, and get the heck outta Dodge."

Even though I believed that as a showgirl I'd made it to the big time and accomplished my dream, those words, coming out of Elvis Presley's mouth, changed my life forever.

By now, sunlight was pouring in through the massive windows. When one of Elvis's people came to tell him it was time for him to go to bed, I felt like he was a little boy being reprimanded by his father. He led me to the large marble foyer and, in front of his "handlers," wrapped his arms around me and kissed me long and tenderly. Instead of expe-riencing the moment, all I could do was think, "Oh my god, oh Jesus, oh god! I'm kissing Elvis Presley! This can't be happening!" It was so surreal that I was sure at any moment I'd wake up alone in my bed at home. When we finally came up for air, he let go of me, stepped back, and said, "Take care of yourself, Cassandra. And don't you forget what I said." As he was literally being pulled by one of his goons to the door of his bedroom, he touched his fingers to his lips, then pointed them in my direction. The door opened and closed, and as I stood staring after him, I distinctly heard the sound of giggling girls coming from inside his room. Hmmm.

I stood in the foyer, knees weak, unable to move or breathe, staring at the door behind which Elvis had just disappeared. One of the guys who had wrangled him took hold of my arm and escorted me outside into the glaring fluorescent light of the hallway.

"Why don't you just sleep here tonight," he suggested, probably noticing I looked way too tired, dazed, or drunk to drive. "We've got plenty of room." He accompanied me down the hall to a room where a young boy, one of Elvis's cousins, I later learned, was sound asleep in one of two twin beds. I crawled into the empty bed, clothes, makeup, and all, and fell sound asleep. Sometime in the late afternoon, my eyes sprung open. What was I doing alone in a hotel room? "Oh, yeah..." The events of the night before came streaming into my head and, for a moment, I wondered whether I'd been hallucinating. Once I convinced myself that it had really happened, the very next thought that popped into my head was, "Find a vocal coach!"

On my way out of the hotel, it was all I could do to not stop strangers in the International's lobby and shout at the top of my lungs, "I just spent the night with Elvis!" I walked past the long line of people waiting to get tickets for his show that night and felt so smug I thought I'd explode. I then drove through the scorching desert heat as fast as I could to tell someone, *anyone*, what had just happened. I immediately hunted down Buddy and Sterling and told them the incredible story. Their reaction was the one I wanted. They knew how I worshipped Elvis and were as thrilled and blown away as I'd hoped they'd be. They recommended I see their vocal coach, Violetta Hall. I practically flew to the phone and called her to set up my first voice lesson.

Coincidently (or not?), Jerry Jackson was working on a new dance number dubbed "Les Lesbiennes" for *Vive*. An audition was coming up for a singer to "intro" the number, and it was open to all the girls in the show. I worked and worked on the song with Violetta, spending a lot more money than I could afford, but it paid off. I was beyond elated when I got the part, and along with it a raise. Thank you, Elvis!

The new number was intended to promote the edgier, hipper "Le Crazy Horse" vibe of the show. As a saxophone began a slow, seductive wail, I strolled alone onto the dark stage, lit cigarette in hand, into a pool of light. I wore a long, tight, black pinstriped skirt and jacket, with a white button-down shirt, red necktie, and black fedora with my long hair tucked up inside. In my best low, sexy voice, I crooned the signature Sophie Tucker tune, "A Good Man Is Hard to Find." As the song ended, the other girls entered dressed in the same '40s gun-moll getup I was wearing, and I joined them in a slow, sensuous striptease. First, we whipped off our skirts and tossed them to the side, exposing black garter belts and stockings. Then the neckties were loosened and flung away. Finally, we unbuttoned our cuffs and collars and, at the dramatic "climax" of the number, tore open our Velcro shirtfronts to expose our breasts. All the while, Pat Gill, the lead dancer, was being roughly shoved around the stage from girl to girl, each one systematically pulling off pieces of her flimsy, pink chiffon gown. At the end of the number, all the girls closed in on the frightened-looking lead nude. We threw her back, removed our hats, and tossed our long red, brunette, or blonde hair over her writhing, naked body as the stage lights dimmed to black. It was a hit! Apparently nothing turns people on like a good all-female gang bang.

CHAPTER 11

IT'S NOT UNUSUAL

Vegas was a never-ending three-ring circus. The story I'm about to tell has become a pretty well-known piece of folklore ever since I was on *The Howard Stern Show* and blabbed about the whole embarrassing episode on national radio. To get me on the show as a guest, Mark, my husband and manager at the time, told them the smarmiest, most sensational story he could possibly come up with about me. Cut to a few months later and there I was in the green room of Howard Stern's New York City studio at 6:00 a.m. chugging whiskey to get up the nerve to answer the questions I knew were coming.

I was a fan of the Howard Stern Show. I enjoyed listening to the rude things he said to other people, but I wasn't happy about being in the hot seat. It was at the height of Howard's popularity and both he and Robin, his sidekick, couldn't have been nicer or more gracious. They made me feel as comfortable as possible beforehand, including having "Earthdog Fred" bring me a glass full of "Jack" to steady my nerves. When I arrived Howard said, "Damn, woman. You're old, but *I'd* bang you!" Coming from Howard, I took it as a huge compliment.

Ever since the day my interview played on Howard's show, guys have been approaching me with a smirk saying things like, "Tom Jones, huh?" and I can feel my face grow hot while I smile and do my best to act like it doesn't bother me. Ugh.

In September of 1970 I took the one and only vacation I had during my stint as a showgirl to celebrate my birthday with my family and friends in Colorado Springs. As soon as I got there, I made the rounds of all my old nightclub haunts, and just to make sure everyone knew I was now a showgirl in Las Vegas, I wore extra-revealing clothes and almost as much makeup as I plastered on for one of my shows. I ended up at Kelker Junction and ran into a friend. The last time I'd seen Joe, he'd painted my bikinied body with Day-Glo flowers and paisley designs so I'd look extra groovy under the black lights while dancing on my pedestal there. He was a hyphenate—artist-construction worker-biker—who I'd been aware of since the age of ten. Back then he was a hot, greasy-haired hoodlum who was dating the big sister of my grade-school friend April. One afternoon, April and I hid behind her parents' BarcaLounger and watched her sister and Joe make out on their pink-and-red-flowered sofa. Hearing their groans and seeing their clumsy groping and fondling made me strangely excited, confused, scared, and sick to my stomach all at the same time. It was the first time I'd seen anything like that, and it would give me a lot to ponder over the summer break between fifth and sixth grade.

A late bloomer, I was the last girl in my class to get her "monthly visitor." When my period still hadn't shown up at age fourteen, my mom assured me that some kind of cancerous tumor must be eating away at my female parts and took me to the doctor. Our family general practitioner—Dr. Paap, I shit you not—announced that I needed to be on the pill to jump-start my period, and I was thunderstruck when my mother actually agreed to it. To her, a former nurse, a doctor's dictum was equal to the word of God, so she accepted his decree and I left, prescription in hand. Those were the days when it seemed that every adult woman was on the newly liberating birth-control pill, and like the good Girl Scout I still was, it was reassuring to "be prepared," even though it would be several more years before it would come in handy.

Joe was quite a bit older than me, in his mid-twenties, with longish, curly brown hair and an adorable gap-toothed smile that exposed two dreamy dimples. At one point, he and his English bulldog, Tubby, lived next door to my family in a little cottage behind our neighbor's house. Joe was cute, funny, and charming, so there was never a shortage of girls coming and going from his place. I'd known him so long that I felt very comfortable around him, like an old family friend. I found out much later that he'd boffed both my sisters. It wouldn't surprise me to find out he'd done my mom, too. He was that irresistible.

When 2:00 a.m. rolled around, Joe and I wound up at the house he shared with a couple of other bikers from the Sons of Silence. I must have decided it was finally time, because without much fanfare, we ended up in Joe's bed, repeating the groaning, grasping scene I'd witnessed so many years before at my friend April's house—and before I knew what was happening, we were *doing it*. I think. It didn't feel like much, really. Later, he did a pencil sketch of us that captured that particular moment in time, and that I have to this day.

AND WE WEREN'T EVEN DRUNK!

Having sex hadn't turned out to be at all like I'd imagined so many years before during my "sexual awakening" in the back seat of my mom's Ford Fairlane. Where was the rapturous, romantic encounter that Barbara Mason had crooned about on the radio? I sure didn't hear bells or angels' voices. I chalked it up to the fact that Joe and I were just "buddies" and knew each other too well for sex to be that exciting, but I had to wonder whether someone's equipment had malfunctioned, either mine or his, because, honestly, I didn't feel a thing!

The Peggy Lee song "Is That All There Is" came to mind and played over and over in my head for days afterward. All the deep fear and anxiety I'd had about fucking had apparently been unfounded. Of course, it had been my parents who had put the fear of God into me about sex: pregnancy, disease, filthy, dirty, disgusting, ick ick ick! Down deep I was so relieved to have the whole thing over! All those years of worrying and waiting and being snubbed for being a prick-tease were behind me. I wanted to kick my own ass for putting it off for so long and making it into such a big, scary deal. I was livid that I'd wasted all the incredible opportunities I might have had with the likes of Jimi Hendrix or, who knows, even Elvis!

But back to Tom.

When I returned to Vegas from Colorado, Buddy and Sterling offered to take me to Caesar's Palace to see Tom Jones, the hottest act on the Strip. Tom was in his prime. His songs were all over the charts and everyone in the country was flipping out over him. I didn't know much about him and wasn't a fan of his music, with the exception of "What's New Pussycat," which had that swingin' London sound I loved. He was a lot older than the singers I liked, but I went along to see what all the fuss was about—and I was stunned! With that powerful voice, skintight pants, and shirt unbuttoned to his navel showing off his hairy chest, I decided he was the hottest, most charismatic performer I'd ever seen (after Elvis, of course). I couldn't believe a guy could gyrate and swivel his hips like that, especially an "old" dude. No wonder women in the audience were throwing their room keys and panties onstage!

I can't remember how I ended up backstage after the show. Maybe Buddy or Sterling accompanied me or maybe I just used the gate-crashing groupie tactics I'd learned as a kid, but I somehow found myself among a gaggle of adoring fans crammed into Tom Jones's plush Caesar's Palace dressing room. I did my best to mingle and look sexy, maintaining a casual "oh-yeah-this-is-just-me-hanging-out-in-Tom-Jones's-dressing-room-I-do-this-all-the-time" attitude. I kept one eye super-glued to Tom's sharkskin-encased ass. He made the rounds as my eyes bored into the halo of damp brown ringlets that brushed the ruffled collar of his shirt. He shook hands with the men and charmed the ladies with a peck on both cheeks—so continental! Then it happened. I looked up just in time to see him sauntering in my direction. He stopped right in front of me, giving me the head-to-toe with a lopsided grin. I stared slack-jawed into his handsome face with its straight nose and manly chin shaded in the sun-kissed glow of Man Tan bronzing gel. In that famous husky Welsh accent of his, he asked, "And who are you, love?" I caught a faint whiff of his cologne—English Leather? Jade East? I couldn't tell, but I knew it was expensive. It was all I could do to keep my knees from buckling under me. I somehow managed to exhale my name and I must have gotten it right because he replied, "Cassandra? Beautiful name for a beautiful lady." I made a quick backward glance to make sure he wasn't talking to someone behind me. "Care for a champagne cocktail, then?" he asked, eyes boring into mine. Yes, I nodded. He seemed to turn in slow motion and made his way through the crowd in the direction of the makeshift dressing-room bar, glancing back once to make sure I hadn't disappeared. I watched his broad, muscular shoulders ripple beneath the thin, white shirt he wore as he disappeared into the hazy, smoke-filled room. In my mind, everything went silent. The only sound I heard was the blood pounding in my ears. My mouth was so dry my lips stuck together, which was probably a good thing. I was so excited I might have let it fly open and announce in some kind of Gomer Pyle voice, "Well, gooooollly! Tom Jones is gittin' me a draaank!" The flocked wallpaper glowed a fuzzy burnt orange in the gold lamplight of his dressing room. A half-smoked Virginia Slim lay smoldering in the melamine Caesar's Palace ashtray next to me.

He returned holding two brimming champagne glasses and, with a sharp tilt of his white-boy Afro, motioned me toward a love seat in the alcove behind us. He plopped down next to me, leg resting against mine, and began to make small talk.

"So, you live in Las Vegas then, or you just visitin'?" I was afraid to look at his face. Afraid I might pass out.

"I live here. I'm a showgirl at the Dunes," I replied, casting my eyes downward to stare at one of his black pointy-toe boots framed by orange shag carpeting.

A slightly tipsy man in a gray business suit swept up to us.

"Hey Tom, great show!" he effused. "Say, would you mind signing a program for my wife? I'll get laid every day for the next year!" Tom let out a subtle sigh, stood up, smiled, and graciously scribbled his name.

I grinned up at the man and took another big gulp of my drink. Tom topped off my glass from the bottle of Dom that had been delivered to him, so thankfully there were no interruptions in the administration of my liquid anxiety medication. He sat back down next to me and placed a hand on my thigh. I took another hit of bubbly courage. We continued to chat as the night wore on and the crowd thinned out.

"Well, baby, looks like the party's over," Tom breathed in my ear. "I've just heard the most amazing song today. You've gotta come up to my room and have a listen." Honestly, he could have said, "I've got the most gigantic pimple on me arse. You've just gotta come up to my room and pop it!" and I would have trotted right along with him. I have to hand it to him for at least giving me the option of saying no.

Just as we reached the door of Tom's penthouse suite, a husky-sized, frizzy-haired boy several years younger than me came wandering down the hall with a sandwich in one hand and a tall glass of milk in the other.

"Hullo, Da'," the kid mumbled. There was an awkward moment of silence. Tom's Man Tan suddenly went pale. He turned his back on him and fumbled with the door key.

"Oh, uh, this is my son, Mark." Tom said brusquely, gesturing in the boy's general direction.

"Hi there," I slurred, giving a little wave as I stumbled over the threshold into Tom's room. The fact that this kid might have a mother somewhere never crossed my mind. Oops.

I lounged on the horseshoe-shaped couch while Tom slipped a cassette into his player. I heard the song that I'll forever link with him, "The First Time Ever I Saw Your Face" by Roberta Flack. I'd never heard it before, and it turned me on as much as it seemed to turn Tom on— musical Spanish fly.

We began kissing to the slow, seductive song that oozed from the recorder and the next thing I knew, I was in Tom's bed and he was on top of me. It was pretty well known from the skintight pants that Tom Jones was famous for wearing onstage that he was well endowed. There were rumors he stuffed his pants with socks. Well, I'm here to tell you he didn't.

Cut back to me on the bottom and Tom Jones on top, banging away. Even though I'd had more than my share of champagne, it wasn't enough to dull the searing, stabbing pain I was feeling between my legs. This wasn't supposed to be happening! It wasn't anything like the time before with Joe.

"Stop, stop! You're hurting me!" I cried. I pushed him off me and sat up, clutching a pillow to cover my chest.

Tom leapt to his feet beside the king-size bed. I couldn't help staring at his huge hard-on which now drooped toward the floor, looking as dejected as the expression on his face. "What the hell is wrong with you?" he asked.

"I'm a virgin!" I blubbered, pointing to the bloodstains on the sheet as evidence. Okay, I know. That maybe wasn't *technically* true, but it was the best answer I could come up with.

"Oh, really. You're a Las Vegas showgirl and a virgin?" He snorted, rolling his eyes. "D'ya really expect me to believe that?"

I felt so ashamed and humiliated that I began to bawl. "I just want to go home!" At least he was gentleman enough to arrange for a car, but he definitely wasn't happy.

My dream date had turned into a nightmare, but it didn't put a damper on the excitement I felt. Even though the night had ended on a decidedly down note, during my ride home I couldn't believe I'd actually "been" with *the* Tom Jones! When I got back to my place, I woke up my roommates to tell them the news and they were almost as astonished as I was.

Despite the pain, the blood, the humiliation, I still suffered from the delusion that so many young women feel after their first time. Finally— this was true love. Tom and I would be married in a fabulous Las Vegas wedding ceremony at the Little Chapel of the West and I would become Mrs. Tom Jones! That night at work amid daydreams of Tom and me on our honeymoon, it became apparent that no amount of tamponage would stem the tide of blood leaking out of me. Jennifer insisted that after the show I head straight to the hospital emergency room.

I remember my face burning as I recounted the embarrassing details of what had happened, graciously leaving Tom's name out of it. I was given a shot to numb the area, which was almost worse than whatever went on after that. They categorized it as some kind of "hymeneal injury." A few stitches later I was as good as I was ever going to be. Oh God, am I really sitting here writing about my cooze?

I quickly recovered from the physical pain, and the very next night, like the clueless kid I was, returned to Caesars Palace after Tom's show. I was so excited about seeing my future husband that I could hardly breathe. In my mind, I saw myself enter Tom's dressing room. He would see me from across the crowded room and time would stand still. We would rush into each other's arms in slow motion and he would shower me in kisses, apologize for the night before, and beg my forgiveness.

But when I entered his dressing room, my rainbow-colored fantasies disintegrated before my eyes and my heart was broken into a million little pieces. There he was, *my* man, caught red-handed, snuggled up on *our* loveseat, making out with not one, but *two* girls—his backup singers, the Blossoms! Before he got the chance to come up for air and spot me, I turned, tears stinging my eyes, and stumbled for the door, completely and utterly devastated. It's hard to believe, even for me, that I could've been that naïve at the ripe old age of eighteen, but although my body belied my innocence, I was still inexperienced, both physically and emotionally.

For the next week I drove all the girls in the dressing room crazy. Between my uncontrollable sobs, I played Tom Jones's song "I Who Have Nothing" over and over and *over* again on my portable cassette player, drowning in my own sorrow. After three nights of that, Kathleen, the brassy blonde from Jersey, stomped up to my dressing table. Fuming, she grabbed my player, jerked the cassette out of the machine, unraveling the thin, shiny tape, and threw it with all her might across the room. "Get the fuck over it, awready!" she shouted. And I did.

I wish I could say that was the end of the Tom Jones saga, but there's a very pathetic addendum to this story. Several years later, I drove from LA to Vegas for the weekend with my best friend and fellow struggling actress, Lynn Guthrie. We managed to get backstage after seeing Tom's show. At the first opportunity, we wiggled our way through the crowded dressing room to say hello to Tom.

"Hi Tom!" I chirped, setting myself up. "Remember me?"

Just being this close to him again caused the color to rise in my face and sweat to bead on my forehead. The room felt suddenly hot and airless. Tom's fans pressed in against me from every side, jostling for position.

"Of course," he sneered, looking me in the eye. "You're the one with the scars on your back." His cruelty that night was a lot more painful than the stitches.

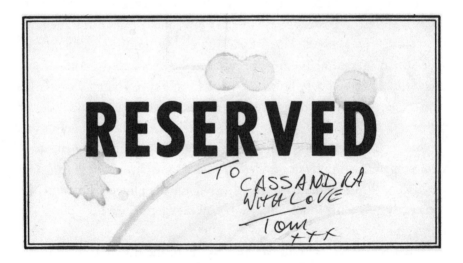

Not long after the Tom Jones experience, I realized that Vegas had lost its charm. The thrill was gone. After more than a year, dancing in the show had become a robotic ritual that I was forced to endure two or three times a night. On stage I now stared straight ahead, grimacing a fake smile while I thought of a laundry list of things I had to do after the show—like for example, the laundry. Top that off with the knowledge that my closest friends, Buddy and Sterl, were leaving the show and moving on to bigger and better things in Paris, and I knew in my heart that Elvis had been right—Vegas was no place for a teenage girl. I'd been the youngest showgirl in town, and I sure as hell didn't want to be the oldest. Now was a good time for leaving Las Vegas.

CHAPTER 12

ROME IF YOU WANT TO

A Roma in cerca di Cassandra

DA LAS VEGAS, sono passati al Lido di Parigi, questi due cantanti ballerini americani: Buddy West e Sterling Clark. Nel nuovo show che sarà presentato il 10 dicembre ai Champs Elysées rappresenteranno la nuova corrente musicale americana, l'Hard Rock music, in attesa di iniziare le prove ai primi di novembre sono passati per Roma a trovare una compagna di lavoro, Cassandra Peterson, che a Roma sta interpretando dei films. Come cantanti ballerini sono abbastanza quotati in America, per aver partecipato ad alcuni dei più famosi musical, «Funny Girl», «Sweet Charity» e «Hello Dolly». Sono stati scoperti da Julia Prowse l'ex fidanzata di Frank Sinatra, ed hanno partecipato a parecchi shows per la televisione americana. Vengono da Los Angeles e sperano di poter lavorare anche per la TV italiana in una qualche futura «Canzonissima».

Once Buddy and Sterling were settled in Paris and had begun rehearsals for their new show, *The Lido de Paris* on the Champs-Élysées, they convinced me to get my butt over there and try out. I packed up my place; sold my car, TV, and what little furniture I'd acquired; and headed for France.

Buddy and Sterling had rented a large, charming house in Le Perreux-sur-Marne, a suburb of Paris, taking the train into town daily to rehearse. I moved into the cozy, sloped-ceiling attic room.

They introduced me to Miss Bluebell, the famous dance mistress for the *Lido*, and I was granted an audition. She was well aware of *Vive Les Girls* and was impressed that I'd been in the show. But despite that, I didn't meet the five-foot-ten height requirement to be one of the famous Bluebell Girls, and no matter how Buddy and Sterl begged and cajoled, she wouldn't budge.

Weeks went by while I hung out at the house on the outskirts of Paris, wondering what to do and where to go next. I loved staying with the boys but knew I couldn't freeload indefinitely—I was blowing through my savings and would have to find work sooner than later. By now, Sunny had also left *Vive*. She came to Paris for a visit and joined us in the house in Le Perreux. Soon, I talked her into coming with me to Rome. I convinced her we would find work there, and if we didn't, the Italian men would more than make up for it.

We bought our train tickets and made plans to leave France on January 1. New Year's Eve was spent watching the *Lido* show, then celebrating with the boys at the famous Georges V hotel. High on Dom Perignon, I went to sleep in my little attic room for the last time. Sometime during the night, much to my surprise and elation, Buddy slipped into bed with me and we made love for the first and only time, bringing my longtime crush to a dream-fulfilling "climax."

First thing New Year's Day, while Buddy slept, Sunny and I said our tearful goodbyes to Sterling and left for Rome. I listened to "(I Can't Live If Livin' Is) Without You" by Harry Nilsson on my little tape recorder, thought of Buddy, and cried all the way to Italy.

Arriving in Rome was an awakening. Walking down the ancient

cobblestone streets, past the ruins and the beautiful decaying buildings, made me feel better than alive. The sounds, the tastes, the smells were all so delicious and familiar. Whether sitting in a little bar sipping cappuccino or strolling past a fountain in a grand piazza, I had the distinct impression that this was where I was meant to be. I explored the ancient city streets for hours on end and it felt like coming home.

Sunny and I found a tiny, but comfortable room in Pensione Ginevra, not far from the Via Veneto, on Via Quintino Sella. It was a second-story walk-up above a coffee bar, where I went every morning for warm, freshly baked *cornettos*. The pensione was also home to the Italian family who owned it, Signora and Signore Fabrizi and their teenaged son, Picci (pronounced "Peachy"). They lived in a cordoned-off area consisting of a kitchen, bathroom, and one bedroom that they all shared. The other four bedrooms were rented out nightly. Sunny and I slept in a cozy room with two twin beds and shared a bathroom with the other residents. The place was modest in the extreme, but the family was warm and welcoming and the intoxicating smells of homemade Italian food wafting from their kitchen at all hours of the day gave it a homey feel.

Sunny and I met another guest staying at the Pensione—an older Black man, probably in his thirties, named Eduardo—who happened to be an excellent guitarist from Brazil. We came up with the idea to form a singing duo and talked him into accompanying us. After getting a short repertoire of songs together, we landed a gig at a nightclub nearby. It didn't pay much but provided us with enough lire to keep a roof over our heads and buy a little food. The gig ended abruptly when Sunny got fed up with living hand to mouth, crammed into a tiny room with me. Declaring she was homesick, she headed back to the US, leaving me on my own.

But my time alone in Rome didn't last long. Another former *Vive* showgirl, Maria Gambotti, soon came to visit from Corsica where she now lived. Despite the Italian last name, Maria spoke only French and English, which didn't help us much when it came to navigating the city. She arrived in her little car, a Cinque Cento that looked like a sardine can but came in handy for tooling around Rome and its environs.

One evening, Maria and I went to Trastevere, the "old" section of

Rome. As we walked down the quiet, narrow streets, the sound of our heels reverberating off the ancient buildings, we heard a commotion up ahead. Bright lights pierced the dark sky, and we could see that a crowd had gathered. Following the sound and light we discovered a film crew shooting a movie—exciting! We edged our way through the gathering to get a closer look. There among the crew, running to and fro moving cables, setting props, and hollering out instructions, was a familiar face from Las Vegas, Stuart Birnbaum. Maria and I instantly recognized him as the film student who had interviewed us in Vegas for a documentary he was making about showgirls. Small world, right?

We waved our hands in Stuart's direction and squealed his name. He was as surprised to see us as we were to see him. He explained that he was there working as a student director on the film *Roma*, directed by Federico Fellini. My jaw dropped. *The* Federico Fellini? The same Federico Fellini who had directed *La Dolce Vita, 8 1/2*, and *Fellini Satyricon*? I was stunned when Stuart assured me it was the one and only.

"Would you like to meet Signore Fellini?" he asked. Seriously? E il Papa cattolico?

"Yes!" we shouted in unison.

A few minutes later, there we were, shaking hands with Federico Fellini himself. He cut an imposing figure and seemed larger than life, but was gracious, soft-spoken, and flattering.

"Deed-a anyone ever tell-a you dat you look-a like my wife, Giulietta Masina, when she was-a young?" he said, staring at me pointedly.

Honestly, at that moment I had no idea who the heck she was or how she looked, but that didn't stop me from answering, "Oh! Yeah. All the time!" Fellini went back to his directing duties and left Maria and me standing there, dumbfounded. A few minutes later, Stuart was back. The words that came out of his mouth nearly knocked us over.

"Mr. Fellini asked if you'd like to be extras in the scene we're setting up?" Before you could say "porca miseria," we were in a wardrobe trailer changing into evening gowns and having our hair and makeup done. We were playing guests at a boxing match, taking place in the center of a piazza. I blended into the background while Maria got a nice close-up, standing up and screeching, "Kill him! Kill him!" while the boxers duked it out. Much to our delight and surprise, after a very long night, we were actually paid! We were so thrilled to work in a real film, making money hadn't crossed our minds. It wasn't much, but it was enough to pay for a few more nights at Pensione Ginevra.

Several days later, Maria headed back to Corsica to take care of her ailing mother, and I was once again on my own in Rome. Stuart and I had exchanged numbers and, before long, I got another call from him asking whether I'd like to work as an extra in a few more scenes. He didn't have to ask twice; I was there! Night after night, for almost thirty days, I showed up on the set. Fellini shot a sequence in which I rode on the back of a motorcycle, my arms wrapped tight around a super-hot Italian guy, zipping through the streets of Rome, past some of the more famous sights: Piazza di Spagna, the Roman Forum, and the Colosseum. Nice work if you can get it, right? I later played a hooker in a '40s bordello scene and a student in a '60s riot. I worked on *Fellini's Roma* every night for a month and ended up as a mere flash of red hair in the finished film but had a great time and made enough to keep myself alive for a few more weeks.

Our last shots took place at Cinecittà, Europe's largest film studio, on the outskirts of Rome. I somehow wound up at lunch in the commissary sitting at a long table with some of the cast, crew, and Signore Fellini himself. I was in awe to be in the presence of such greatness and had the good sense to keep my mouth shut and just listen. Someone at the table mentioned he'd heard they were hiring extras for another movie shooting on the lot, a bizarre, avant-garde film called *Salomè* starring the famous German model Verushka and written and directed by Carmelo Bene. I immediately looked into it and soon returned to Cinecittà to play a cornice (or was it a "buttress"?), hanging my bare ass over the edge of a building. The beautiful Black actress who played the same role, but on the opposite corner of the facade, glanced over at me at one point, rolled her eyes, and said, "If anyone asks me what I was doing last night, I ain't sayin' *nothin'*!"

Feeling lonely and a little homesick, I convinced my parents to allow my sister Melody to come over and stay with me, and they bought her a one-way ticket as a belated high school graduation gift. I was happy to see someone from home, especially someone who spoke English, and I was excited to show her around Rome. She shared my room at the pensione and soon I was able to get her some "extra" work too. As redheads we were a popular pair!

A few film gigs came our way, mainly in spaghetti westerns or horror films, where I sometimes got to deliver a line or two. I was offered a part as a Catholic nun in a major international film, *I Diavoli* (*The Devils*) from director Ken Russell, but when I discovered that the part entailed not only nudity but also having to shave my head, I reluctantly declined. I mean, naked is one thing, but baldness—no, my brother! One film Melody and I worked on together, *All' Onorevole Piacciono Le Donne*, was coincidently directed by legendary gore-meister Lucio Fulvi. It was filmed in an ancient monastery in the mountains and Melody and I played Catholic *sorelle*, sisters. We slept in tiny, freezing medieval cells for a week. Method acting.

* * *

Melody and I went from one little acting gig to another, but we were having fun and, most importantly, keeping a roof over our heads. But a month after she arrived, my sister hooked up with Massimiliano, an out-of-work, English-speaking Italian she'd met at our favorite hangout, Club Yellow, and off she went with him, despite me begging her not to leave.

The low point of my stay in Italy—actually one of the lowest points of my life—happened around this time. I also met a guy at Club Yellow who I liked. Franco was good-looking in a mafioso sort of way, dressing impeccably in expensive suits, crisp white European-cut shirts, and lots of gold jewelry. He was so much more worldly and charming than the other guys I'd met there, and soon he was taking me to the fanciest restaurants in the city for some fantastic Italian meals, which was a nice break from my usual diet of mozzarella and *suppli*, fried rice-balls. After dating a short time, I began staying over with him occasionally in his creepy basement apartment.

Franco spoke Italian only, and my poor language skills must have impeded my sense of character judgment, because it wasn't long before I made a strange discovery. Every night, around 3:00 a.m., Franco would creep out of bed, get dressed, and silently leave the apartment while I pretended to be asleep. One night, after I was sure he'd gone, I climbed out of bed and began snooping around. I snuck into the empty second bedroom and opened the door to a large closet. The rods were jam-packed with dozens of fur coats, and the shelves held boxes and bags full of high-end jewelry. I stood for several minutes, staring at the luxurious loot, wondering what it meant. Was Franco really a burglar? That's the only conclusion I could draw.

When he returned to the apartment just before dawn, I confronted him in my best, very limited Italian. He flipped out and charged toward me, flailing his arms with dramatic Italian flair and shouting a string of words I couldn't decipher, except for a few phrases: *non dire niente*—"say nothing"—and *ti ucciderò!*—"I'll kill you!"

I fell hard onto the bed. The blow came out of nowhere, striking the side of my head and sending me reeling backward. The room went black and I saw a tiny white-gold fireworks display behind my eyelids. It's true, you really do see stars, I remember thinking. I heard the blood rush into my ears, whoosh, whoosh, whoosh, as pain throbbed in my temples.

The heels of his expensive Italian boots clicked back and forth across the tile floor with resolved purpose. "Franco?" I called. My voice echoed through the sparsely furnished apartment. Somewhere, the sound of a distant siren blared, then grew faint. The door slammed so hard I felt shock waves shudder through the mattress.

I sat on the edge of the bed for a moment, massaging my temples. When I felt steady enough, I grabbed my things, stuffed them into my bag as fast as I could, and headed for the door. It wouldn't open. I tried again, tugging, pulling, jiggling the lock. It still wouldn't open. I sat down and waited. Would he come back? And if he did, what then? I soon fell into a restless sleep.

When I woke up, the room was beginning to grow dark and Franco still wasn't back. I realized there was no phone in the apartment. As night approached, I tried yelling for help at the top of my lungs, but no one answered, no one came. I used a hairpin I'd found in the bottom of my purse and a knife from the kitchen to try to pick the lock, but the door wouldn't budge. Because it was a basement apartment, the only opening to the outside was a window well topped with a layer of thick glass brick underneath a sidewalk. I could see blurry images of people hurrying by above me, but no matter how loud I yelled or how hard I banged on it with a kitchen saucepan, no one reacted. After four days I'd gone through almost every bit of food that I could find in the kitchen cabinets and was getting more and more scared and desperate by the minute. Then, in the middle of the night, I awoke to the sound of someone unlocking the door. I held my breath. My heart pounded so hard it felt like it would burst through my chest. It was Franco's partner in crime, Mario, a chubby little chain-smoking gangster, dressed in black. He looked at me but didn't speak. I lay there staring at him, scared to death of what might happen next. Suddenly he threw the door open.

Vai!—"Go!"—he commanded. Still wearing my clothes and shoes, I bolted out of the apartment without my purse or overnight bag. I ran down the brightly lit hallway and up the stairs as fast as my legs would carry me, not turning to look back once. When I reached the outside, I kept running, down dark streets and narrow passages between buildings, intermittently ducking into doorways and peering around corners to make sure he wasn't following me. When I finally felt safe, I stopped to catch my breath and broke into sobs of relief. My heart pounded. The cold winter air burned my lungs and my sweat felt like icy fingers running down my spine. Now I had a new problem. Where the fuck was I? I had no idea what part of Rome I was in. I had no money, no phone numbers, no passport. I was starving. I'd eaten almost nothing for the past two days. I wandered the streets until the sun came up. By morning, I was reduced to standing on a corner bumming change, something I'd done back in my hippie days in Colorado Springs when I'd needed cigarettes, but now I was much more desperate. I eventually got enough lire together to buy a loaf of bread. Using a combination of the few Italian words I knew and my best charades-playing skills, I managed to glean enough information from the Roman locals to catch a series of buses back to Pensione Ginevra. The relief I felt when I arrived quickly dissolved when Signora Fabrizi informed me she'd had to give my room away because I hadn't paid that week. She'd kept my clothes, toiletries, and most importantly, my passport, which she'd safely stashed in her room for me, hoping I'd return. Before I left, she let me use the family's phone to call the only number I could find scribbled on a scrap of paper at the bottom of my suitcase—Gerta, an English-speaking German girl I'd met at Club Yellow.

"Pronto?" a stranger answered. I shoved the receiver toward the *proprietaria*, who was hovering nearby. There was a brief exchange in Italian, then she cupped her hand over the receiver and tried to explain that we'd reached the phone in an apartment building lobby, and someone had gone to look for my friend. Several minutes went by before Gerta came to the phone. I explained my predicament, and *hallelujah!* she invited me to stay with her. The kind Signora gave me enough money for the bus and hugged me goodbye. I must have said "Grazie" a hundred times.

After dragging my gigantic suitcase on and off three buses, I finally arrived at Gerta's apartment building on the outskirts of Rome. The relief I'd felt when I'd learned I had a place to stay dissolved before my eyes. I had no idea there was such a seedy, run-down area in the city. I stood on the sidewalk, staring up at several gray, multistory cement buildings, probably built after the war for fast, cheap housing, in an area that tourists never see. In America we'd call it "the projects." Broken wire fencing, graffiti, and trash seemed to be the hallmarks. As if the building wasn't bad enough, after making my way to Gerta's apartment, I found that it was even more dismal. The only furniture was a dirty, bare mattress on the cold cement floor. There was no electricity or heat, and the door didn't lock. It became obvious she was squatting. By some miracle there was water—freezing cold, but actual H_2O. Although there weren't many niceties, like toilet paper for example, the toilet actually flushed.

When the sun dipped behind the building, the apartment went dark. Gerta lit a candle, sat on the mattress next to me, and began digging through the clothes in my suitcase.

"Cassandra, do you haf any segsy clothes mit you?" she asked. Illuminated by the candlelight, her hard-edged face peered out from beneath dark, stringy bangs, giving her a tough look that belied her supposed twenty-four years.

I hesitated for a moment, wondering what she was up to. "Uh, yeah. I guess. Black satin hot pants and a midriff top?" Remember, it was the early seventies. "Yah! Gut!" she exclaimed. It seemed Gerta had a plan to make us some money. "Get dressed! Vee going out."

We left the apartment decked out in our sexy best, which wasn't that great, but apparently did the trick—so to speak. We hung around on a street corner until a car pulled up and offered us a "ride." In her fluent Italian, she told the male driver we were available for a *ménage à trois*— two for the price of one! She must have been the ultimate scam artist because she convinced the guy to meet us later that evening at a place she named, but in order to secure us, she somehow talked him into paying half the money up front, the equivalent of fifty dollars. Of course, once we got the dough, we disappeared. It felt pretty damn sleazy, but we were young, desperate, and hungry. I reconciled my behavior by reminding myself that the guys we were conning weren't exactly angels either.

After a few days of performing our scam, I woke up late one morning, or possibly afternoon, to an empty apartment. Gerta was gone. So were all her things—and mine. Every cent I'd made, every piece of clothing I owned, all gone. Out of the kindness of her heart, or possibly just because they were dirty, she'd left the clothes I'd been wearing the night before, and thank you Jesus, my passport.

I wasn't about to continue the "fake hooker" scam on my own—way too scary and dangerous—but once again, I found myself without food or money. I had to find a job, and fast. Somehow I made it back to the center of Rome and spent hours wandering into clubs to see whether I could land a job waitressing, which I knew would be a long shot with my limited Italian and even more limited waitressing skills, but I had to try. I finally came upon a place that featured "hostesses." The manager, a heavily made-up, world-worn woman, explained the job to me in Italian and I did my best to follow along. It seemed like it mainly entailed drinking champagne and dancing with customers, which sounded pretty sweet to me.

As a hostess, I'd receive only a minimal salary but could make a lot more by talking patrons into buying champagne and "dance tickets." Sounded easy. It wasn't.

I started the evening with eight or nine other ladies, much older than I was, hanging out at the bar waiting for customers to show up. The club smelled of cigarette smoke and years of spilled cocktails. The men who came in were mainly old, overweight foreigners, so it wasn't nearly as fun as I'd imagined it might be. I spent every evening forcing down cheap champagne (when the client wasn't looking, I was able to dump most of it into one of the strategically placed fake plants that had been conveniently located around the club) and, despite the signs posted in several languages that translated to "No inappropriate touching allowed," blocking determined hands from creeping onto my various body parts. The songs they piped in were almost always slow, sexy ballads, of course, so every dance became a virtual wrestling match. I'd gone from manifesting the movie *Viva Las Vegas* to living out the film *Sweet Charity*! With the money I made, I couldn't afford much more than food and bus or cab fare, so every night I wore the only outfit I owned—a skin-tight, spaghetti-strapped, maroon jersey dress that grazed my ankles—washing it out and wearing it again the next night, which got old fast.

After work, I'd return to Gerta's dark, ice-cold apartment alone, on the verge of puking from the cheap champagne and even sicker from the shame and humiliation I felt doing what I had to do to survive.

My next-door neighbors were three enormous Maasai tribesmen from Tanzania. As if they weren't scary enough just based on the fact that they were all well over six feet tall, their faces were covered in elaborate scarification, making them look like they were wearing permanent scary Halloween masks. With no lock on my door, having three strange, gigantic, foreign men living next to me who could walk in at any moment, day or night, scared the living hell out of me. But once I got to know them, they became my guardian angels. They spoke beautiful English and turned out to be kind and gentle souls, often bringing me delicious exotic food they'd made. They also assured me they were always keeping an eye on me and my apartment, which made me feel a lot safer. Nobody in their right mind would fuck with these guys!

I don't remember how long I worked at the "dime-a-dance club." It seemed like forever, but was probably only a few weeks. Somehow I miraculously reunited with Melody, and a few days later we found ourselves walking down the tourist-jammed streets near the Fountain of Trevi, bemoaning our sucky lives and pouring our sad stories out to each other. Her situation was as bad as mine. She'd broken up with Massimiliano because he'd given her a black eye during an argument. Just like me, she had no money and no place to go. Suddenly, out of nowhere, looming head and shoulders above a boisterous crowd of autograph seekers, we spotted my Vegas roommate's boyfriend, Wilt Chamberlain! For those of you who are too young to know who he is, Wilt "the Stilt" Chamberlain, at seven-foot-one and over 300 pounds, was sometimes referred to as the strongest athlete ever. He was called the most dominating and amazing basketball player of all time and holds dozens of unbroken basketball records to this day. Melody and I got his attention, then plowed our way through the crowd. This was *crazy*! I mean, what were the odds? The next thing we knew, we were having lunch with the world-famous basketball star in a posh restaurant and wolfing down the best food Melody and I had eaten in months. We regaled him with tales of our adventures, sugar-coating them so he wouldn't think we were quite as desperate as we really were. After lunch, "Uncle Wiltie," which is what I'd always called him, got in his limo and headed for the airport. Before he left, he hugged us both, wished us luck, and discreetly slipped each of us a hundred dollars' worth of lire.

Feeling like we'd just won the lottery, we high-tailed it back to good old Pensione Ginevra. The Signora, although happy to see us, explained they were full up. But if we didn't mind, she'd squeeze us into a large closet she had at less than half the price of a regular room. We were thrilled because that meant our money would go twice as far! The room fit a twin bed only. When we opened the door, we crawled directly onto the bed, which Melody and I shared, and crammed our stuff underneath it. That didn't last long. Melody's boyfriend, Max, tracked her down, and despite my warnings, she took off with him again.

CHAPTER 13

ARRIVEDERCI, ROMA

The next time I saw Melody, her skin was covered in sores and she looked emaciated and deathly ill. She refused to tell me anything and wouldn't let me take her to a doctor, no matter how much I begged. I was scared out of my brain and had no idea what was going on with her. I had no choice but to call my parents, tell them she was sick, and plead with them to wire money to buy her a ticket home, which they did. They were furious at me for not taking better care of her, but what could I have done? She was an adult and I couldn't control her. I was having enough problems of my own, which I certainly didn't let them know about. Putting her on the plane back to America was a huge relief.

Safely ensconced back at Pensione Ginevra, I received a call from someone I'd met while working at Cinecittà, famous Italian singer-songwriter Memo Remigi. He told me about friends of his who had a band that was looking for a female vocalist. Their previous singer, also an American girl, was getting married and going back to the US. He gave me the number of the bandleader and I set up an audition for the next day.

"I Latins '80" (pronounced Ee Lateens Otanta) was a touring band specializing in a pop/funk/bossa-nova sound similar to Brasil '66—hence, the name. The band members were Franco Marcangeli on keyboards, Lino Ranieri on bass, Wilfred Copello on drums, Rosalba di Marzo on vocals, and Vincenzo Barbera on lead guitar and vocals. Much to my surprise and elation, I auditioned and got the job! I shared singing duties with Rosalba, who was twenty-one, same as me, and we immediately became best friends. The guys were excellent musicians, seemed like good people, and were paying me to sing, so I couldn't have been happier!

A couple of weeks of rehearsals in Rome and we hit the road, traveling city to city from Catania in the southern tip of the "boot" to Bergamo in the north. Their music wasn't exactly my cup of tea, but they allowed Rosalba and me to cover some American rock and pop tunes, which we sometimes translated into Italian. In between songs by popular '70s Italian female artists like Mina, I got to sing "Yesterday" by the Beatles and "Ain't No Sunshine When She's Gone" by Bill Withers, which Rosalba and I changed to "Comè Buio la Città" (roughly translated to "How Dark Is the City"). We generally played one- or two-night gigs at large venues, then packed up the van and headed to the next town. Visiting so many beautiful places and immersing myself in the sights, sounds, and culture of Italy was a huge bonus. Once in a while we'd land a job that would last a week or two, which gave me an opportunity to explore, have a life, and sometimes even have a romantic rendezvous, however short-lived. In Lake Lugano, the band opened for jazz great Herbie Hancock, and he and I engaged in a very sexy make-out session in a broom closet after the show, which ended abruptly when Vincenzo discovered us and insisted I get into the van to head to the next town.

Rosalba and I usually shared a room, and once in a while, her Neapolitan mamma would join us on the road, cooking scrumptious Italian meals for the band. I vividly remember her staring at me, bug-eyed and mouth agape, when I told her I didn't know how to cook. Worried I'd never catch a husband, she literally *forced* me to learn. It turned out to be one of the best things that ever happened to me, because cooking Italian food later became a passion of mine, and still is. During the long hours in the van, driving across the county, Rosalba helped me learn to speak Italian—a lifesaver since no one in the band, including her, spoke more than a few words of English. Not being able to express yourself is a great incentive to learn a language!

During a month-long gig at the beautiful rooftop garden of the Casino di Sanremo, my parents maxed out their credit cards and came to see me in the band—their first and only trip abroad together. Rosal-ba's mamma and papa were visiting at the same time, and even though our parents couldn't understand a word the other said, they all ended up bonding over big bottles of Chianti. On my parents' last night in Italy, Rosalba and I discovered that the male members of the band were being paid exactly double what Rosalba and I were getting. (I guess pay inequality isn't exclusively an American issue.) After a year of touring with the band, the combination of being pissed and hurt about my pay and a rare wave of homesickness prompted me to walk out between sets, grab my suitcase from our apartment, and join my parents on a plane back to the US. I wonder whether the band is still waiting for me to come back from the break. I kept in touch with my dear friend Rosalba and visited her and her family many times over the years.

CHAPTER 14

LA WOMAN

Returning to the US after all that time in Italy was a culture shock. Everything in my hometown was so ... *un-European*! There I was back in Colorado staying with my mom and dad, which wore thin in no time. I had no idea what to do with my life or where to go next. The only thing I was sure about was that I didn't want to stay in Colorado Springs living with my parents at the ripe old age of twenty-two.

Three weeks after getting home, I got a call from my pal Jerry Jackson, from my *Vive Les Girls* days, asking whether I was interested in doing a new show he was mounting in Florida called—you'll love this—*Fantasies of Love au Naturel*. Jerry offered me the part of "Lead Nude," and also promised me a singing number in the show. This was quite a step up from showgirl in both stature and pay, and I leapt at the chance. After just three weeks at home, which was two-and-a-half weeks too long, I was off again on a new adventure.

Working at the Playboy Club, *the* hot spot in Miami Beach in those days, was like a six-month-long paid vacation. Unlike the grueling hours I'd had in Vegas, the Miami shows ended at a reasonable hour each night, so I was actually able to have a life. Everyone in the cast got snazzy free accommodations at the hotel and free meals in the restaurants, so all the money I made, I socked away for later. The show opened to rave reviews, I got a ton of press, and we played to packed houses for the entire run. With the beach right outside our door, there was always a lot of partying and a *lot* of cocaine. It was the '70s in Miami after all, and coke was everywhere. You couldn't meet someone without them pulling out a vial and offering you a line. I was already so hyper I couldn't stand getting any speedier than I was, so I managed to steer clear of it for the most part, but it became an issue for a couple of the other girls, who were let go and replaced mid-run.

I had two memorable numbers in the show. In one, I dressed as a call girl, wearing a Day-Glo orange wig, spiked heels, and a sparkly orange micro-minidress. I stood under a street lamp in a pool of light on the dark stage and sang the Burt Bacharach hit "Walk on By." One by one, the other girls joined me onstage wearing only feather boas; garter belts and stockings; purple, green, or pink afros; and a snatch to match—actually merkins, which, in case you don't have any drag-queen friends, are little wigs for your pubic area. When the song was done, I stripped out of my dress and joined the other girls in a "sexy whore" dance number employing cane-back chairs. Black light made it a super-psychedelic showstopper.

My other memorable number was an Aladdin-themed number called "The Sultan's Dilemma" in which I was featured wearing a harem-girl costume and got the chance to show off my infamous tassel-twirling talents. This was the first time I'd ever worn tassels attached to pasties instead of a bra, which was both good and bad—not having my breasts connected made spinning them in different directions a lot easier, but after a tassel flew off one night and landed in an audience member's drink, I had to start using rubber cement to keep them in place. By the end of the run, my nipples were raw, bloody, and incredibly painful. There really *is* no business like show business.

During the Playboy Club run, I had a chance encounter with handsome actor and future Jaclyn Smith ex, Dennis Cole. We ended up going out (and in) the week he was in town. No sooner had he left when I fell for the lead singer of the show, Matt Vernon, and the feeling was mutual. He was cute, young, and funny, and a talented singer to boot. I knew he was fresh off a relationship with a guy, but I'd never let those little details stop me before. It was clear he appreciated women and especially me. When the show closed, Matt asked me to come back to Los Angeles with him and, without much thought as to what I would do once I got there, I followed him.

In a live-in relationship for the first time, Matt and I split the ninety dollar a month rent on his tiny, one-bedroom bungalow at the top of Beachwood Canyon, an eclectic, Bohemian neighborhood in Hollywood. A few months after I moved in, the rent was raised to $125 and we seriously thought it was the end of the world. How were we *ever* going to make enough to pay that kind of outrageous price? I'd be willing to bet that same house goes for something in the $3,000 range now.

We were happy setting up house together, and even though Los Angeles was the last place I wanted to live, I was so gaga over Matt that I didn't care. Up until now, the only time I'd ventured into LA had been with my parents when I was twelve, on one of our many summer vacations. My mom had to make a stop in the downtown garment district to buy fabric for her costume shop, so my sisters and I were instructed to lock ourselves in the car while my parents ran inside. They had parked in a seedy alley behind the store and I remember staring out the window at the murky brown sky, the tall buildings that made me feel lost and insignificant, and the hobos who staggered by, muttering to themselves. I was definitely not in Kansas anymore. Despite my horoscope in *Cosmopolitan* magazine that said Los Angeles was my "lucky city," I'd made up my mind that I would *never* live there.

But here I was in the City of Angels, living in the shadow of the world-famous Hollywood sign and running through my savings. Matt and I discussed our plans for the future and we both agreed that at our age, we were getting a little long in the tooth to continue careers that would take us on the road singing and dancing. Despite the fact that I'd never taken a single acting lesson in my life, if you don't count my failed high school drama class, with Matt's encouragement, I set my sights on an acting career.

Cut to my first big interview. Matt suggested I go through the

Agents Directory, call every agent in it, and set up as many meetings as possible. It was discouraging as hell. When an agent asked what my credits were, all I could tell them was I'd played Emily in a high school production of *Our Town* (which was a lie; I'd only done a couple of scene studies from it) and that I was an ex-dancer/singer/showgirl. They were not impressed. Day after day I made calls, but not one agent was willing to meet with me. Until finally, one day, an agent was interested. *Very* interested. He was so nice on the phone! He even offered to come to my apartment to do the interview. Was that lucky or what? An hour later, a red-faced, overweight man arrived at my door, huffing and puffing after climbing the millions of stairs to our place.

He impressed me by talking about all the famous clients he represented, then opened his briefcase and took out a mimeographed scene to read. It took place on the beach, so naturally, he asked whether I had a swimsuit I could slip into. Skeptical, I wondered aloud whether that was really necessary, but he assured me it was and convinced me that if I wanted to be a professional actress, I needed to take direction. Intimidated and feeling stupid, I conceded and ran into the bedroom to change. I know what you're thinking: how dumb could you be? I'm asking myself the same question as I sit here typing. But what can I say? I was young and desperate. I wanted to become an actress, and according to this "showbiz authority," this is how you did it. After all, he was a seasoned pro and I was brand-new to Hollywood. What the fuck did I know?

Moments later, I found myself sitting on the sofa in a bikini reading the part of the female character while this sweaty slug played the part of the "leading man." It went fine until the end when I read, in parentheses: (THEY FALL TO THE SAND IN A SENSUAL EMBRACE, KISSING PASSIONATELY). I finished my last line of dialogue and leapt off the couch.

"Didn't you see the directions there at the end?" he asked.

"Oh, uh…no. What directions?" I lied.

He looked at me like I was a freakin' idiot and huffed, *"They fall to the sand in a sensual embrace, kissing passionately!"* I just stood there staring at him like a deer in the headlights. There was no way in hell I was going to make out with Jabba the Hutt.

"Well?"

"Well…what?" I replied, playing dumb.

The conversation went on like this for a minute or so until he hauled his huge ass off the couch and came toward me. I backed away as fast as my quivering legs would allow.

"I'm sorry," he said, throwing his arms up in frustration so I couldn't help but notice the massive sweat stains in his pits. "But it doesn't look like acting is the career for you. Maybe you should stick to what you know best: being a *showgirl!*" He spat the word out like it was the lowest of the low. I remained mute, glued to my spot in the corner of the room. He grabbed the "sides" from the couch, stuffed them into his briefcase, and lumbered out the door. I watched from the window, half naked and blubbering like a baby as he trundled down the steps, taking my dreams of becoming an actress with him.

When Matt got home that evening, he found me packing my bags for Colorado. Lots of hugs and a rousing pep talk later, he convinced me to stay.

After being with Matt for almost a year, I decided to move on. That decision was prompted by me coming home early one afternoon to find him *in flagrante delicto* in *our* bed with an infamous male network exec! I figured it was best that I get my own place and managed to scrape together enough money to rent a dinky single apartment on Hollywood Boulevard.

While living alone in my first LA apartment in 1974, I was finally able to get my Screen Actors Guild (SAG) card, a nearly impossible catch-22 hurdle that has been known to deter many an actor from pursuing a career. According to union rules, you can't work in TV or film without a SAG card, but the catch is that you can't get a SAG card without first working in TV or film. As fate would have it, during a quick trip home to Colorado to visit my family, my friend Jerry Jackson happened to be there staging a musical act for actress Goldie

Hawn. Jerry asked whether I'd mind taking her around town to shop and see the sights, which I happily did. She was a doll, and we had a really fun time. Upon learning I was a struggling actress, she was kind enough to give me the name of her friend Sam Denoff, writer of such well-known TV classics as *The Dick Van Dyke Show* and *That Girl*. I called him first thing when I got back to LA and, out of the kindness of his heart, and I suspect as a favor to Goldie, he hired me to do a "one-liner" on his newest sitcom, *Lotsa Luck*, starring Dom DeLuise. Thanks to Sam, I began the process of getting my SAG card and becoming "legit."

Sam also introduced me to a good-looking single producer friend of his, David Yarnell. Although David was quite a bit older than me, he was kind, funny, and charming, and we began dating. He knew how broke I was, so he threw a job my way on a show he was producing in Las Vegas called *The Bachelor of the Year Awards,* starring several male showbiz and sports figures, like David Brenner, Jim Brown, Bobby Riggs, and (yikes!) OJ Simpson. My part was called "The Feather Girl," and I wore a PG version of a showgirl costume, prancing onstage to present the award in each category. After all, somebody had to do it. Even though my relationship with David eventually fizzled out, we remained friends and he hired me as a production assistant on his next project, *Don Kirshner's Rock Concert.* It was a dream job! Not only were the hours flexible, enabling me to go on auditions for acting work, but I got to meet tons of bands, like REO Speedwagon, Edgar Winter Group, Ashford and Simpson, Mott the Hoople, the Commodores, Linda Ronstadt, and others. I did every job that needed doing, including pressing pants, photographing the bands onstage, getting them food, and doing their makeup if they requested it. On my budget, I could afford only one neutral color of base for my makeup kit, which I used on everyone, no matter what their skin tone. The show also featured stand-up comedians, and every time I've run into Arsenio Hall since, he reminds me of how I turned him an ashy gray color for his TV debut. I got to reconnect with old "friends" like Steve Miller, snort coke with the Pointer Sisters, see Rick James's dick, and in general, have the time of my life! Also, *Rock Concert* is where I met my friend Dawna Kaufmann, who worked there as a receptionist and would later help change the course of my life when she suggested auditioning for *Movie Macabre*.

In our spare time, Dawna-ski and I became budding entrepreneurs. When we weren't working on *Rock Concert*, we did things like track down the new all-female band the Go-Go's at the Starwood club in Hollywood and pitch them on the idea of us managing them, which unfortunately (for us, not them) didn't happen. We came up with all kinds of ideas for shows to sell and produce, *Mr. & Ms. Sex Appeal* and *The Ms. Nude America Pageant* among them. We pulled some money together and took a trip to New York City, where we combed nightclubs like CBGB and the Mudd Club for new acts and spent an afternoon with Brooke Shields and her mom trying to convince them that Brooke should sign on to host a show we'd come up with called *Women of Rock*. None of our projects ever materialized, but in spite of it, Dawna went on to become a successful television writer, producer, and true-crime journalist, and I ended up doing pretty well for myself, too.

One night while I was still living in my little Hollywood Boulevard single, Matt asked me to come along with him to a Christmas party at Zsa Zsa Gabor's house. I have no idea how he snagged an invite, but it was exciting to go to my first big "Hollywood" party. I was blown away by the guest list, mostly older Hollywood actors I recognized from the movies, but it wasn't some stuffy party full of old fuddy-duddies. There were trippy psychedelic lights, loud disco music, and lots of hot, young actors, too. There was even a "human Christmas tree"—a guy wrapped in colored Christmas lights standing perfectly still on top of a ladder, naked but for a flesh-colored jock strap. There was also a lot of drinking going on and the distinct smell of pot in the air.

I met Zsa Zsa, who chirped a brief "Hello, dahling!" while flitting from room to room hosting the festivities, after which Matt and I parked ourselves on a throw pillow–laden mattress under the "Christmas tree," probably so Matt could stare at its ass. We soon struck up a conversation with a good-looking guy who shared our mattress. He introduced himself as Bobby and seemed like the quiet and reserved type, but after sharing a joint with him, he opened up and we had fun laughing and chatting. Out of nowhere, Matt suddenly decided it was time to go. Although Matt and I were no longer a "thing," I suspect it had something to do with Bobby and me getting a little too friendly. I didn't feel like leaving, because the party was just getting started, but Matt insisted I come with him. Reluctantly, I said goodbye to Bobby and we headed to Matt's car, bickering all the way. We were both a little drunk and stoned by this time, and our arguing became louder and more heated as we went. By the time we reached his Volkswagen "Bug," I told Matt I was staying and would find a ride home, but he wasn't having it. He yanked open the passenger door, jerked me hard by the arm, and attempted to shove me in. As I struggled to loosen his grip, out of nowhere came a hand. It grabbed his arm in midair, spun him around, and slammed him against the car. Bobby to the rescue!

"You okay?" he asked, still pinning Matt up against the Bug.

"Yes, yes, I'm fine! Just let him go!" I pleaded, not wanting to be responsible for Matt getting the crap beaten out of him. Although shorter than Matt, Bobby had a strong, athletic build and looked like he could definitely do some damage. Bobby loosened his grip long enough for Matt to hop into his car and speed away as fast as one could in a '64 Beetle. I stood in the middle of the street wondering what to do next when a cab pulled up and Bobby said, "This is me. Hop in. I'll give you a ride home." I was more than happy to oblige.

"How can you live in LA without a car?" I asked.

"Oh, I'm only here for a couple days. I live in New York." We pulled up to my apartment and like a true gentleman, he got out and walked me to my door. "How about dinner tomorrow night?" he asked. I accepted and scribbled my number on a scrap of paper. No kiss, just a sweet goodbye and an "I'll call you tomorrow."

True to his word, I found a message from him on my phone machine the next afternoon. When I dialed the number he'd left, I was surprised to hear an operator answer with, "Good afternoon. Bel-Air Hotel." Fancy-schmancy!

"Uh, room 264 please."

"Mr. De Niro? Yes, right away."

We made plans to have dinner and he said he'd get a cab over to my place and we'd go from there. When he arrived, he came in and I offered him a glass of cheap wine. We sat on the convertible sofa that doubled as my bed and picked up where we'd left off the night before. From our previous conversation I already knew he was an actor, so we had something in common. I asked what he'd done and he told me he had just worked in two films—*Bang the Drum Slowly* and *Mean Streets*—neither of which I'd seen. He was excited to tell me he had just been offered a role in the Godfather series, *The Godfather II.*

"I'm playin' a young Marlon Brando! Can you believe that? Marlon fuckin' Brando!" I was impressed! We talked a little more, drank a lot more, and long story short, never made it out to dinner. He left for New York the next morning and that was the last time I saw him, but it took almost a week to wipe the smile off my face.

Another evening, Matt took me for a drink to the home of a mutual friend, Richard Caruso, a handsome ex-circus performer and all-around bon vivant. On the way there, Matt said, "There's a guy who'll be there tonight that you're going to *love*!" And boy was he right. Bill Cable was a stunning six-foot-two body builder, model/actor, and sometime tree-trimmer with dark ringlets of curly, face-framing hair and movie-star good looks. From the second Bill and I laid eyes on each other, we were hooked. Throughout the night we stealthily flirted up a storm, and before he left, he slipped me his number. We hooked up the next night at my place, made hot, sweaty love, and not a week passed before Bill asked me to move in with him. Even though I was crazy about him, it was a hard decision. The fact that he lived in a tree was off-putting. Yep, a real, live tree. A few years before, he had played the part of Tarzan in a low-budget film shot in the Amazon, and apparently it had gone to his head. He'd built a one-room tree house from odd bits of wood, glass, and corrugated metal in the hills on the west end of Hollywood Boulevard. Head over heels in lust with him, I eventually agreed to move in and gave up my apartment. The tree house was about the size of a one-car garage. To get into the place you first had to slide twenty or so feet down a hillside to the trunk of the tree, while grasping onto a rope that Bill had conveniently tied to a telephone pole at street level. When you reached the trunk, you were then faced with climbing up a rope ladder and squeezing yourself through a tiny trapdoor in the floor. The only furniture to speak of was a huge, king-size bed Bill had made from thick tree limbs, which was so high you almost needed a stepladder to get into it. Hanging by chains from a tiny platform at the end of the bed was a small TV set. Nearly every inch of the walls and bed were draped with the skins of rabbits, coyotes, wolves, and deer that Bill had collected over the years. The ceiling was covered in mirrored tiles and out of a huge picture window at the head of the bed, a spectacular panoramic view of LA spread out below. It was a romantic bachelor pad to say the least. But practical? Not so much.

We hung our clothes on branches and our electricity was delivered via a very long extension cord that Bill had rigged up to a power line. A garden hose pulled through a hole in the wall was our shower, courtesy of an unknown neighbor. Behind a wooden partition was a Port-a-Potty that Bill occasionally hauled away to the dump in his army-green camouflage-painted pickup truck with the "chaw" stains down the driver's side. In the center of the room, beneath a metal flue leading to a hole in the roof, was a firepit made from rocks and sand that served as our stove and heat source. Okay, there were challenges, but the upside was that there was no rent or utilities to pay.

According to Bill, after a brief stint in the LA Police Academy, he'd been kicked out for dating a stripper and became a mercenary. He had some pretty gnarly scars that served as proof. He was obsessed with *Soldier of Fortune* magazine, and although I was never really sure how much of his past was true, what *was* true was that he kept an arsenal of every type of gun, rifle, and weapon imaginable, including a rocket launcher and a few hand grenades, stored under our bed.

Bill had modeled for famous photographers Jim French and Ken Duncan, and his friends included actor Roddy McDowell and directors George Cukor (*My Fair Lady*) and John Schlesinger (*Midnight Cowboy*), both of whom we occasionally house-sat for, taking full advantage of their indoor plumbing. Bill's best friend and tree-trimming buddy was Marlon Brando's son, Christian. Christian was a doll—handsome and sexy like his dad, but not the sharpest tool in the shed. For one thing, he had never learned to read. He once doused his pubic hair with lighter fluid and was preparing to light it on fire to kill the crabs he said he'd contracted from a well-known Russ Meyers film actress, when Bill stopped him in the nick of time. Bill would later loan Christian the gun that he used to murder his half sister's boyfriend, Dag Drollet, at Marlon's Mulholland Drive home. Bill was pulled into the trial proceedings and was lucky not to wind up in jail himself. Christian ultimately served five years in prison and sadly died of pneumonia in 2008 at the age of forty-nine.

When he wasn't at the gym working out, Bill stayed home writing a screenplay, an unpaid job that took up the lion's share of his time. At night we watched cartoons and old episodes of *Our Gang*, which he loved. He called me Petey, after the Little Rascals' dog (and short for my last name), and I called him Boo-Boo, after Yogi Bear's sidekick.

Every once in a while, he would land a modeling job or a tree-trimming gig that would cover his truck payment and keep him in Kodiak chewing tobacco and groceries for a few weeks. I often found myself giving tours of our "house" because none of my friends or fellow workers could believe I actually lived in a tree unless they saw it with their own eyes.

I went on acting and modeling interviews most days, which made negotiating the trapdoor and rope ladder in a tight skirt and heels especially challenging. At night I worked as a hostess and coat-check girl at Emilio's, a high-end Italian restaurant on the corner of Highland and

Melrose Avenues. There, when I wasn't busy avoiding Emilio's grabby hands, I got to practice my Italian with the waiters and watch Hollywood stars come and go.

One of my favorite stories involving Bill happened one night after leaving Emilio's at 2:00 a.m. As I walked across the street to my car, a carload of gang-banger types pulled up alongside me, hooting and hollering. Doing my best to ignore them, I jumped into my car, slammed the locks down as quickly as I could, and peeled out. After I'd gone a few blocks, I looked in my rearview mirror and there they were. Stomping down on the gas pedal, I sped through Laurel Canyon and into the hills toward home. But no matter how many twists and turns I took, there they were, still on my tail.

When I got near the tree house, I blasted an "S.O.S." on my horn and kept going, praying that Bill would pick up on my honks for help. I continued circling around on the narrow winding streets, the carload of guys on my ass, blasting my horn as I passed our tree for the second time. The third time I approached, I screeched to a halt. There was Boo-Boo, wearing nothing but a loincloth, swinging down from the roof on a rope attached to a limb. All that was missing was Tarzan's famous yell! He was brandishing an AK-47 while clenching a bowie knife between his teeth. When he landed in the middle of the street, he shot a rapid-fire round of bullets into the air, just above the creeps' car. I watched, eyes bugging out of my head, as the Chevy slammed into reverse and disappeared in a cloud of dust and exhaust. It was definitely one of the more surreal moments of my life.

Bill and I were deeply in love, but after a year of playing "You Tarzan, Me Jane," I put my foot down. Either we moved into a real house with running water, heat, and all the other modern conveniences of home, or I was out of there. Although he wasn't thrilled, he finally agreed, and we moved into a 1920s storybook cottage apartment building on Formosa in West Hollywood that had been built by Charlie Chaplin.

In 1976, an old boyfriend from Vegas, Dane Clark, got in touch with me. He had gone from Vegas dancer to Elton John's hair-and-wardrobe person. Dane invited Bill and me to come to Elton's concert the next night at the Universal Amphitheatre and his private party afterward. We were thrilled! After the concert, Dane took us backstage to meet

Elton, who was immediately taken with Bill, as pretty much all gay men were. For the private party that followed, an entire carnival had been set up on the Universal back lot. Dane was the one who delivered the news to me that it was "boys only," and I was disinvited. Bill and Dane went off with Elton and his entourage, leaving me in the parking lot, and, boy, was I pissed!

In 1977, Dane went to work as wardrobe supervisor for Queen. This time I had the good sense to go to the show on my own. I

loooooooved Queen, so getting front-row seats to see their show at the Forum was a dream come true! Their performance was as spectacular as anything I've ever seen, and afterward Dane escorted me backstage to meet the band. A couple of hours later, I joined everyone as they piled into the limo for the trip back to their hotel. The limo was overflowing with guys, so I ended up on Dane's lap, where, after quite a few cocktails, we resumed our former crush, flirting like mad. Everyone was having fun, laughing, and continuing the party that had begun in the dressing room—except for Freddie Mercury, who had suddenly gone quiet. When we arrived at the hotel, Freddie jumped out of the car and left without a word to anyone. I was disappointed but chalked it up to him being exhausted after such an energetic performance.

Roger Taylor and Brian May were interested in shopping for antiques while in LA and quizzed me about where the best stores were. I offered to take them shopping the next day on Melrose, and much to my surprise they accepted. It didn't seem to bother them a bit that they had to ride all over Hollywood in my old Volkswagen Bug. I was blown away watching them pick out items in the hundreds and even thousands of dollars, then having them shipped to England. We had a fun day together and I couldn't get over how sweet and down to earth they both were.

Interesting side story: after the movie *Bohemian Rhapsody* came out in 2018, I did a little research and came across an article that mentioned Dane. Not only did he do Freddie's wardrobe, but he also did Freddie! The whole cold-shoulder treatment by Freddie suddenly came into focus. I wasn't surprised, though, because I'd heard Freddie had a penchant for giant schlongs and Dane wasn't referred to as "Great Dane" for nothing.

He later gave me a copy of Queen's most recent album, *Jazz*, signed to me by all four members: John Deacon, Brian, Roger, and, yes, even Freddie. It was one of my most treasured pieces of memorabilia until my husband sold it. I recently tracked it down and found the collector who had bought it at auction in Canada, having no idea that the "Cassandra" it was signed to was me.

While in Vegas, one of my favorite shows had been performed by a comedy group called The Good Humor Company that featured a writer/performer named Joe Danova. The show was unlike anything I'd seen before, so much more hip and happening than the other old-timey, Vaudeville-style comedy shows on the Strip. I was so impressed that I went to see them as often as I could and soon became friends with Joe and the cast. After seeing my comedy bit in *Vive*, Joe asked me to join the group, but I was unable to get out of my contract at the Dunes, so it wasn't an option.

Somehow, years later, Joe tracked me down in LA. The Good Humor Company had disbanded and he was hard at work on a new show called *The Boob Tube Review*. This time nothing was going to stop me from being a part of it. When Joe got a firm commitment from Harrah's Hotel, I joined the show, said a temporary goodbye to Bill, and headed to Reno, Nevada. The word "boob" in the title referred to TV and not my anatomy, so although I wore some skimpy costumes, for the first time I was doing a live show where all the naughty bits were covered. It felt like a step in the right direction.

The show featured parodies of popular commercials that we taped beforehand and played on TV screens between live musical and comedy numbers. The cast included dancers, singers, and musicians, along with rotating acts that were plugged into the middle of the show. One of them was the comedy duo of Al Franken and Tom Davis. Despite their humble beginnings, they went on to become one of America's best-known comedy-writing teams with *Saturday Night Live*. Al also became a US senator, so they did pretty well for themselves. Tom and Al were both brilliant and funny and I loved hanging out with them, usually at the local hot springs, soaking in the mineral water after our two nightly shows. They were big nerds, so of course we got along great, so much so that they worked me into one of their bits. In the sketch Al played a TV weatherman. I was his assistant, who came onstage carrying a large plexiglass weather map. I held the map in front of me, clearly displaying my body in a sexy, tight-fitting dress, while Al did the weather forecast, scribbling on the map with his Day-Glo marker. As his weather forecast progressed, he became more and more distracted by my body. He described two "big fronts" that were moving in up north and drew big circles directly over my breasts. He then went down south and drew in "rainstorms," lots of tiny lines which formed a "V" over my crotch. The bit ended with him getting so worked up that he drew a series of long, spurting lines coming from the tip of the Florida pan handle. Okay. Not sophisticated humor, but we all have to start somewhere.

Years later I took my friend Jack White to one of Al's campaign fund-raisers in LA. Al pretended not to know me, which was embarrassing to say the least because, of course, I'd blabbed to Jack about how Al and I had worked together and been such great friends. Jack and I made dona-tions to his campaign nonetheless, and I was thrilled when he won. I guess when you become a senator you need to back away from your past. Too bad he also backed away from questionable allegations of sexual misconduct.

Fabian Forte, teen heartthrob from the '50s, was also booked for a month in Harrah's, in alternating shows. Although his celebrity had long since faded, he was still cute as hell and I immediately homed in on him. We began a torrid little affair, which definitely helped pass the time. A decade later, after I became Elvira, I accidentally won "A Date with Fabian" at a pajama party thrown by my brilliant friend, songwriter Allee Willis. It was basically a publicity stunt to promote a new zine, but we still had a fun,

if slightly awkward, time driv-ing around the San Fernando Valley posing for pictures in front of landmarks like Bob's Big Boy.

The Boob Tube Review had a successful run, but eventu-ally the producer, Dick Foster, and Joe came to a parting of the ways. (I knew things weren't good when Joe had T-shirts made for the cast that showed Mickey Mouse holding a lol-lipop with a caption that read, "Dick Foster Sucks!") After four months, the show folded, and I hightailed it back to Hollywood.

It was now 1974 and once again I found myself back in LA. One evening I got a call from Joe Danova, who was also living there, asking whether I'd like to join him and his partner, Allen Perlstein, to go see a group of improvisational actors called the Groundlings. I didn't know what comedy improv was exactly, but I always had fun with Joe and Allen, so I was happy to go along for the ride.

That night, when we arrived at the rundown thirty-seat theater in East Hollywood, I had no idea what I was in for. The show blew my mind! I couldn't believe that a group of actors actually got up on stage in front of an audience and put on a show that they basically made up as they went along—just like I had for the neighborhood kids! I knew at that moment that I was somehow going to become a member of that group. It would take another few years for me to make the commitment, but the Groundlings were never far from my mind.

CHAPTER 15

❧

YOU'LL NEVER WORK IN THIS TOWN AGAIN

There's no place like Hollywood when it comes to sexual harassment. Although the entertainment industry certainly doesn't have a corner on the market, it seems to be so rampant here because of the way it's set up. Women trying to make a living in the career they've chosen are asked to interview by baring their soul, and sometimes their breasts, to get a job. It puts women in an especially vulnerable position.

During the '70s, when I was auditioning, men seemed to be the only ones in charge of hiring actors. And for the most part, they still are. They were the casting directors, agents, and producers who had the power to make your career if you did what they wanted or break it if you didn't. Having been a former go-go dancer and showgirl, I was used to being treated as a sex object by men, so I already had a leg up. No pun intended.

When you're desperate to pay your rent, buy food, and make car payments, unscrupulous men may dangle a carrot (or their penis) in front of you and imply the unspoken question, "What will you do to get this job?" I'm definitely no prude, but I never stooped so low as to exchange sexual favors for any job. It's something that wouldn't allow me to live with myself if I had, and it cost me a lot of acting jobs over the years. By the way, it also doesn't work. I've never heard a story about a talented actress who fucked her way to the top.

It fills me with so much hope and pride that women are finally able to speak out about the treatment we've had to endure from men. Women have always had to worry about the damage to their livelihoods, not to mention loss of their dreams and aspirations, which could result from resisting men's unwanted advances or, God forbid, reporting it. These days, men are finally having to think very seriously about the potential damage to their own careers that engaging in this type of sexist behavior may cause. One way or another, it *will* catch up with them, and karma's a bitch.

I'll just cite a few of the close calls I've had that I know many of you female readers will sadly relate to. If I recounted every story of sexual harassment or assault I've endured, this book would be as long as the New York City phone book (remember those?).

Beginning in the second grade, I began to realize the world wasn't a safe place for girls. On my way to school one day, I remember a man pulling his car alongside me and asking whether I'd like a ride. I'd already been prepped by my parents to *never, ever get in a car with a stranger*, so I shook my head "no" and picked up my pace. He continued to cruise alongside me, offering me candy if I'd get in his car. Now, I'll never know for sure if he wasn't just a nice man wanting to do me a favor, but that day I listened to my gut, and it told me to run like my life depended on it, which it possibly did.

There was another incident when I was twelve. My parents rented a pasture and stall for my horse, a block from our house. It was owned by a grandfatherly widower in his seventies, who lived alone next door. One afternoon when I went to feed Apache, Mr. Bruning was there. He offered to help pitch some hay and alfalfa, a favor I gladly accepted. But when he called me into the dark, claustrophobic shed, I found him with his pecker out of his pants and in his hand. "Come over here and just touch it," he said. I froze, terrified. My legs turned to Jell-O, but I still managed to turn and run all the way home. I never told my parents because I knew they'd be angry. Not at him. At me. They thought the world of Mr. Bruning and I knew they would take his side. I kept my mouth shut and did my best to avoid him from then on. My parents couldn't understand why I would never visit poor, old Mr. Bruning, who was all alone because his wife had died and none of his ungrateful children ever came to see him. Hmm, I wonder why.

In seventh grade, when my friend Kathy Hall and I exited the gates of South Junior High, a man in a convertible pulled up next to us to ask for directions. We approached the car and Kathy began blabbing away, when I happened to glance down and notice he was pulling his putz. I grabbed her arm and dragged her back into the schoolyard.

Miraculously—seriously—miraculously, I made it through my teen years without getting raped, although I had some very close calls. I learned over time to never walk alone at night, to never park in dark areas, to always check to see whether anyone was hiding in the back seat of my car before getting in, and to keep an eye in my rearview mirror to make sure no one was following me. It's great to grow up feeling like you're being hunted, right girls?

Once in Hollywood, I was eventually lucky enough to land a commercial agent. I was thrilled when I got called in on an audition for Colgate-Palmolive, a big national brand. I stood in front of a roomful of "suits" from the advertising agency, pretending to take a shower. I did as they asked and sensually rubbed a bar of Palmolive soap all over my clothed body while "oohing" and "ahhing" with every ounce of emotion I could muster. Much to my surprise, I got a call back. I was absolutely *ecstatic* because a national commercial like this could pay my rent for a year! My antennae went up a little when I learned it would take place at 7:00 that evening, but hey, this was a professional commercial for a huge national brand. I was just being paranoid.

I arrived to find a darkened office building. I pushed the intercom button and, a moment later, a friendly man's voice answered, gave me directions to his office, and buzzed me in. I walked down the empty corridor. There wasn't another soul in sight. The door to his office stood open and there, sitting behind a big desk, was one of the men from the earlier audition. He was in his forties and wore horn-rimmed glasses and a suit and tie. Seemed legit to me. After I took a seat opposite him, he began asking me casual, friendly questions about myself.

"Where did you grow up?"

"How are things going here in Hollywood for you so far?"

"Do you like giving blow jobs?" I nearly fell off my chair.

"Do you like to give blow jobs?" he repeated, rising to his feet. Below his shirt and suit jacket, he was completely naked. Shaken, I jumped to my feet and headed for the door as fast as my feet would carry me. As I literally ran down the dark hallway, my commercial aspirations in the dumper, I heard him yell these very words: "You'll never work in this town again!"

There were incidents that were a lot more serious. When I was working for *Don Kirshner's Rock Concert,* I spent a lot of time hanging out at the Rainbow Bar & Grill, right across the street from our offices. My excuse was that I was checking out bands that had potential to be on the show, but I was usually just trolling for rock stars, a habit left over from my groupie days. One night I met a cute guy and, after a few drinks, invited him back to my apartment because the bar was closing and neither of us was ready to call it a night. Once in my apartment, we each had another drink and talked. After he slammed his beer, it was clear he was bombed. I definitely was no longer feeling the chemistry. "Well, I've got to get up early tomorrow," I said, standing and giving an exaggerated yawn. I made moves to usher him to the door. He apparently *was* still feeling the chemistry, however. "Aw, c'mon," he slurred. "What about I stay over?" He draped both arms over my shoulders and attempted to give me a sloppy kiss. "No, really," I insisted, trying to squirm out of his grip. "We can get together another night." Before I knew what had hit me, I was flat on my back on the floor and he was on top of me. I struggled against him, but he put one hand on my throat, and pulled the other back, balling it into a fist. "Do you want me to punch your fuckin' teeth down your throat?" he growled. Terrified, I went silent and limp as a rag doll while he pulled my dress up and fucked me, giving a few rough thrusts before shooting his wad. He stood up and glared at me while zipping his jeans. "If you ever say a word about this to anyone, you'll be sorry," he said as he stalked out the door. "Don't forget, I know where you live." I lay on the floor for what seemed like forever, unable to move. Eventually I dragged myself into the shower, where I sat under the warm running water, sobbing and shaking.

Was I to blame? After all, I'd invited a man to my apartment. I'd had drinks with him. I knew people would say I "asked for it," so calling the police didn't seem like an option. Silly me. I believed, and still do, that when a woman says no, it means no, even if she's standing in front of a man stark naked. As the lyrics to one of my favorite female rap songs so eloquently put it, "No means *no* muthafuckah! Are you deaf in yo' ear, muthafuckah!?"

The other episode involved my friend, "Uncle Wiltie," who I'd run into once or twice at the Playboy Mansion since moving back to LA.

In Las Vegas, whenever Wilt was in town, he and Sunny frequently slept over at the house I shared with her and our other roommates, and spent a lot of time hanging around the pool. I got to know him and liked him a lot. He was flirty, although always respectful, but he did have a big ego to go along with his big body and his big career. He was smart, interesting, and funny, and *damn* was he *big*. He towered over us at seven-foot-one. We took a picture together by our pool one time and in it I look like a munchkin, only coming up to a little above his waist. It was crazy how big he was—not just tall, like his friend Lew Alcindor (aka Kareem Abdul-Jabbar), who I'd met with him on a couple of occasions, but *huge*, weighing in at 300 pounds. My entire outstretched hand fit just inside his palm.

Wilt had always flirted and kidded around with me, but he was never pushy or rude. He was rich, good-looking, and famous, so he had girls coming out of the woodwork. He hardly needed to force himself on anyone like me. I was somehow always able to deflect his advances by joking around, and he'd always laugh and slough it off. I'd known him for so long, I trusted him and felt very comfortable around him.

His new custom-built home in Bel Air at the top of Mulholland Drive became a massive party house in the '70s and he invited me to them on a few occasions. I always took a girlfriend along and we would have a great time—good food, plenty of booze, and always an impressive list of sports figures and celebrities in attendance. He loved giving tours of his house and showing off his custom-made 2,200-pound front door, kitchen cabinets that came up to my chest, and even his *super* king-size bed. With the push of a button, the biggest TV screen I'd ever seen automatically rose from the footboard, and another button opened the bedroom ceiling to the night sky. I'd never seen anything even close to this kind of crazy technology, so I was pretty damned impressed.

The third time I went to his house for a party, my friend bailed on me at the last minute, so I went alone. An hour or so into the party, he asked whether I'd ever seen the closet he'd built for his collection of basketball jerseys from the various teams he'd played with over the years. As I shook my head no, he led me through his bedroom and into his closet, which was roughly the size of my single apartment. I stood marveling at the rows of size-fifteen shoes while he pulled jerseys off the rack—the Philadelphia Warriors, the Harlem Globetrotters, the LA Lakers—and laid them out on the center island for me to see. "Wow!" I gasped, trying to look impressed even though I didn't know a thing about basketball. Suddenly, with no warning, he grabbed me from behind, gripped my neck with one gigantic hand, and shoved his sweatpants down with the other. He slammed my head down on his erect penis, came in my mouth almost instantly, then stood there smirking while he pulled his fancy sweats up and tucked himself into his pants.

"See? That wasn't so bad, was it?" he asked.

I didn't respond. My face burned with anger and humiliation as he chuckled to himself on his way out of the closet. It all happened so fast I was still in shock. Trembling, I made sure he'd gone, then ran into his bathroom, locked the door, and puked into his giant-size toilet. I rinsed my mouth out, splashed water in my face, and did my best to pull it together enough to walk out through the throng of partygoers without bringing attention to myself. I slunk through the kitchen, past the catering staff, and out the back door to my car like I was the one who had committed a crime. As women often do, I blamed myself and felt a deep sense of shame, embarrassment, and utter stupidity.

Why didn't I try to scream, fight back, or get away? When a seven-foot-one, 300-pound man has his hand wrapped around your neck,

The Petersons: August, Dale, "Boxer," Dorton, Lorrayne, Lyle, and Ivah.

My mother, Phyllis, age eighteen.

Daddy and his Singer truck down on the farm.

With Mother and Daddy, 1952.

With Melody and the bad Christmas kitty, 1955.

Queen of Halloween,
1957.

Fishing with my
dad.

Me (on the right with a Toni perm) on one of our many infamous vacations.

Melody, me, and Nyliram, 1960.

With my sisters, Melody and Robin. I gave Mel that awesome haircut!

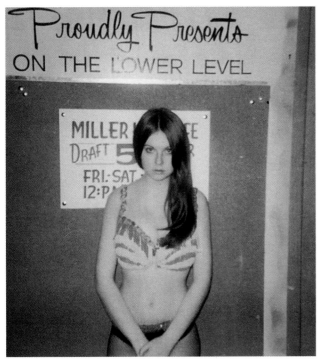

Club A-Go-Go,
1968. "Lower
Level" says it all.

Drawn for me by Keith
Relf of the Yardbirds.

Viva Les Girls.

My Las Vegas soul mates, Buddy Vest (left) and
Sterling Clark (right).

Las Vegas with "Uncle Wiltie."

I Latins 80, my pop/funk/
bossa-nova band in Italy.

Tassel twirling in *Fantasies of Love au Naturel.*

Boo-Boo and Petey.
(Photo by Ed Mangus)

Mama's Boys. Check out
Robert's abs!

With Travis in
P-town.

Inspiration and film goddess, Ann-Margret.

With writing partner and alter ego, John Paragon.

The Groundlings, 1980. (From left to right, top row: Doug Cox, Teresa Burton, Suzanne Kent, Catherine Bergstrom, Paul Reubens, Phyllis Katz, John Paragon, Shirley Prestia, Phil Hartman, "Hendo" Hendrickson, Tim Stack, John Moody, Joan Leizman. Center: Randy Bennett. Bottom row: Me and B. J. Ward)

First day on the job as Elvira. Hadn't quite figured out the shoes, stockings, and belt yet.

At KHJ-TV with my trusty Orange "bug."

Transforming
from Cassandra to
Elvira.

Elvira's first big public appearance at a mall in Azusa, California.

Knott's Scary Farms Halloween Haunt. You can tell by the dancers' costumes it's 1982.

My dear friend and ally Robert Redding, 1983, wearing the makeup he created for Elvira.

With my hero, Vincent Price.

Forrest J. Ackerman, legendary editor of *Famous Monsters of Filmland*. Hey, Forrey, watch the hands!

Briarcliff Manor.

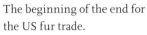
The beginning of the end for the US fur trade.

Horror Hosts: Zacherley, John Stanley, Ghoulardi (Ernie Anderson), Joe Bob Briggs, and Elvira.

Team Elvira: Scott Marcus, T, and me.
(*Photo by Chris Ameruoso*)

T. *(Photo by Jeremy Samuelson)*

Me and Vinny the Pee, 2020.

there's really not a lot you can do. Should I have reported him to the police? Are you kidding? What chance do you think a former showgirl/out-of-work actress would have against a sports superstar?

Thankfully, I never saw or heard from Uncle Wiltie again. When his book came out in which he bragged about having sex with more than 20,000 women, I had to wonder how many of those women actually *consented* to having sex with him.

I kept this suffocating secret to myself, and over the years, the memory faded from my mind. However, one day in 2003 when I was watching TV, I heard the news that another prominent NBA basketball star had been accused of grabbing a nineteen-year-old female by the neck, forcing her over a chair, and raping her. Sitting there in front of the television, I felt the blood drain from my face. I began to hyperventilate and shiver uncontrollably. All the fear and shame I'd felt came rushing back as if the Wilt incident had happened yesterday instead of years before.

The player later claimed it was consensual and went on with his charmed life—multimillion-dollar contracts, product endorsements, and accolades from fans. The female victim who was brave enough to speak up was portrayed as a mentally ill slut. Her reputation was smeared, and she received hate mail and death threats.

It's virtually impossible to communicate to a man how deeply these experiences affect a woman's sense of self and every other aspect of her life, but let me try.

Put yourself in our high heels for a minute, boys. Imagine you find yourself at home alone with the electrician or handyman you've hired. He happens to be a hundred pounds or so heavier and several inches taller than you, and in his spare time, he's a wrestler. He seems like a very nice dude and before long, you strike up a conversation. Perhaps you even offer him a beer and shoot the shit with him. Now it's getting late and you need to say "adios," but he's got other ideas. Before you can say "where's my butt plug," he's got you bent over your desk with your pants down around your ankles, ramming his rod up your poop-chute. Now, really, does that seem fair? After all, when he started flirting with you, you politely asked him to leave. And when you hollered "No!" dozens of times, he totally ignored you.

Of course, I'm using a man as the attacker here because, (a) we all know this would never, *ever*, happen with a woman as the perpetrator, and if it did, it would be a fantasy come true for most guys; and (b) in general, only another man could be bigger and stronger than you and make you feel like you don't have a fighting chance.

So, do you get it now?

Maybe this fantasy victim will try to teach his son that women deserve the same respect as men. Or maybe he'll be more aware of the signs of sexual harassment if it happens to his wife, girlfriend, mother, or daughter.

Sorry to say, but I'm not that special when it comes to being sexually harassed, molested, or assaulted. In fact, I'm one of the lucky ones. I'm a staunch #metoo supporter and have always called myself a feminist. But I also like being the object of men's attention. I sure as hell picked the wrong career if I didn't! I've always been attracted to men and like knowing men appreciate and are attracted to me. Sex, when it's consensual, is a normal, healthy part of a woman's life and something I've always enjoyed.

But as a woman, especially one who worked in nightclubs and casinos, it's often been challenging. Just putting up with the unwanted whistling, insults, and catcalls young women experience daily is annoying enough, but when it descends into groping, grabbing, fondling, or kissing without permission, you can understand why I've surrounded myself with gay men most of my life. I'm not going to play the victim, however. I hope that spilling my guts about some of the traumatic situations I've gone through will allow other women to feel like they're not alone. I hope I'll live to see a day when men's desire or perceived right to commit sexual violence will no longer be an issue. Not because of the fear of punishment, but because men learn to respect the rights and humanity of women.

And maybe, if there's one straight man out there reading this book, you'll realize the terrible damage men can do when they perceive women as somehow "less than."

CHAPTER 16

MAMA'S BOYS

I'd taken acting lessons from various drama coaches and acting teachers since arriving in LA. The classes took a lot of time and money, both in short supply, but it was something I felt I needed to do if I wanted to fulfill my goal of working in showbiz. I eventually landed at Lieux Dressler's Patio Playhouse in the San Fernando Valley. Not only was it more affordable than the big Hollywood acting schools, but it was a small group of students, which was more comfortable and made me feel like I was getting more time and attention. I immediately took to Lieux, a plucky little redhead and former *General Hospital* actress who taught the class. There were several guys in the class, but only two other girls: Lynda, a former Miss World USA; and Debbie, a younger girl who wore braces and glasses, and sported an uncontrollable, frizzy brown 'fro. She was always accompanied to class by her mom, who comprised an awkward, one-woman cheering section. Debbie had a characteristic throaty voice that made her stand out from the crowd. She was a natural and always blew everyone away when she did scenes. Lynda and I were the same age and got along well, despite a little friendly competition in class. We also bonded over the fact that she'd had the same nasty experience with the very *same* tubby agent who had come to my apartment and tried to put the make on me. Lieux became our hero when she declared war on him and helped us get his name taken off the SAG-AFTRA list of approved agents. A couple years after I left the class, I was surprised and happy to see Lynda Carter on TV, starring in her own series, *Wonder Woman*. She obviously had some pull because she cast little Debbie Winger as her sister. Debra, of course, would go on to star in films like *Urban Cowboy, An Officer and a Gentleman,* and *Terms of Endearment.*

I was starting to get more and more frustrated with the direction my career was going, or more specifically, where it *wasn't* going. Every time I got an agent, got a new headshot and résumé, and began going on auditions, a job that paid "real money" would come up and I'd find myself back on the road. Did I want to be an actor? A singer? A dancer? I had no focus. All I knew was that I wanted a career in show business.

Once again back from another gig on the road and settled in LA with new resolve, I got a call from Joe Danova. He was determined to keep the *Boob Tube Review* alive and had come up with an idea for another version of the show that would feature me. Within weeks we began rehearsals on our newly created show, *Mama's Boys,* which consisted of myself, six gay men, and, for a short time, a token straight guy. They were all talented singers, dancers, or actors, and, what a couple of them lacked in singing or dancing ability, they made up for in pure *hot*-ness!

Joe Danova, tall and thin, of Portuguese descent with a handlebar mustache and bald head, was a very talented comedian. When it came to business, however, that's where his talent ended.

Joe Croyle was a handsome singer and pianist. He was our only straight guy and didn't have a homophobic bone in his body, despite all the crazy queer crap he had to put up with.

Bobby Howland was a cuddly little teddy bear of a man, only five-foot-two with a perfect muscular physique, and the gay crowd *loved* him! We always had him done up in lots of black leather and studs and not much else.

Jim Raitt was the nephew of singer John Raitt and cousin to Bonnie. An incredibly talented pianist, he accompanied us on ballads and was brilliant at coming up with charts. He also sang harmony with his gorgeous tenor voice. He was a chain-smoker and had a nervous knee that never stopped bouncing, whether playing the piano or sitting still.

Richard Herkert, the best singer of us all, was a Eurasian with beautiful feminine features. He played a Japanese newswoman named Tricia Toyota in one sketch that was a big crowd pleaser and sang a rendition of the 1929 tune "My Mother's Eyes" that never failed to bring down the house and make the audience weepy.

John Palmer was from Texas, and in addition to playing small parts in the show, he was also our lighting-and-sound man. He had a slight Southern accent, and with his blond hair and mustache, bore a striking resemblance to a young Robert Redford. He was more composed and sophisticated than the rest of us and I often got the feeling that he was the only "adult" in the room.

Next to Bill, I thought Robert Redding was the most beautiful man I'd ever seen, and in fact, he and Bill had posed together in a layout for photographer Ken Duncan years before. Robert was six-foot-five with blond curls and a tan, muscular body. He was a beautiful singer and dancer and did impeccable impersonations of Katharine Hepburn and Bette Davis that were showstoppers. Robert and I became as close as two people could be. In truth I was madly in love with him, but despite a lot of kissing and cuddling, our relationship never quite strayed into "lover" territory. He did my hair and makeup and picked out my costumes. But more importantly, he believed in me much more than I believed in myself and encouraged me to do numbers in the show I would never have done otherwise. "Bad Mary," my nickname for him, had so much faith in me and my abilities that he instilled a sense of confidence in me that I'd never have had if it wasn't for him.

Our first shows were in San Francisco where we were welcomed with open arms. Bette Midler had paved the way with her performances at the Continental Baths in New York City, and *Mama's Boys* was perfectly poised to fill the burgeoning need for gay-centric acts at the many discos popping up across the country. The show alternated between musical numbers and comedy sketches. I sang everything from current hits like, "Don't Go Breakin' My Heart," in a duet with Robert, to old-timey ballads like "It Had to Be You." In one sketch, a parody of the soap opera *General Hospital*, I played sexy Nurse Joy Jello, with Joe Danova as the doctor.

Me: Doctor, doctor, you have a thermometer behind your ear!
Joe: Oh no! Some asshole has my pen!

Some of the boys did quite a bit of drag throughout the show, when they weren't busy looking like sexy hunks. Between each number, we played prerecorded comedy parodies of popular commercials on TV monitors scattered throughout the club. The audience loved them, and it gave us time to change costumes in whatever iffy backstage accommodations had been provided.

After San Francisco, we did a month-long run in San Diego at the Ball Express, then headed to Studio One in West Hollywood, the granddaddy of all West Coast gay clubs. After a month there, our poor straight guy, Joe Croyle, dropped out—probably because he couldn't deal with so much gayness. Either that, or he got a real job that paid. We loaded up a couple of rented trucks and headed across country on our US tour, the boys pulling triple duty as entertainers, drivers, and roadies. We traveled from city to city, one big, colorful family, getting paid only enough to cover motels, food, and gas, but we were all having so much fun we didn't care. I became one of the boys, sharing clothes, showers, and beds.

The discos in the '70s were *wild* and the boys were up to their asses in men! Quaaludes, alcohol, and poppers were passed around like candy and it wasn't unusual to wake up in the morning with a stranger or two in our beds. When I woke up one morning with one of the boys *and* a drag queen dressed as Diana Ross, I actually considered cutting down on the partying. We were the belles of the gay balls, but despite glowing reviews wherever we went—Chicago, Dallas, Washington DC, Detroit, Atlanta, Fort Lauderdale—we somehow only made enough money to get us to the next gig.

We ended one run of shows in Atlanta by not getting paid at all. Joe naively agreed to get paid when the two-week gig was up instead of asking for money up front. When he demanded the money, the gay-mafia club owners ran us out of town at gunpoint. We stayed in a roach-infested motel, eating PB&J sandwiches and Cup O'Noodles until Joe could line up our next gig in Fort Lauderdale. After our scary Atlanta adventure, Bill joined us as roadie/bodyguard, which kept me especially happy, made us feel safer, and helped everyone's morale. Naturally, he was a big hit with the boys.

In '76, we played the famous Village Gate in New York City's Greenwich Village, once home to performers like John Coltrane and Aretha Franklin. We opened just after the Grammy-nominated "Let My People Come," an explicit musical about sex, performed the last of their record-breaking 1,167 shows. We had a good run at the Village Gate but a hard time making ends meet. It's expensive to live in New York City, people! We spent our days there trying our best to survive. Nerves were becoming frayed and there were rumblings from a couple of the boys about quitting. Just when we thought we wouldn't make it another day, Joe came through with a gig for us at a popular gay venue in Provincetown, Massachusetts.

I'd never heard of the place, but soon found out that for a "fag hag" like myself, it was like I'd died and gone to gay heaven. P-town was the best-known Mecca for the gay crowd on the East Coast and was a welcome change from the dirty, chaotic streets of New York. The month of June in the quintessential picturesque New England town at the tip of Cape Cod was refreshing and beautiful. Stretches of white, sandy beach ran for miles, and the light, the ocean, and the dunes were magical.

Mama's Boys arrived in P-town just in time to take part in the big Pride Parade festivities. Joe got ahold of an old classic Ford flatbed truck and we rode atop it, wearing lots of black leather and silver lamé to make sure the town knew we'd arrived. We rented a huge, two-story Cape Cod house a block from the beach, which belonged to a family who had raised seven kids there, so for the first time in forever we didn't have to share a bed (unless we wanted to). After our experience in the Big Apple, we felt like we'd landed in paradise. Twice a night we performed to packed houses in the crowded upstairs room above the Post Office Café and Cabaret in the heart of town. I'd never seen so many gay men in one place at one time! We got to schmooze with the other acts in town, gay icons like Jim Bailey, a friend from my Vegas days; Wayland

Flowers and Madam; and drag royalty like Craig Russell and Charles Pierce. Watching these ultra-talented performers and hanging out with them was the experience of a lifetime. (In *my* book anyway. And, after all this *is* my book.)

In the late '70s, P-town was one big, crazy, nonstop gay party, and for once we were actually making enough money to take us beyond survival mode. Our nights off were spent cooking big lobster dinners before hitting the bars to celebrate our good fortune. Sunday afternoons were spent at the Boatslip tea dances, rocking out to fist-pumping disco music on the beach while we swilled mimosas. One night we all got our hands on a new drug called MDA and went to see the first *Star Wars* movie—quite a surreal experience! The benches, or "meat rack," in front of the town hall served as a late-night, last-minute pickup spot for the boys after the bars closed. Bill and I never knew who or what we might run into in the house when we woke up the next day.

At one point, Joe was arrested after being caught under a pier on a public beach performing some kind of gay act—and not the one we were performing at the Post Office. Our show came to a screeching halt for the three weeks he was in jail, which found us all scrambling for enough money to maintain the lifestyle to which we'd become accustomed. Jim Raitt and I were able to land a short-term gig singing to a mostly straight tourist crowd at Vorelli's restaurant on Commercial Street. With Jim accompanying me on piano, I got to sing some of my favorite ballads.

On August 16, 1977, just as I was leaving for work, came the shocking news that Elvis Presley had died. I couldn't believe my ears—Elvis was *never* supposed to die! I thought back to the short time I'd spent with him and was broken-hearted. I had a hard time believing that someone as staunchly antidrug as he had been could have died of an overdose. But I'd been around long enough to understand how it happens when you're a money-making machine for others. From that night on, I added the Joan Baez song "Never Dreamed You'd Leave in Summer" to my repertoire and dedicated it to Elvis. I always had a hard time making it to the end without getting choked up. He was truly one of the greatest artists that ever lived, and the impact he had on the world, and on me personally, was profound.

Over the years, I felt Elvis had gone from an edgy, revolutionary rock-'n'-roll rebel to his manager the Colonel's puppet, churning out the banal, sappy shit that appealed to the masses and brought in the big bucks. There was no way the Colonel and all the people who relied on Elvis as their meal ticket were going to let that "golden goose" slip through their hands. Enter the drugs—*legal* of course, prescribed by a doctor: uppers when he was tired, downers when he was buzzed, pain pills if he hurt—like so many performers before and after him. When every ounce of creativity had been stripped from his bones, he became tired, fat, apathetic, and more than likely, too zonked out to give a damn. Driven by his management's demands, the King of Rock had become the King of Schlock—another great American tragedy.

Sometime near the end of summer, my three-year lovefest with Boo-Boo began to wear thin. We argued about everything, and his hanging around the house all day doing nothing was getting on my last nerve. I could understand him not wanting to come to work with me at the Post Office every night because our audience was made up of mainly gay men, and Bill's former job as a Colt model under the pseudonym "Stoner," plus his *Playgirl* cover and layout, made him a serious dude magnet. I began going in to work early every evening and staying there until the bars closed just to get away from him. With too much time on his hands, and apparently other body parts, I began hearing rumors of him with another girl. I confronted him, which led to a *huge* fight. As luck would have it, my parents, whose hobby it was to follow me from town to town in their Winnebago, happened to be in P-town. Bill, with no money and no place to stay since I'd kicked his ass out of the house, caught a ride home with my mom and dad, and that was the end of Petey and Boo-Boo.

In the meantime, between sets at Vorelli's, I'd begun hanging out next door at Front Street, the happening high-end restaurant for the artsy New York crowd. I struck up a friendship with the handsome, charming bartender, Travis Cresswell, and before Bill's side of the bed was cold, Travis and I were an item. Coincidentally, it turned out that the girl Bill had been cheating on me with was Travis's ex. It's a small world after all.

After Bill left, I began spending most of my time at Travis's three-story, saltbox-style house on the water. Cookie Mueller, an actress from John Waters's early movies, ran a clothing store on the street level of the house and Travis and I stayed on the second floor. Also staying at the house for the summer were Travis's brother and his friend, acerbic director Ron Link, who was up from New York staging a preview of the play *Women Behind Bars*. I vividly remember looking out of our second-story window one morning and seeing something that looked dead, white, and bloated lying on the beach. It turned out to be Divine. The notorious actor/drag queen was starring in Ron's production for the summer, so the first thing I had to look at every morning was this enormous hunk of blinding-white human flesh wearing nothing but a string bikini bottom, taking his daily sunbath. It was *not* a pretty picture. Seriously, it could ruin your whole day. The several times I attempted to join him, on *our* deck, by engaging in conversation or offering him food and drink, he'd just grunt something indecipherable, or worse, completely ignore me. This was a dagger to my heart—*all* gay men loved me, goddammit! Why, why, *why* didn't Divine? I guess I should just get over it and count myself lucky I wasn't eaten.

Labor Day 1977 arrived and our glorious gay summer in Provincetown came to an abrupt end, and with it, *Mama's Boys*. For nearly a year and a half we'd been together 24/7. The boys had become my brothers, my helpmates, and my supporters, and I loved each one of them so much that I wasn't sure how I was going to live without them. We said our tearful goodbyes, vowing to never lose contact with one another as long as we lived, a promise that, with the exception of Joe, we kept. The boys went their separate ways—LA, Dallas, New York—Joe promising to revive the show, but that never happened. No one had an inkling that in a few years, Provincetown, and all our lives, would be ravaged by the scourge of AIDS.

At the end of our run, Joe assured each of us that he'd have our costumes, equipment, photos, and personal belongings put on a truck and hauled back to LA, but because he apparently "forgot" to pay the bill, it was all auctioned off somewhere in the Midwest. We were beyond livid! It was later discovered he'd incurred a huge debt and had been borrowing money all along the way from friends, his ex, and even his parents, whose retirement savings he lost. Joe was talented and well-meaning, but as I mentioned earlier, definitely not a businessman. None of us ever heard from him again. He miraculously survived the AIDS epidemic and, I later learned, passed away in Florida in 2004.

With the arrival of the first chill of fall weather, the Boston and New York crowds abandoned Provincetown almost overnight. I moved my meager belongings from the house on Bradford Street that I'd shared with the boys to Travis's other house, a tiny, daffodil-yellow Victorian cottage on the beach.

In the '70s, nearly all the P-Town businesses closed their doors for fall, winter, and part of spring. One by one, the restaurants, movie theater, and stores drew their shutters as the days grew shorter, darker, and colder. As fall approached, Travis went from bartending to his real gigs: lobster diving and building custom homes. Driving rain battered our little cottage and nor'easters whipped the waves against the deck. I was left alone all day to sit in the cold, damp house or wander the empty, wind-swept streets. In the beginning, I enjoyed having a break from work for the first time ever. I read, wrote letters, and cooked Travis's leftover lobsters in every conceivable way, for breakfast, lunch, and dinner, until I couldn't even *think* about eating lobster again for years afterward. Being a very career-oriented person (workaholic?), I realized this wasn't going to work. I loved Travis, but as anyone who's endured a winter in Provincetown pre-1980 will tell you, they were boring as hell!

Together we came up with a plan: I would move to New York full-time to continue my acting career and Travis would join me on weekends. I still had access to the subleased apartment that Bill and I had rented during our *Mama's Boys* stint and was able to renew it at the hard-to-believe rate of $325 a month. Travis and I moved into the lovely but tiny brownstone apartment on Central Park West and 87th. Two of my boys, Robert and Jim, now a couple, were also living in the city, which was a godsend because I didn't know a soul there. However, unable to find showbiz work, the financial strain of living in the Big Apple became too much for them, and they soon moved back to LA. It broke my heart to see them go again. The only upside was that Robert was able to pass his day job along to me. I became the new espresso bar girl at Fiorucci's, a very trendy Italian clothing store, at 125 East 59th. The pay sucked but the perks were insane! Not only did I get to drink free espresso and cappuccinos all day for the first time since returning from Italy (hard as it is to believe, in the days before Starbucks, all you could find in the US was weak-assed American coffee), but Fiorucci's was like the daytime Studio 54, credited with inventing everything from designer jeans to Madonna's career. It was excruciating to be surrounded by beautiful, hip clothing that I could never hope to own, even with my employee discount, but working there was like a crazy, nonstop party. Much to my delight, the store was frequented by the A-list. I got to serve and sometimes briefly chat with the likes of Andy Warhol, Jackie Onassis, Lauren Bacall, and Truman Capote, to name a few.

But the best thing to come out of the job was meeting my friend Joey Arias. Joey was, and still is, a unique and quirky performance artist and a New York City fixture. We hit it off immediately. At the time, he was Fiorucci's star salesperson. Not only did he dance and model clothing in the windows on East 59th Street, but he loved to stage outrageous PR stunts, sashaying around the store in his tight, gold designer jeans and exaggerated pompadour hairstyle, helping make Fiorucci's a destination. In another bizarre, it's-a-small-world connection, it turned out that Joey had also been one of the founding members of the Groundlings in LA, which I would eventually join. Years later, Joey would make quite an impression on fans of *Elvira, Mistress of the Dark*, in a small but memorable cameo as the Charlie Manson–esque hitchhiker I pick up on my way to Falwell.

While in New York, I was forced to work two regular jobs to cover my expenses. In addition to days at Fiorucci's, I landed another job at night waiting tables at Reno Sweeney's, a cabaret in the lower East Village that has been described as the '70s "center of the universe" when it comes to the cabaret revival scene. Again, it didn't pay much, but I got to see all the popular acts that performed nightly, like Jane Oliver and a very young Bernadette Peters, which almost made my crappy waitressing gig worthwhile.

Working two jobs left me with only mornings to look for an agent and go on auditions, the reason I'd moved to New York. I pored over *Backstage* magazine, New York's equivalent of *Variety*, and went on crowded cattle calls for dancers and singers. Weeks and months passed without landing even the smallest showbiz gig. I was exhausted, essentially working three jobs and getting more and more discouraged. Every day I walked to work all the way across Central Park in the snow, heat, or rain to get to Fiorucci's by 11:00 a.m., then left at 5:00 p.m. to make the long subway trek to Reno Sweeney's. I served food and drinks until 1:30 a.m. and then made the three subway changes from the lower East Side back to my apartment. The one time I took a cab home, because I was too tired to walk another step, it ended up costing me more than I'd made the whole night.

As a lone woman, waiting for the train on the lower East Side at 2:00 in the morning wasn't such a treat, either. I was nonstop paranoid, worrying that one of the ranting homeless men would shove me onto the train tracks, where I'd die like Anna Karenina. One night while waiting for my train, exhausted and half asleep, I heard what sounded like heavy breathing behind me. I whipped around just in time to find a hobo jerking off on the back of my rabbit fur jacket! I threw the jacket on the ground and shivered all the way home. Guess that's what I get for wearing fur.

Travis continued to visit me most weekends, but with little time and even less money, I hadn't been able to socialize or make friends in New York. My lone female friend, Martha, another struggling actress, would sometimes meet me for meager breakfasts at a cheap Greek restaurant on Amsterdam, where we'd commiserate over our mutual lack of acting work. After leaving New York, we lost touch, but twenty years later I ran into her at a party in LA. After our joyful reunion, she introduced me to her new husband—Joe Esposito, Elvis's road manager! Spooky, huh? They were a lovely couple, and we resumed our friendship and kept in touch for many years until first Martha, then Joe passed away, both much too young.

New York is no place to live if you don't have money. Even though I was working around the clock, I barely made enough to cover my half of the rent, plus a few bucks left over for food and essentials like deodorant and Midol. Months went by and I hadn't even gotten a nibble as far as performing went. But one icy fall morning, I went on a call for a backup singer and dancer for a show based on Elvis Presley's life—and was elated when I actually got a callback. "Elvis's spirit is looking out for me!" I remember thinking. I felt like I'd aced the audition and had the job in the bag. I was asked to come back the next day and was so excited I couldn't sleep all night! Unfortunately, when I arrived, they gave me the bad news that I hadn't made the cut after all but they wanted to tell me in person. I was crushed. I walked out of the studio into a brutal late October storm and bawled at the top of my lungs all the way home. Passersby stared at me with the same look of revulsion and pity that I gave the wild-eyed transients in the subway station.

The next morning, I woke up on my mattress on the floor of my lonely, ice-cold apartment. It was almost November and the landlord *still* hadn't turned on the furnace for the building. Underneath my inadequate blankets, I wore every piece of clothing I could get on my body. When I woke up that frosty morning, my face still puffy from crying, I found myself staring straight into the soulless little black eyes of a giant cockroach parked on my pillow. I snapped! I jumped up, crammed everything I could fit into my two shabby suitcases, and headed out the door and down the snow-covered streets to the airport. I figured if I had to be broke, at least let me do it in LA where I wouldn't freeze to death! For the first time, I used the credit card my parents had given me years before for emergencies, charged a one-way ticket to LA, and never looked back.

Travis was understandably upset, although I'd heard rumors about him with a pretty young blonde in Provincetown, so I didn't feel *that* guilty. I still loved him and was sad to leave, but at that time, and for most of my life, I put work before relationships. Over the next few months Travis made every effort to visit me in LA, but as time went by and because long-distance relationships are next to impossible, we drifted apart. We remained the best of friends, however, visiting each other over the years, until his death in 2010.

CHAPTER 17

DO YOU BELIEVE IN MAGIC?

Once I was back in LA, my friend Allen Perlstein, who by this time had broken up with his partner, Joe Danova, was kind enough to let me stay with him until I could find work and get back on my feet. Allen helped me land a job working with him during the Christmas rush at Propinquity, a popular gift shop in Boystown, and I eventually saved up enough money to rent a nondescript single apartment in my old stomping ground, Beachwood Canyon.

To make ends meet, I signed up with Hugh Hefner's Playboy Modeling Agency and began going on interviews. Despite the name and the fact that many of the girls were ex-centerfolds, the jobs we went out on had little to do with *Playboy* magazine. They usually entailed wearing short, sexy outfits and working as convention hostesses or modeling for movie posters or romance-novel covers, but mainly posing alongside car parts, washing machines, or you name it. My most memorable jobs were being Ann-Margret's body double on the movie poster for the film *The Twist* and wearing a silver lamé bikini while standing in a "Vanna White pose" next to the Voyager II spacecraft at NASA's Jet Propulsion Lab in Pasadena. I also worked as a hostess at the American Film Market for Sid and Marty Krofft, creators of H. R. Pufnstuf, and legendary producer Samuel Z. Arkoff, whose company, American International Pictures, had produced so many of my best-loved horror films, like *The Pit and the Pendulum*, *Premature Burial*, and *The Tomb of Ligeia*.

Once in a while I'd land a job for *Oui* magazine, another Playboy publication, which required posing topless. Perhaps the biggest mistake

I made in my twenties was posing nude for a husband-and-wife photography team, who bullshitted me into doing what they said was a "test shoot" for *Penthouse* magazine. They guaranteed it would *never* be seen anywhere publicly. Seemed safe to me! God knows, I had no problem posing topless, but I drew the line at showing pubic hair (this was back when girls still *had* pubic hair). Promising the photos would be tasteful and not show anything I didn't want to reveal, they managed to talk me into getting completely naked, "so your underwear won't accidentally get in the shot." Like the trusting moron I was, I did the shoot, signed the contract, and collected a small fortune—what an easy $500! I never saw or heard from them again, and as far as I knew, that was the end of that—until 1981 when I became famous. Those photos, pubic hair and all, appeared in every sleazy men's magazine on the stand and there wasn't a damn thing I could do about it. The advent of the Internet compounded matters, and I realized I'd made a very stupid mistake with long-lasting negative consequences. Although tame by today's standards, they were embarrassing and ultimately cost me a lot of work.

During my time with Playboy models, I also got to work as a hostess for Lorimar Motion Pictures' annual showcase for international distributors that took place at the La Costa Resort and Spa near San Diego. During the weeklong event, the venue hosted more than 300 distributors from around the world who attended to view Lorimar films and make deals. My bosses were Merv Adelson and Lee Rich, who ran Lorimar at the time. Stars like Jon Voight and Al Pacino were there promoting their upcoming films, and after a little eye contact passed between Jon and me, he asked for my number. Back in LA, Jon, who had just finished filming *Coming Home* and was still *so* handsome, called and we ended up spending a romantic night at his house making love on a bearskin rug in front of a roaring fire—so theatrical!

I was later hired by a director I'd met at the Film Market to work as a production assistant and photographer on a commercial starring Raquel Welch. She was the most beautiful woman I'd ever seen; however, she wasn't the kindest, at least to me. The whole day she treated me like her personal slave, making crazy demands that kept me running.

First, she wanted fruit. We were shooting at a home high up in the hills of Bel Air, so getting to a store was quite a trek. When I returned with an array of every fruit available, she got angry because there weren't any kiwis. I sped back down to town, running from one store to another, only to discover that, during winter in the '70s, kiwis were impossible to find. When I returned kiwi-less hours later, she was furious. She demanded I go out and buy her some magazines. "Which ones would you like?" I asked. "I don't know! Get them all!" she snapped. Frustrated, I drove to a magazine stand and came back with a trunkful of everything from *Ladies' Home Journal* to *Popular Mechanic*. Turns out she had good reason to want me out of the way. Her slimy French husband, who spent the day hanging around the set, was making passes at me and every other woman within spitting distance whenever Raquel turned her back. The moral? Beauty doesn't always equal happiness.

The same director hired me again to shoot photos at the press junket for the box office flop *Meteor*. Even though the movie sucked, I had a fantastic time spending the day in a helicopter shuttling up and down into the Barringer meteor crater in Arizona and taking photos of the movie's stars, Natalie Wood, Martin Landau, and Sean Connery (who I'd met back in my Vegas days when I shot a brief scene in the Bond film *Diamonds Are Forever*, which featured some of the showgirls from *Vive Les Girls*). We spent a fun day together and I got some great shots.

It was time to reevaluate. I had no money, no real career, and no boyfriend. What was I doing wrong? Why was I here again? It suddenly felt like my whole life had been a huge waste of time. I became depressed and had moments when I seriously considered doing myself in. A friend suggested a couple of books to me that became game changers: *The Power of Your Subconscious Mind* by Dr. Joseph Murphy and *The Science of Mind* by Ernest Holmes. Coincidentally, I later learned that a dog-eared, highlighted copy of that book sits on Elvis's desk at Graceland. The basic philosophy is this: "The law of action and reaction is universal. Whatever you impress upon your subconscious mind is expressed in your life experiences. Therefore, you must carefully watch all ideas and thoughts entertained in your conscious mind." Many years later, *The Secret* would echo a similar philosophy and become wildly successful.

I'm not a religious person. Between my Jehovah's Witness grandma scaring the literal bejesus out of me with her fire-and-brimstone talk, and my parents, who never attended church but still forced me to go to Sunday school every week, I was turned off to religion big time. When I was a kid, sitting through endless repetitions of Bible passages at Sunday school was living hell for me. The only image that stuck with me was watching the smiling teacher slap some cutout felt figures of Jesus, a few sheep, and a couple dogs that looked like Lassie on a cloth board while we recited the Lord's Prayer in unison: "Surely goodness and mercy shall follow me all the days of my life and I shall dwell in the house of the Lord forever." I decided the two collies were named Goodness and Mercy and that they would follow me for the rest of my life, which I have to say gave me a sense of security. After a short time of being coerced into attending Sunday-school classes, I got smart. When my parents dropped me off at the little white clapboard Presbyterian church not far from our house, I walked in the front door and straight out the back, where I'd climb down to the creek and catch and release tadpoles for the next hour. I'm all for everyone practicing whatever religion they want as long as they (a) don't try to foist it off on me; and (b) don't berate, deride, beat, maim, or kill anyone who doesn't believe exactly the same way they do.

Despite all this, I consider myself a spiritual person and believe in a power greater than myself. Dr. Murphy's and Ernest Holmes's philosophy resonated deeply. Based on both the spiritual and scientific, their philosophy had already worked for me so many times in my life that I couldn't ignore it. Just a couple examples: believing I could be a showgirl in Vegas and my encounter with Elvis—hellooo!? I'd always known that what I dreamed of, what I desired and believed in, came into my experience. Here was a book that put my feelings into words and spelled it out: if you desire something and truly believe and feel it's your reality, it will come to pass. That works both ways, by the way—good and bad—so it's critical to watch your thoughts and words.

A quote of Ernest Holmes that really resonated was, "You are like the Captain navigating a ship. He must give the right orders, and likewise, you must give the right orders (thoughts and images) to your subconscious mind, which controls and governs all your experiences." It went on to say that a person without a specific goal in mind is like a ship without a compass. How will you ever reach your goal if you're floating around in circles without a map or a specific destination in mind?

Reading that passage, over and over again, I decided I had to be a lot more specific about what I wanted. I made a vow not to leave LA again for another traveling show, no matter how bleak my finances became. From then on, I would focus on acting, and even more specifically, on comedy acting. I promised myself that I would no longer go on any interviews or accept any jobs that weren't for comedy roles.

The first thing I did was write down the specific things I wanted in painstaking detail, beginning with a good long-term acting job and a lasting romantic relationship. I read my list every night before bed, then tucked it under my pillow. The next thing I did was go to the Groundlings Theatre and sign up for classes.

CHAPTER 18

THE GROUNDLINGS

By this time, the Groundlings had moved to their current digs on Melrose Avenue in Los Angeles. I'd gone to see one of their shows again and was even more impressed than before. The troupe was full of brilliant comedians, but Phil Hartman as the film-noir detective Chick Hazard; John Paragon as the back-flipping Mr. Entertainment; and Paul Reubens as Jay Longtoe, a tiptoe dancing, chain-smoking Native American lounge singer, stood out. Groundlings became my new "rock stars." I had no idea how they did what they did, but I knew I had to learn. I signed up for classes, and for the next four and a half years, ate, breathed, and slept the Groundlings. On weeknights I learned the ropes and on weekends we were expected to do everything from man the box office to scrub the toilets. There was a lot to learn: to be a good improvisor you had to listen carefully and always say *yes*! (Which, as you've probably surmised from reading my book so far, I almost always did anyway.) We learned to support the other actors onstage, not hog the limelight, and be specific—why say "car" when "Ford Pinto" is so much more interesting?

After a year of classes, I became a full-fledged Groundling. I was lucky. Back in the early '70s the process was easy-breezy: give them your money, take the classes, and if you were halfway funny, voila! You were a Groundling. In 1975 Laraine Newman had been plucked off the stage by NBC to become a founding cast member of the new comedy show *Saturday Night Live*. Little by little other cast members became successful actors, writers, and producers, and the Groundlings' reputation exploded. The show became the hottest ticket in town and, as the years went by, the process of becoming a Groundling became much more challenging. Students have been known to take classes for years, and even then there's no guarantee they'll make it into the main company.

It was an amazing time to be a Groundling. In addition to Phil, John, and Paul, my group included Edie McClurg, Lynne Marie Stewart, Tress MacNeille, and so many other incredible comedic actors. Everything Phil, John, and Paul did on stage was comedy magic and I idolized them. I remember a specific moment when I was still taking classes: I stood in the lobby of the theater and stared at John and Paul, who were off in a corner talking to each other, and thought to myself, "I'm going to become their best friend." Sounds creepy, doesn't it? But that's what I wanted more than anything.

John and I discovered we had a lot in common. We'd both grown up in Colorado, had bedrooms in the basement, drove orange Volkswagen Bugs, and were Beatlemaniacs. In fact, we'd both learned to do perfect forgeries of the Beatles' signatures and sold them to kids at school as the real thing. Great minds think alike!

Performing in the shows on weekends could be either fantastic or horrifying. Everyone fought for a slot in the show. There was an amazing amount of love and respect for one another but also a lot of jealousy and backbiting. Sometimes you came up with a good character or sketch and got a lot of stage time, and sometimes you didn't. We each fought, struggled, and clawed our way into the show every weekend. For better or worse, I didn't really worry about it much. I kept myself as far away from Groundling politics as possible. I'd fallen into the role of the Groundlings "sex symbol," which was just fine by me. Whenever anyone needed a voluptuous girl in their scene, I was there. I kept my locker stocked with lots of wigs and provocative costumes so I was always prepared. On most nights, I showed up to the shows wearing a short skirt or a low-cut top and had to sneak past Edie McClurg, a former teacher from Kansas City, as I made my way backstage. If she happened to catch a glimpse of me in her makeup mirror, she would scold me. "You're not going out there in *that*, are you?" or "I hope you're going to wear a *bra!*" When it came to casting Chastity Pariah, the overbearing, self-righteous moral compass of Falwell in *Mistress of the Dark*, Edie was our first choice.

Paul eventually mounted *The Pee-wee Herman Show* at the Groundlings, based on one of his many characters, a strange man-child standup comedian. John played Jambi the Genie, a head in a box who grants wishes. Phil played the crusty old seadog, Captain Carl, and the talented Lynne Marie Stewart played Miss Yvonne, the most beautiful woman in Puppetland. I, on the other hand, dressed in a child's gingham dress and pigtails and helped out every night as an usherette. Unfortunately, there wasn't another part for a sexy-girl character. Deservedly, Lynne had already snagged that spot.

Strange but true, for someone who ended up making her career playing a definitive character, my weakest suit in the Groundlings was developing one. My two strongest characters, if you could even call them that, were "The Dog Lady" in a "commercial" for a dog-grooming store, and staying in my comfort zone, playing a sexy ingénue with Groundling Teresa Burton. In the sketch, we both showed up at an audition for the same part, wearing identical rainbow-striped dresses, sunglasses, and Farrah Fawcett hairstyles. The first thing we did was point at each other and squeal in unison, "I like your dress!" My character was unique in that she had a heavy "valley girl" accent, something that had only recently been made popular by Frank Zappa and his daughter, Moon Unit, in the song of the same name.

Taking a cue from Paul's success staging a special late-night show, another Groundling, Randy Bennett, came up with an idea for a show based on a hilarious sketch he'd written about his backwoods family in Texas. He called it *Waco* and brought me onboard to play his sex-kitten, "white trash" daughter, Waylita (a hybrid of my "parents'" names, Waymond and Olita). Phil Hartman played my boyfriend, Dr. Red Greene, a sleazy, big-city drug dealer. We had a blast performing every weekend and the audience loved it, but unfortunately it never took off the way Pee-wee's show had. During the play, Phil and I had to exchange a steamy kiss each night, so after the play came to an end, we decided it would be a good idea to go on a date. We went out to dinner and had a fun time, as usual, but when it came to kissing goodnight, for some reason it felt so awkward, neither of us could stop laughing. Over and over, we attempted to calm down and catch our breath, then try again, but we just kept bursting into laughter. I guess by that time we'd known each other too long and too well to make anything sizzle.

Each night, the Groundlings show included at least one group improv featuring the whole cast. If we happened to get bad suggestions from the audience or someone in the cast was having an off night, the whole evening could turn into a disaster. Bombing in front of a house full of paying customers was devastating and there were many nights when I left the theater feeling like I wanted to quit show business once and for all. The fear that gripped me during an improvisation that wasn't working was paralyzing. Often, the harder we tried to turn it around, the deeper we dug ourselves in. But if everyone was "up," and the audience wasn't too tired or grumpy, we would *kill*! Almost nothing in the world felt better than that. We often chipped in to buy a large box of wine, and when things were going bad, that sucker was empty by the time the first show ended. Coming in for the second show only, which often happened, was a crapshoot. You could almost smell the mood as you passed down the long, dark, locker-lined hallway to the backstage area. Some nights it took every ounce of strength I had not to turn around and bolt for the door.

As my time at the Groundlings went on, I began to get more acting work. I landed small TV roles on *The Sonny and Cher Show, Tony Orlando and Dawn, Fantasy Island, Happy Days*, and commercials for Dodge Aspen and Axion detergent. I worked on movies like *Coast to Coast* starring Dyan Cannon and Robert Blake and *King of the Mountain* with Harry Hamlin, Joseph Bottoms, and Dennis Hopper. Cheech and Chong populated their first big bust-out film, *Up in Smoke*, with Groundlings and then cast me and several other members of the troupe in their next film, the appropriately titled *Cheech and Chong's Next Movie*. They needed an attractive blonde, brunette, and redhead to parody *Charlie's Angels*, so I was cast, along with Groundlings member

Catherine Bergstrom and the future Mrs. Tom Hanks, Rita Wilson. My famous line as we fled for our lives was "Help me Wamba!" which fans love to quote and embarrass me with to this day.

All in all, the years I spent with the Groundlings were some of the best times of my life. The friendships I forged there have been among my closest and most enduring. Being "in the trenches" with so many funny and talented people created an incredible bonding experience. I credit the Groundlings with giving me the tools and the chutzpah I needed to build my career. As I've said many times over the years, if you can get up in front of an audience without a clue of what you're going to say or do and with the possibility of making a total fool out of yourself hanging over your head, everything else is a piece of cake.

My odds of landing parts were becoming better all the time—and I had proof. I kept a log of my audition-to-job ratio, and instead of getting one job in every thirty auditions, I was now averaging one job in every seven. But good-paying acting gigs were still coming in so slowly I sometimes worried I wouldn't live long enough to realize my dream of becoming a working actor. Now in my late twenties, I was getting *really* tired of wondering where my next paycheck was coming from.

In 1979, while still at the Groundlings, I auditioned for a small role on *B. J. and the Bear,* a popular TV show that capitalized on the CB radio/ trucking craze. When I arrived, I was handed my "sides," and then sat for an eternity studying my lines along with a dozen other hopefuls. When it was my turn to read for the director, producer, writers, and whoever the hell else was there, I entered the inner sanctum: an office full of white men, as usual. I introduced myself and proceeded to read my lines with the casting director.

Once I finished reading, I put the sides on my lap and waited.

"What about the action?" one of the guys asked. Oh no. Here we go again. The "action" at the end of my scene described my character hopping on a motorcycle, speeding off around a racetrack a few times, then crashing and dying.

"Um. How exactly am I supposed to do that?" I responded.

In a cranky voice, whoever-he-was said, "In case you can't read, you're supposed to get on your motorcycle, ride around a track, and crash!"

I stood up, my face burning, and pantomimed throwing my leg over a bike, careful not to flash the beaver—no easy feat while wearing a short, tight skirt. I then squatted down as if I were sitting on a motorcycle and with my arms straight out in front of me and my legs splayed out to either side, attempted to run in a wide-legged circle around the small room. After a couple of laps, I threw myself onto the floor and lay there for a moment with my eyes shut, pretending to be dead—actually, wishing I *was* dead. As I breathed in the faint odor of dirty feet that wafted up from the carpet, I heard the sound of sniggering come from one of the men. *That* was it—I'd had it! I jumped up, basically told them where they could stick their part, and stormed out, slamming the door behind me. I knew what I was doing—burning my bridges for this producer and possibly for the network—but I didn't give a rat's ass. I was getting too damned old to keep debasing myself this way!

The old story about the guy who worked in the circus shoveling elephant shit comes to mind. Someone passes by and, seeing him up to his ass in dung, asks, "How can you put up with such a demeaning job? Why not go into some other line of work?" He replies, "What? And give up show business?" This humiliating episode marked the first time the thought crossed my mind that maybe a showbiz career just wasn't in the cards for me.

I continued to work at *Don Kirshner's Rock Concert*, and one night, I was sent to the Starwood Club on Santa Monica Boulevard to check out a hot new musician who was interested in doing the show. I wore a sexy little red-and-white-striped number I borrowed from fellow Groundling Phyllis Katz, and after the show, I finagled my way backstage to meet Johnny Cougar (who would later revert to his real name, John Mellencamp). Guarding the door of his dressing room was a cute young surfer dude who introduced himself to me as Mark Pierson. Although Johnny was pretty damned adorable, his music just wasn't my cup of tea, which was always a turnoff, so when Mark invited me to go with him to the party for the band at their manager Billy Gaff's house, I didn't have to think twice. Shy and soft-spoken, Mark was in his early twenties, a younger man—tall, tan, and thin with longish blond hair. During the party he waited on me hand and foot, bringing me drinks, lighting my cigarettes (yes, despite Little Richard admonishing me, I still smoked! Yuck.), and fawning over me the whole evening. It's hard to ignore a guy who shows you that much attention! We ended up back at my place for a night of passionate, drunken lovemaking. At some point, I woke up and crept out of bed to use the bathroom, trying my best not to wake him. When I returned, I stopped dead in my tracks and stifled a gasp. The light from a street lamp shone across the bed revealing his tanned, naked surfer's body sprawled across the bed. As I stared at him it hit me like a bolt of lightning—this was the man I'd described on my wish list, the man I was going to marry.

From that day on, Mark and I never spent another night apart. Although we both kept our separate apartments, we stayed at either his place or mine for the next several months and found ourselves falling deeper and deeper in love.

CHAPTER 19

A HOLLYWOOD HORROR STORY

While working at *Don Kirschner's Rock Concert* and living in my split-level, '70s single apartment on Beachwood Drive, I made what I thought would be a quick trip home from the nearby soundstage to iron a blouse for one of the Pointer Sisters and grab another roll or two of film for my Nikon. As I stood at the ironing board, I heard the neighbors in the building next door arguing again. I was used to it by now, but this time it was odd because their fights usually took place late at night. I'd called the police and reported them on two previous occasions because their yelling was so loud I couldn't sleep. Now they were at it again. I took a quick look out my window but didn't see anything unusual. As I continued ironing, the shouting escalated, growing louder and more intense. The yelling turned to a woman's screams—short and sharp at first, then longer and more guttural, like something out of a horror movie. As I grabbed the telephone in my trembling hands and dialed 911, I ran back to the window, phone cord trailing behind me. Like some twisted version of a football commentator, I relayed what I was seeing to the dispatcher. I described a woman, half running, half falling down the stairway from her second-story apartment, tumbling toward the glass front door. She was immediately followed by a man who struck at her savagely.

"He's hitting her…she's screaming…she's down on the floor… she's quiet. He's walking outside. Oh God, I think he killed her! There's blood all over him! He has a rubber glove on. It's all bloody. He's straightening his clothes like nothing happened. He's walking away."

I dropped the phone and ran from my apartment to where she lay.

Outside was a perfect California summer afternoon. The sun was shining and the sky was blue, but nothing looked right.

I stopped abruptly and for a moment just stared at her body, which was spilling halfway in and halfway out of the open glass door. I approached her slowly and knelt beside her. I could smell a sweet, metallic odor that made the knot in my stomach tighten. She was lying on her back, covered from head to toe in blood, her eyes wide open, staring past me into the distance. The only sound coming from her was gurgling that emanated from deep inside her throat. One stylish brown pump stood upright next to her on the stoop. I hesitated, then reached out to feel her wrist for a pulse. She was still warm. I kept thinking this couldn't be real, it had to be a movie.

"Do you think she's okay?" a low voice asked from behind me.

I turned my head slowly and squinted into the bright sunlight at the silhouette of a man hovering over me.

My voice quavered. "I...I don't think so," I breathed. He tossed something into the azalea bushes behind him, removed the bloody glove he was wearing, and dropped it at his feet, then casually strolled off down Beachwood Drive.

One by one, neighbors arrived on the gruesome scene. The police showed up soon after, and then the coroner. I was put into a patrol car and taken to the station where I was interviewed for hours. I was in shock, traumatized by what I'd just witnessed and shaking so violently that my teeth chattered. It's a horrible thing to witness another human being killed so brutally right in front of your eyes, something I hope none of you ever have or will have to experience. When I returned home, the mere thought of going back inside my apartment made me feel nauseous. There was no way I could stay there and not keep replaying that scene over and over in my head. I also knew the killer was still out there somewhere and might come looking for me because I could identify him. I called Mark, who rushed right over, grabbed a few of my things from the apartment, and took me to his place.

The living arrangement was less than ideal. For the next several nights we slept in his twin bed in the tiny apartment he shared with a roommate. A few weeks later, we decided to give up our respective apartments, find a place, and move in together. I wanted to stay in the same Beachwood neighborhood, near my friends. It's where I'd first lived with Matt, and to me, it felt like a small town in the big city. We combed the papers, then drove around the neighborhood in Mark's '76 Volkswagen van checking out rentals. About a half-mile away from my apartment, we came across a man pounding a "Duplex Apartment for Rent" sign into the ground at the top of a long, cypress-lined driveway. At the bottom sat a beautiful Spanish bungalow perched on a hillside overlooking the Hollywood sign. The landlord offered us a tour, but we both knew we wanted it even before we walked through the door. It was the lower level, and although it was only a one-bedroom, one-bath place, it was bigger than anything I'd lived in since leaving Las Vegas. The price was right, so we snapped it up. It seemed almost too good to be true. And in a way, it was.

What I didn't know was that the man who had brutally murdered my neighbor was the reason we were living there. Only after we'd gotten married, I'd become "Elvira," and we'd moved out did Mark tell me what had taken place there before we'd rented it. After the killer left the scene of the murder, he made his way on foot into the hills, where he approached a man walking two small dogs. Pretending he had a gun in his pocket, he forced the man to take him to his home, where he tied him up, grabbed a butcher knife from the kitchen, and threatened to kill him and his dogs if he tried anything. After showering and changing into some of the frightened tenant's clothes, he left. Thankfully, neither the man nor his dogs were hurt, but obviously feeling the same way I'd felt about living in a place that sparked such traumatic memories, he broke his lease and abruptly moved out. We were the lucky couple to rent it.

I later learned that the perpetrator, an African American advertising executive with no prior record, turned himself in to the police not long after the murder. The victim, who was white, turned out to be the daughter of a powerful politician and Texas Instruments executive and the ex-wife of a prominent Hollywood producer. Days after turning himself in, the killer was found dead, hanging from his belt in the cell. The *Los Angeles Herald Examiner* claimed she was murdered during a random robbery. The whole sad story still strikes me as very fishy to this day.

A year after moving in together, Mark and I decided to get married. Our wedding was held in a little church in Green Mountain Falls, Colorado, attended by a few friends, *lots* of my relatives, and both Mark's parents and mine. Deliriously happy and madly in love, we headed to a modest hotel in Aspen for our honeymoon and the beginning of our new life together.

In August of 1981, Maila Nurmi was asked by KHJ-TV to revive her Vampira character for television. I'm assuming that after their initial meeting it was obvious that wasn't an option. Maila was in her sixties and was clearly not up to the task. The TV station came up with the idea of finding a new, younger actress to revive the role. KHJ promised Maila that in exchange for the use of the name, she would receive an executive-producer credit on the show and collect a weekly royalty payment.

That week, I had a meeting with the director of the show, Larry Thomas; the station manager, Chuck Velona; and the program director, Walt Baker; along with Vampira herself, Maila Nurmi.

Vampira had hosted horror movies at the station for a brief period in 1956 and they explained that I would be playing Vampira's daughter. At this time, I had absolutely no idea there was an actual person named Vampira, probably because the show had aired only in the Los Angeles area when I was a child. I was familiar with the character Vampirella from *Famous Monsters of Filmland* creator Forrest J. Ackerman, but I assumed the name Vampira was a generic name for a female vampire. They showed me a few photos they had on hand of her when she was in her prime and I was thrilled that the character she'd played looked so much like one of my childhood favorites, Morticia Addams. Coincidently, Maila and I had a lot in common. She had previously worked as a showgirl and modeled for men's magazines before turning to horror hosting. She'd even worked as a hatcheck girl like me. And according to Hollywood legend, she was a bit of a star-fucker too.

The idea for the Vampira character was born in 1953 when the young ingénue was invited to a masquerade ball and took her inspiration for her costume from Morticia as portrayed in the *New Yorker* cartoons of Charles Addams. She caught the eye of producer Hunt Stromberg Jr., who arranged for her to host horror movies on local Los Angeles television station KABC-TV. Maila's first of three husbands, Dean Riesner, came up with the name Vampira and the show premiered on May 1, 1954.

It was canceled in 1955 and after leaving the station, Maila took *The Vampira Show* to their competition, KHJ-TV, where we now found ourselves. It aired on KHJ for only a few months in 1956 before being canceled again for the final time.

Our meeting that day was seriously awkward. It was plain to see from the photos she shared that she'd once been a very statuesque and beautiful woman, but it was also clear that she'd lived a very hard life. She had only a tooth or two left in her head and she rambled on incoherently about subjects that didn't relate at all to what we were there to discuss. She talked a lot about her relationship with James Dean, but in the present tense, as if it was ongoing. I wasn't all that familiar with James Dean, but I knew enough about him to know he was *dead*. It was sad to see an older lady like her alone and down on her luck. I was happy the show would be an opportunity for her to make some money for the use of the Vampira name.

When the meeting adjourned, the first thing I did to prepare for the new show was go straight to my friend Robert Redding from *Mama's Boys*, who was now living back in LA. In addition to being a performer, he was also a talented artist, so he and I threw some ideas around and he came up with sketches of what we thought the character might look like. The first version we both agreed on was a take on Sharon Tate's character from Roman Polanski's movie *The Fearless Vampire Killers, or Pardon Me, But Your Teeth Are in My Neck*, which had been a favorite of ours. The Sharon Tate look would utilize my own long, wavy, red locks and I would wear a pale-pink tattered gown with "dead-girl" makeup: pale face and lips and dark, sunken eyes. That look didn't fly with the KHJ management at *all*.

"No, definitely not," came the response. "Has to be all black!"

That left us with the more typical vampire look, which was frustrating for both of us, but Robert managed to give it a cooler, edgier '80s spin. He'd recently wrapped a production of *Macbeth* at West Hollywood's Globe Playhouse, playing the witch Hecate, and had researched Kabuki theater books for his look. His makeup turned out to be perfect for me, too.

Robert's favorite performer of all time was Ronnie Spector of the '60s girl group the Ronettes—the original bad girl of rock 'n' roll. Elvira's hairdo was inspired by Ronnie's beehive (only she called it a "knowledge bump") featuring long, black hair cascading from beneath a mile-high bouffant.

We were both a bit shocked that they didn't mind the plunging neckline that Robert had drawn. In fact, their only comment regarding changes to the costume was to ask that we make the slit on the leg a little higher. Ratings were ratings, and local stations back then didn't seem to get much flak from "standards and practices," so what the hell. Coming from my background, I was totally fine wearing a skimpy outfit. From time to time, I was asked in interviews how my parents felt about what I was wearing on TV and I always replied, "Heck, they're just happy I'm wearing *anything*!" Back then, my super-low-cut neckline and long, black nails were so shocking! Today, it seems like every woman on the Grammys and Academy Awards has adopted my look.

The first day of filming almost turned out to be the last. After spending hours in the dressing room with Robert putting the finishing touches on my wig, makeup, and costume, I appeared on set for the first time. Larry and the crew were impressed with the transformation, to say the least. They set me in place to tape the introduction to the show. Just as we were about to begin, Walt Baker burst into the studio.

"STOP THE SHOW!" he commanded. "Maila Nurmi's attorney just called. We can't use the name Vampira!"

Apparently, she was unhappy that the station had cast me, a comedic actress, to portray her character. According to an interview in a 2005 *Bizarre* magazine, Maila wanted thirty-nine-year-old Lola Falana, an African American singer, to play the part. It was easy to see how I might be a big disappointment.

So, there we were, me in full regalia, rented hallway flats propped up, fake spiderwebs blown into place and ready to go. I was completely verklempt—*not another part snatched away at the last minute!* Just as I was about to drag my sorry ass back to the dressing room, I heard a commotion. Larry suddenly turned around and shouted, "Okay, gang. Let's pick another name and get this show on the road!" I breathed a huge sigh of relief—hey, a job's a job—and everyone on the crew began throwing out names. Larry came up with the idea of writing names on scraps of paper, tossing them into an old Folgers coffee can, and choosing one at random. Robert, Mark, and I, along with the cameraman, lighting and sound guys, stage manager, and whoever else happened to be on the set, threw our little scraps of paper into the can. I tossed in the name Cassandra. Thank God I didn't choose *that*!

"El-*vi*-ra?" I grimaced when I pulled the slip of paper from the can. "Sounds like a country-western singer to me," I said, probably in reference to the song "Elvira" by the Oakridge Boys, which had recently been released.

Oh well. That was that. We fired up the ol' fog machine and got back to shooting the intro to the show—me, standing in a doorway at the end of a long, dark hallway, beckoning viewers to join me. Thus began Vampira's long, one-sided feud with Elvira.

The show was called *Elvira's Movie Macabre* and debuted in September 1981, just days before my thirtieth birthday. It ran in the Los Angeles area every Saturday night at midnight and repeated on Sunday afternoons as an alternative to the football games that were airing on all other channels. Our first show featured the 1972 horror snore-fest *Grave of the Vampire*. Mark and I watched my very first episode from home, excited and nervous. Not two minutes after it ended, the calls started pouring in, first from friends congratulating me, then from guys with important questions like, "Are your tits real?" That's when we realized that having my name and number in the phone book was a super-bad idea.

I had absolutely *zero* hopes of the show staying on the air long, much less leading to fame. I was just happy to have a weekly check coming in! Apparently, the station didn't hold out much hope for the show either, because years later, when the show came to an end and I asked to buy the red velvet sofa I'd reclined on, management discovered they'd been paying a weekly prop rental fee for the previous six years instead of buying it outright. I estimate that sofa had about $20,000 sunk into it. I got it for $200—deal of the century!

With Halloween around the corner, among the calls I received from men wondering whether I liked guys with big dicks were calls asking if I might be available for an appearance at their beauty salon, mini-mart, or Halloween party. I accepted a gig to sign autographs at a small convention in LA, which offered to pay me one hundred dollars. Mark and I could hardly believe our ears! *A hundred dollars?*! For doing nothing but signing my *name?* You gotta be kidding!

When the day of the convention rolled around, I woke up desperately sick with the flu. This turn of events was not going to deter me, however. Mark drove me there in his Volkswagen van while I lay in the back, nauseated and headachy. The promoters gave us a hotel room, where I slathered makeup onto my feverish face, which was already so pale that the white foundation was almost redundant. They were also nice enough to place my table right next to the ladies' room, so that while I was signing, I could periodically pop in to puke. The few fans that showed up seemed happy with their autographed photos and each received a bonus with purchase: a free flu bug! I made it through the convention alive and left with a hundred bucks in hand.

My husband, a budding composer (or so I hoped), wrote an eerie organ melody, punctuated by ghoulish sound effects, that was adopted as Elvira's trademark theme song. In the beginning, Larry wrote the scripts for the show. His writing style was pure vaudeville—schlocky jokes and puns that would make even Henny Youngman cringe.

Coming from a Vegas background, I *loved* it! The show always opened with a line or two welcoming viewers to *Movie Macabre* and introducing myself:

> Hello darling, and welcome to *Movie Macabre*…or as we like to call it: rent.
>
> Yes, it's me.…
>
> …that gal in the wig whose talents are big…
>
> …the gal who put the "sick" into classic…
>
> …the gal who put the "boob" back into "Boob Tube…"
>
> …the gal with the yucks who's workin' for schmucks…
>
> …that gal in the dress who al-l-l-ways says yes…except for one time when somebody asked me if I'd ever said no…
>
> …the cute high school dropout who looks like she'll pop out…
>
> Elvira, Mistress of the Dark.

You get the picture.

Each Thursday, I showed up at KHJ to shoot a show (or two, time permitting). Larry was a genius at coming up with hilarious, albeit corny scripts, but eventually, between writing, screening the movies, pulling all the film clips, and editing them into the show, plus directing and producing the whole shebang, it became too much for one guy to handle. I suggested John Paragon come onboard to help with the writing. John was one of the funniest and most brilliant Groundlings ever to grace their stage and Larry loved his work, so he convinced the station to scrape together a little money to pay him.

Paragon would become my writing partner for the next twenty-four years. In addition to writing *Movie Macabre* and all of my many home-video series together, John also cowrote *Elvira, Mistress of the Dark*. He helped write my Knott's Scary Farm Halloween show each year, in which he performed his Latin lover character, Ramone Azteca, which was incredibly popular. He and I collaborated on three Elvira-themed young adult novels, *The Boy Who Cried Werewolf, Camp Vamp,* and *Tran-*

sylvania 90210, as well as a parody of the popular children's book *Good Dog, Carl*, called *Bad Dog, Andy*, about John's very naughty dalmatian. John later became my child's godfather, and we became as close as two friends can be.

The movies on our show usually ran an hour and a half, minus commercials, so we had to come up with anywhere from fifteen to thirty minutes of nonstop yakking. In the case of some of the films that were shot in Italy or Mexico, we had to cut so much nudity and hot, horny girl-on-girl vampire action that we hardly had a film left, so we had to make up a *lot* of time!

The movies were the "crème de la crap." KHJ's parent company, the legendary RKO Pictures, happened to be chockablock with low, low, *low* budget films. Sometimes we got some decent classic horror films like *Frankenstein, Dracula, The Texas Chainsaw Massacre, Peeping Tom, Tales of Terror, The Other, Village of the Damned*, or *Willard*. But mostly we got movies that you could argue were not-so-classic, like *The Wild Women of Wongo, Meateaters, Blackula, Dr. Jekyll and Sister Hyde, The Incredible Two-Headed Transplant, Monstroid, The Navy vs. the Night Monsters*, and *Pigs.*

To give these tired-ass old movies new life, KHJ had figured out that the key to getting new viewers was the addition of a horror host, and lucky for me, I just happened to be crazy about these B-grade and C-grade clunkers!

Every Monday morning, John and I grabbed a couple of coffees and headed to KHJ, where we shut ourselves in a tiny, closet-size room for the better part of a day. A mystery man on the other side of the back wall projected the week's film onto a pull-down screen the size of an old-school TV set. There were no "pause" or "rewind" buttons, so we had to watch and rewatch the films two, three, four times, often jabbing each other in the ribs when one of us started snoring. John and I laughed and joked our way through the films, making cracks about the wardrobe and hair, the monster, the bad acting, and the corny plot, and then jotted down our notes. The shows consisted of an "open," a "close," and eight commercial "intro and outro" segments, with John doing the heavy lifting of actually forming our notes into an intelligible script. The worse the movies were, the easier it was to come up with funny material. Our biggest problem came when I had to host a film that was too classy, like *Peeping Tom*. Fortunately, we didn't have to deal with *that* pesky problem too often.

Another difficult script to write was one in which the movie took its own stab at comedy, leaving us struggling to make jokes on a joke, the perfect example being *Attack of the Killer Tomatoes*—all the good jokes about ketchup were already taken!

Meanwhile, Robert and I ran around town each week begging, borrowing, and buying props and costumes with our very limited budget. When Thursday rolled around, I reclined on my trusty old Victorian sofa in front of a black scrim, candelabras glowing behind me, and delivered my lines. Just to switch things up, Larry once tried an alternate set— me, leaning against a lamppost—but for obvious reasons, management ruled against it.

People often ask whether I improvised my scripts—possibly because they seemed so amateurish—but, *no. Hell no!* All the improvising was done during the writing process and I read every word straight from the teleprompter. We didn't have the luxury of time when it came to shooting the show. The one and only studio at KHJ was available between the News at Noon and the News at Five. We started each taping day at 1:00 p.m. and it didn't matter if we were finished shooting or not, at five minutes to 5:00, we were *done!* The opening scene from *Mistress of the Dark*, where I'm hosting a movie and the weather map drops down in front of my face mid-sentence, wasn't far from reality.

A big problem soon emerged. Without my glasses, I couldn't see two feet in front of me, let alone read a teleprompter ten feet away, no matter *how* big they made the copy. I wore contact lenses, but all the heavy eye makeup and lashes made them unbearable! A dozen times during the shoot, I'd waste precious minutes running to the bathroom to take my contacts out, rinse them, and stick them back in my eyes. That process would screw up my eye makeup, so it would take even more time to redo *that*. Edie McClurg told me about a new experimental surgery for near-sightedness that she and actor Robert Wagner had just undergone called radial keratotomy, the forerunner to LASIK. I immediately signed up for it and underwent the surgery and it was a miracle—I could see without glasses for the first time since third grade! Edie may have single-handedly saved my career.

As the show became successful, we were given a little money to hire other actors. We started by adding Paragon in a recurring role, "The Breather," based on his Groundlings's character "Mr. Ferguson"—a deranged sex-ed teacher who wore a dirty, disheveled suit and tie, thick Coke-bottle lenses in his horn-rimmed glasses, and a greasy face, courtesy of KY Jelly. Breather regularly called me from a phone booth, first breathing heavily into the receiver and then, in his creepy, croaking delivery, telling me a stupid joke, for example:

Breather: "What's the last thing that goes through a fly's mind when he hits the windshield of your car?"
Elvira: "I dunno, Breather. What *is* the last thing that goes through a fly's mind when he hits the windshield of your car?
Breather: "His butt!! Hahahahahaha!!!"

Okay, not the most sophisticated humor, but people loved him!

Over the years we were lucky to get an amazing list of actors who came on the show for little or no money. Some were "reprising" roles from the film I was showing that week, like my old flame Fabian Forte in *Kiss Daddy Goodbye* and Johnny Crawford (*The Rifleman*) in *Village of the Giants*. Other actors included John Carradine, fellow Groundlings Paul Reubens and Laraine Newman, John Astin (*The Addams Family*), Ed McMahon (*The Tonight Show*), Barbara Billingsley (*Leave It to Beaver*), Cheech Marin (Cheech & Chong), Mark Mothersbaugh (Devo), Hervé Villachaize (*Fantasy Island*), and comedian Arsenio Hall (playing the head of the NAACP—the Negroes Alliance Against Crappy Pictures). Larry Thomas reached out to Vincent Price to see if he might consider doing a quick appearance on our "Halloween Special" and to our shock and amazement, he said yes! At the time he happened to be appearing locally in a play called *Diversions and Delights*, based on the life of Oscar Wilde, and if we would allow him to plug it, he would agree to do the show. I couldn't believe it! "Vinny the P," my childhood hero, was actually going to be on *my* show! I was so nervous during the taping I could hardly get the words out, but he was charming, funny, and down-to-earth and quickly put me at ease.

One of the perks of being Elvira was that with the black wig and major makeup I wore, no one recognized Cassandra Peterson, so I could continue to go out for "legitimate" acting roles to boost my income.

I was still working as a temp in mind-numbingly boring office jobs, and the first inkling that I might be onto something came not long after the show aired. I mentioned to my boss at whatever insurance office I was working at that day that I'd landed a gig on a late-night TV show and was no longer available to work on Thursdays. Being a lowly insurance dude, he was clearly impressed and asked what the show was. When I told him I was Elvira, I thought he'd shit his drawers! Word traveled fast, because by the end of the day a steady stream of guys was flowing in from other offices to ogle me. When I left the office, I passed a group of construction workers outside who screamed and giggled like little girls. Was I actually becoming "famous"?

In May 1982, *Movie Macabre* was among the first wave of TV shows ever to be broadcast in 3D. Along with my segments, we aired the Vincent Price 3D classic *The Mad Magician*. Because 3D television technology was new and fairly experimental, shooting my segments of the show was painstakingly slow and difficult and took *forever!* We shot on a weekend starting around noon and ended at noon the next day, with a quick break or two to eat and pee. Naturally, we had to get in as many 3D jokes as possible. I opened Snakes in a Can, played with paddle-balls, blew party "blowouts," and of course, lunged my chest toward the camera as many times as possible, milking the 3D effect for all it was worth—ew, bad pun. Two point seven million pairs of cheesy cardboard 3D glasses were sold through 7-11 stores in Southern California where the show aired. At three bucks a pop, somebody was making a crap-load of moolah and it wasn't me. I was still being paid my regular weekly salary. Was I bitter? You could have made lemonade out of my spit. I'm *still* wondering where the other $8,099,650.00 went!

Paragon and Mark collaborated on a song that was featured in the show, appropriately entitled "3D TV." It was later released on vinyl through Rhino Records with another John Paragon original on the flip side, "Trick or Treat." Mark played recording engineer, while Paul Reubens and John—as my backup singers, The Vi-Tones—stood in our bathtub with the shower curtain drawn to give the record that special "bathtub of sound" effect that was so popular in the early '80s.

The night the 3D show premiered was beyond exciting! Mark and I invited over as many friends as we could pack into our living room and even scraped together the money for a new, larger TV set for everyone's "viewing displeasure." Of course, KHJ didn't give me any 3D glasses, so the afternoon of the premiere I schlepped down to the nearest 7-11 to buy them for us and our guests. When I got there, I couldn't believe my eyes—there was a long line of people outside the store waiting to buy the glasses! Feeling comfortable that I wouldn't be recognized, especially since I wasn't wearing makeup and had my hair up in curlers (I know. I'm sorry.), I took my place in line tucking my hands under my armpits to conceal my long black nails, and prepared to wait. Moments later, a mobile news van from a competing station pulled up and a reporter hopped out and shoved a microphone in my face. "Are you waiting in line to get glasses for Elvira's upcoming 3D show?" she brayed. Before she could see my nails or hear my voice and put two and two together, I turned, bolted to my car, and headed out to track down another store. How humiliating would it have been to find out that Elvira was waiting in line because her employers were too cheap to comp her a few pairs of the damn things? Sheesh! I later read in the *LA Times* that the demand for the 3D glasses was so great that the supply ran out long before the lines died down. There was even a story about a guy leaving a 7-11 being robbed at gunpoint by someone who took only his 3D glasses!

Even though I didn't make any money on the 3D broadcast, *Movie*

Macabre's ratings went through the roof, and the next thing I knew, I was invited to appear as a guest on *The Tonight Show* starring Johnny Carson. At the time there was only one talk show that mattered and this was it. Appearing on *The Tonight Show* was a career-defining moment and everybody knew it. They specifically asked me to do the interview as Cassandra, something that has rarely happened since. It would be the first time the television audience would see me out of Elvira drag, and, without my alter ego to protect me, I was scared shitless! I searched the stores for the perfect thing to wear, spending almost two weeks' salary on a dress. The night I went on, I was *so* nervous I thought I might hyperventilate and pass out! The producers introduced me to Johnny as he was getting into makeup, and he couldn't have been nicer or more encouraging. "You'll be fine," he said. "Just relax and be yourself." When I was actually on the stage, seated next to him, he led me through the interview, his years of expertise making me look good every step of the way. The high point came when Johnny asked what my favorite movie I'd hosted had been. I answered, "The Head with Two Things... I mean, *The Thing with Two Heads*!" It got a huge laugh and Johnny milked it for all it was worth by just staring at the audience with that signature deadpan look of his—a Carson trademark. During the following commercial break, I leaned over and whispered to him, "I'm so sorry...I didn't mean to say that!" He looked at me with a sly grin and said, "Don't bullshit a bullshitter, honey," knowing full well I'd planned it. In the years that followed, I went on to guest on *The Tonight Show* as Elvira with hosts Joan Rivers, David Brenner, and Jay Leno, sharing the sofa with Vincent Price, Dionne Warwick, Pee-wee Herman, and Betty White, among others.

Much to everyone's delight, *Movie Macabre* plugged along, week after week, and the ratings continued to grow. I think I was more shocked than anyone else! It seemed that not only did Elvira have a great set of boobs—she also had "legs."

Dressed as Elvira, I did local newspaper, TV, radio interviews, and my first professional photo session, and made my first public appearance at a shopping mall in Azusa. Whoo hoo! In 1982, I also received a local LA-area Emmy award nomination, which, even though I didn't win, seemed unimaginable.

When *Elvira's Movie Macabre* was well on its way to becoming a cult hit, Maila Nurmi resurfaced—this time to sue me for stealing her character. She'd dug up a lawyer, willing to work on a contingency basis, by placing an ad in a local newspaper that read, "Vampira to sue Elvira—Interested attorneys please inquire below." She filed a lawsuit naming KHJ-TV, Larry Thomas, and me, personally, as defendants. What really chapped my ass is that I didn't steal her character or anyone else's. I was just a "gun for hire," not involved in the terms of whatever agreement she'd made, or hadn't made, with KHJ, but that didn't seem to matter.

After Mark and I were forced to borrow $35,000, which was promptly thrown down the dumper on lawyer's fees, Maila never showed up in court and the judge ruled in our favor, stating, "*likeness* means actual representation of another person's appearance, and not simply close resemblance." Maila herself had claimed in a 1994 interview with *Boxoffice* magazine that Vampira's image was based on the Charles Addams character of Morticia from the *New Yorker* cartoons—hypocritical much?

Unfortunately, the Vampira saga didn't end there. She would continue to haunt me for years, sometimes sending tough-looking punks to my various appearances to heckle and threaten me, and once even shove me. When I was on the verge of signing a deal for a *Little Elvira* cartoon show on one of the major networks, Maila mailed their attorneys nude photos of me as Cassandra that she'd dug up in an obscure men's magazine. The cartoon show was promptly canceled.

But for all the trouble she caused me, she was still television's first horror host and I owe her a debt of gratitude for paving the way for me and all horror hosts to follow.

In late '82, Mark and I were invited to a party at the Hollywood Hills home of Eric Gardner, manager of singer/musician Todd Rundgren, an artist I'd idolized since his days in the Nazz in the '60s. I wouldn't have missed a chance to meet him for the world! On top of getting to hang out with Todd, who became a friend—and Richard Butler from the Psychedelic Furs, who was drunk, stoned, or both and behaved like a total douche—that evening marked the night we began discussions with Eric about the possibility of managing me in partnership with Mark, who, being new to the biz, lacked the experience Eric brought to the party, so to speak. Eric began his career in the early '70s coordinating tours for groups like the Grateful Dead, Jefferson Airplane, and KISS. In 1974 he shifted to talent management with his company Panacea Entertainment, and in addition to Todd, managed musicians like Steven Van Zandt as well as Bill Wyman of the Rolling Stones. Since moving from New York to Los Angeles with his wife, Janis, he'd been looking for a vehicle that would allow him to expand into the world of film and television, and I was that ride.

Halloween 1982 found me performing a month-long show at the Southern California amusement park Knott's Berry Farm, which, during the month of October, transforms into the Halloween Haunt, the largest and longest-running Halloween venue in the country. I replaced the former host, radio personality Wolfman Jack, to perform onstage in Knott's 2,000-seat Good Time Theatre. Dancing and singing was something I hadn't done in years, but I had a blast doing the show and was reminded why there's nothing quite like the thrill of performing in front of a live audience. Knott's Scary Farm became a seasonal gig for Elvira that would continue, on and off, for twenty-four out of forty years.

For a year, I'd worked on *Movie Macabre*—the number one–rated show on KHJ—acting, writing, and buying costumes and props, and at the end of the week picked up my skimpy paycheck. Mark had negotiated a minor raise in 1982, up to $500 a week, but KHJ wouldn't budge beyond that. Shocked that KHJ owned all the rights to the Elvira character, Eric made getting them his number-one priority. Thanks to some deft negotiating on his part, and with the help of attorney Vance Van Petten, we soon owned the rights. After a long history of corporate misconduct, KHJ's parent company, RKO General, was ordered to surrender their remaining broadcast licenses in 1988, including that of KHJ, which was sold to the Walt Disney Company, becoming KCAL. If KHJ had retained the rights to the character, Elvira would have disappeared down the dark hole of history along with the station.

With a little help from Mark's generous parents, we were able to buy a house in the Los Feliz Oaks neighborhood, just down the hill from the duplex apartment we'd been renting. It was nothing fancy, no pool, no gates, just a modest, middle-class, three-bedroom home on Park Oak Drive, but it was a place of our own and we were ecstatic.

It was a magical time. Mark and I were more in love than ever, and becoming successful added to our feelings of happiness and well-being. We adored our new home, our dogs and cats, cooking for friends, and throwing parties. I replaced my Volkswagen with a BMW and Mark exchanged his van for a Mercedes station wagon, both used, but big improvements over what we'd been driving.

The first year at KHJ passed in a crazy whirlwind of newfound fame. I'd gone from a struggling actress to a celebrity. Life was turning out in the way I'd always dreamed it would.

In 1983 we released *Elvira Presents Vinyl Macabre—Oldies But Ghoulies Vol. I* through Rhino Records, this time an album of classic Halloween hits like Bobby "Boris" Pickett's Halloween classic "Monster Mash" and one of my favorite weird songs of all time, "It's Halloween" by the Shaggs. Each song was bookended with Elvira's signature snarky comments.

I flew to Atlanta to film a small part in the movie *Stroker Ace*, starring Burt Reynolds and Loni Anderson. Burt and Loni were still blissful lovebirds back then, and they, along with director Hal Needham and actor Jim Nabors, treated me like a star. Although Jim, as his Gomer Pyle character in *The Andy Griffith Show* was a favorite of mine growing up, the scene between the two of us was awkward, to say the least. I played a kind of Elvira-human hybrid, wearing Elvira's hair and makeup, but dressed in a high-collared, knee-length blue dress, attempting to pick Jim up in a bar—a formidable task.

Settling into our very first home, Mark was now comanaging me full-time, so we added an office above the garage that made our house feel more like a home and not a workplace. Through fans, we acquired two adorable rottweiler pups who we named Vlad and Bela, and along with our cats, Renfield and Hecate, we started to feel like a family.

My career continued to ramp up. March 9, 1984, was declared Elvira Day in Los Angeles, and I attended a ceremony where I was given a plaque by then-Mayor Tom Bradley. I received the 22nd Annual Count Dracula Society Award from founder Dr. Donald A. Reed and, while at the awards ceremony, spent a very festive hour in my limo drinking and chatting with *Fahrenheit 451* author Ray Bradbury, whose books were among my favorites. MTV hired our newly formed production company to write and produce a six-hour Halloween special, doing comedy bits in between their year-end countdown of best music videos, and I made lots more TV appearances including on *The Today Show* and *Entertainment Tonight* and another guest spot on *The Tonight Show*. This time, I appeared as Elvira, and the show was hosted by comic David Brenner (who was surprised to learn I'd worked with him years earlier on *The Bachelor of the Year Awards*). I was excited as could be to discover that Vincent Price was also a guest that night. When I told David that Vincent had been featured in many of the Edgar Allan Poe–themed movies on my show, Vinny replied, "You're right, Elvira. Those were some po' pitchures, they were!" (I've used that line so many times over the years, I should have paid him royalties!) For almost a decade, it seemed like every time there was a talk show, an awards ceremony, or a movie premiere with a horror theme at which Vincent was a guest, I was there, too, so we saw a lot of each other. We became friends until his death, writing letters back and forth, some of which I hear are archived in the Smithsonian. He also taught me to cook fish in my dishwasher. Just throwing that out there.

In 1984, I attended the Grammys, and while backstage, got the chance to meet Michael Jackson. During the show that evening, he'd won a record eight Grammy Awards for various songs from his album *Thriller*. I hadn't seen him since he'd performed as a child in Vegas with the Jackson Five, and I was slightly intimidated by how tall, handsome, and larger than life he appeared. "I love you, Elvira," he breathed in his high-pitched, whispery voice as I shook his begloved hand. "You should have done that voiceover in 'Thriller.'" Michael Jackson was telling me I should have been in "Thriller," one of the best-selling singles of all time?! Get the fuck out! Stifling a yelp from the rhinestones that were digging into my flesh, I wanted to scream, "Damn straight I shoulda been!" but instead murmured politely, "Oh, that would have been fun!" Years later, when Rod Temperton, the prolific genius who wrote "Thriller," passed away, I read an article in the *New York Post*, claiming that Temperton had initially suggested Elvira to record the spooky spoken-word segment of the song. Instead, producer Quincy Jones decided to hire his wife's friend's husband, who just happened to be Vincent Price. Well, I guess if I had to lose out to someone, my idol would be my first choice. But I still have to wonder sometimes how "Thriller" would have changed the trajectory of my career.

Becoming famous was quite a rush, but it wasn't all champagne and limousines. Don't get me wrong, being invited to Hollywood parties and premieres, hanging with other celebs, offers of all the cocaine I could snort, and having everyone make a big fuss over me was *fun*. But little by little the loss of privacy crept in and I began to feel overwhelmed. I went from a "no one" to a "someone" so quickly it made my head spin.

I received bags and bags of fan mail, which I loved reading and did my best to personally respond to. There were flattering and moving letters from adults and children alike. As you might expect, there were also tons of letters from every branch of the military, from bikers, and from lots and lots of prison inmates. I once got a Christmas card signed by dozens of prisoners from the Chino State Prison in California and, on the same day, received a card signed by dozens of the men who put them there, the Los Angeles Police Department. There were even fan letters from clergymen. Yep, at one time or another I got fan letters from someone in almost every branch of the religious establishment, including Catholic priests, Jewish rabbis, monks, preachers of every denomination, and a lovely card from a convent signed by each and every one of the Sisters of the Immaculate Heart of Mary. Among the overwhelmingly kind, funny, sad, interesting letters were always a few creepy and slightly disturbing ones, too. Like photos of men you would *never* want to see naked. One went beyond that, however, making threats and describing, in detail, violent things he'd like to do to me. He followed me from appearance to appearance, sent threatening letters to my husband, and often planted himself outside the post office where we picked up the fan mail. We reported him to the LAPD's stalking unit, and that's the point at which alarms were installed in our house, our two rottweilers were guard-trained, and our street number was painted on the roof so the police could spot our house from the air in an emergency.

At the same time, my family was in turmoil. My sisters, Melody and Robin, who'd had drug and alcohol issues since their teens, were descending deeper into their addictions. I'd loaned them money time and time again and begged them to enter rehab on my dime, but nothing seemed to help. The few times they did agree to go to rehab, they stayed for only a short time and then relapsed. As anyone who's had a friend or relative with addiction issues knows, there's little you can do to help if the person isn't willing to help themselves. Drugs and alcohol would plague Melody and Robin their whole lives, and they both spent time in jail and on the streets, with all the horror that entails.

As if that wasn't depressing enough, the AIDS epidemic was just beginning to rear its ugly head. The first time I heard anything about the deadly virus was when I stopped by a local bar on Hollywood's Eastside to see my friend David Meyer. David was a successful photographer who had shot the photo spread and cover of Bill Cable in *Playgirl* magazine years before. He also co-owned a bar, so I always knew where to find him.

"David's not here today?" I asked the substitute bartender.

"No. Out sick. Pneumonia."

I was shocked. I'd seen him just a week before and he was fine.

"Pneumonia? You're kidding, right?" I said. "Did he have a cold?"

"Nope. He just got sick. Said he'd be back in by next weekend."

I left, concerned but not freaked out. I'd heard that Joey Arias's friend Klaus Nomi had recently come down with pneumonia, too, and decided it must just be going around. I returned to the bar the following weekend hoping to catch David, and from the look on his co-owner's

face I immediately knew something was very wrong. His voice breaking, he said, "David died." Nothing could have prepared me for that
response. What the hell? He was a healthy, fit, young guy. Things like
that didn't happen.

Over the next few weeks, I began hearing rumors about the new
"gay pneumonia." Then people started talking about something they
called "gay cancer," but I was sure someone must be working on a pill or
a vaccine to take care of it. I just prayed to God that no one else I knew
would get sick before a cure was found. The occasional news report or
a story from a friend about another man dying of a mysterious virus
struck terror into my heart, not only for my friends, but for myself, too.

In the meantime, not a day went by that I didn't see or talk to Robert
Redding. Then one day he called to tell me he had shingles. I got a sick
feeling in the pit of my stomach because I'd heard that shingles was one
of the many diseases that people with HIV were getting. I accompanied
Robert to the hospital to get some medication and the doctor on duty
suggested he have a blood test. It confirmed what I already suspected:
Robert had AIDS.

His brother, Dan, Mark, I, and all Robert's friends leapt into action,
calling every person we knew in the medical profession and reading
every bit of information we could lay our hands on for any news of
something, *anything*, that might help. Robert tried everything possible
to boost his immune system—vitamins, herbal tonics, special diets—
vowing he'd beat this thing. But over the next months, he went from
a strapping six-foot-four-inch muscular hunk to a dried-up shell of a
man, weighing almost half his normal weight. When he was treated for
one disease, another would pop up—Crohn's, Bell's palsy, Kaposi's sar-
coma, and on and on. He was now spending more time in the hospital
than at home, and it left me feeling desperately helpless and scared. It
wasn't bad enough that Robert already felt like a pariah because of his
disease, but most nurses and doctors were afraid of treating patients
with this new, baffling virus and wore something akin to a hazmat suit
when they entered his room. Some just flat-out refused to treat him.
When I visited him in the hospital, all I could do was crawl into bed with

him, hold him, and do my best to make up for them. I kept my "happy face" on when I was with him, but the pressure of keeping my emotions inside led me to go home every night, pour myself a drink or two—or three—and cry myself to sleep.

As a young, previously healthy man and your typical starving artist, Robert had no insurance, so it was up to his friends and family to do what we could to set him up with various AIDS services, which helped financially by paying a portion of his medical bills and keeping a roof over his head.

Mark and I offered to throw a fundraiser at our home to raise money to pay some of his mounting bills. Robert was such a talented genius in so many areas—art, music, theater—that he had many well-known and affluent friends who loved him, including writer Christopher Isherwood and his partner, artist Don Bachardy, director Randal Kleiser, and singer/songwriter Brenda Russell, who were all graciously willing to help.

On a warm August afternoon, I was in my backyard planting flowers in pots in preparation for the benefit that night, when I suddenly stopped dead in my tracks. An overwhelming sense of Robert's presence surrounded me. At the risk of sounding too "woo-woo," I gazed up at the sky and smiled, a warm, loving feeling enveloping me. I was snapped back to reality when the kitchen phone rang. It was Robert's younger brother, Dan, calling to say that Robert had just passed away. Even though I knew how ill he was, I wasn't prepared for the news. All this time I kept hoping against hope that *something* would come along and save him. The party became a wake, and one of the hardest things I've ever had to do was greet each of his friends at the door with the heartbreaking news of Robert's death.

I fell into a deep depression after Robert was gone. He was so much a part of my life, and of Elvira, that I really didn't know what I was going to do without him. It was a dark time. The AIDS epidemic kept growing and growing, with no end in sight. I still kept in touch with all the guys from *Mama's Boys* and was shaken and deeply saddened to learn that first John Palmer, then Jim Raitt, then Bobby Howland, were dying. I heard that Buddy Vest, my crush from my Las Vegas days, had passed, and my first serious boyfriend, Matt Vernon, was sick. Robert's brother Dan, who was also an ex-boyfriend and someone I'd been close to for years, discovered he had AIDS and died by suicide, and my gorgeous, talented friend and "Halloween Haunt" choreographer, Alan DeWames, became ill and soon succumbed. With my dating history, it was nothing short of a miracle that I somehow escaped the virus.

Every few days, I crossed off another name in my address book. This disease was so horrific that it's impossible to describe the tragic loss and seething rage I felt seeing so many friends' and loved ones' young lives cut short.

As time went on, my sisters and the AIDS crisis, in combination with my newfound fame, began to take its toll. My own drinking increased and I began to use cocaine more and more frequently to get "up" for appearances. I gradually became afraid to leave my house. For the first and only time in my life, I started having panic attacks. I developed what, in hindsight, I believe was agoraphobia. I became extremely paranoid, and if I had to go somewhere, I kept my eyes glued to the rearview mirror, sure that someone was following me.

The breaking point came one day as I was grocery shopping at the local Mayfair Market. Someone was following me; I was sure of it. No matter what aisle I turned down, I caught a glimpse of a man prowling around each corner. By the time I reached the checkout counter my heart was pounding so hard I became dizzy and was short of breath. The last thing I remember was the cashier saying, "Miss? Are you all right?" before waking up on the floor with paramedics hovering over me.

This was the cue that I needed help. For the first time, I began seeing a therapist regularly and keeping medication with me in case of another panic attack. Over the next year I learned to cope with the anxiety, curbed my alcohol consumption, and cut the drugs out altogether.

The TV offers kept coming in. In 1984 I did my first episode of *The Fall Guy* with Lee Majors and guest stars John Carradine and his three sons, David, Robert, and Keith; and a second one a year later with Chris Humphreys and Vincent Schiavelli. That same year I was asked to do an episode of *Bloopers & Practical Jokes,* hosted by Ed McMahon and Dick Clark, and my third appearance on *The Tonight Show,* this time with Joan Rivers as host.

On a plane back from Florida, where I'd been hired to lead the "Parade of Villains" at Walt Disney World, I happened to sit directly behind the legendary comedian Bob Hope. Summoning all my nerve, I introduced myself, letting him know what an honor it was to meet him. Of course, I was familiar with Mr. Hope's work, having seen him in films and on TV my entire life, so I was a bit intimidated. He was very polite and gracious, but when I explained that I played the character Elvira, his face registered a blank. Suddenly his wife, Dolores, piped up: "My sister and I are big fans!" She elbowed her hubby and decreed, "Bob, you need to have Elvira on your next special." Mr. Hope, in perfect-husband mode, smiled, nodded, and said, "Yes, darling," and I assumed that would be the end of it. But a week later I got a call from his production company asking me to be on the first of two *Bob Hope Specials* I would appear in.

In 1984, Cheech Marin, who had become a friend since my appearance in *Cheech and Chong's Next Movie,* featured Elvira in the music video for his popular novelty song "Born in East LA." That same year the home-video series I hosted, *ThrillerVideo,* was released and sold more than 200,000 copies, and Elvira Day was declared in Atlanta, Georgia. I even became a figure in LA's Movieland Wax Museum. Elvira was on a roll!

Then in 1986, in a game-changing move for Elvira, Mark and Eric landed a deal to syndicate *Movie Macabre.* Our little local TV show expanded to the national television market, making Elvira the first horror host ever to be televised throughout the US. That year we also produced and hosted our second MTV special, "Elvira in Salem," and Elvira appeared as a comic-book character for the first time in twelve issues of *Elvira's House of Mystery* from DC comics. The show was still taped at KHJ, so of course had the low-budget look of being shot in somebody's basement, which I believe endeared Elvira to fans across the country all the more. Viewers in each town assumed Elvira was their own local horror host. After all, how could a show made in Hollywood look so incredibly cheesy? Despite the occasional complaints about my cleavage, our biggest audience was in the Bible Belt. Figures, right?

When the station manager made a rare appearance on set, we always knew it wasn't to deliver good news.

"You're going to have to do something about that neckline," Walt would intone. "We got another complaint about the cleavage."

"Oh, right! No problemo!" I'd reply. I wouldn't do anything to change it and the following week he'd be back.

"Did you fix the dress?"

"Yep, all good!"

And that was the end of that until the next complaint.

After a billboard went up in one Southern city featuring Elvira seductively sprawled across it, the local television station that had sponsored it received a dozen complaints, so they slapped a black "censored" banner across the offending body parts and then received hundreds of complaints.

CHAPTER 20

BOOBS 'N' BEER

Back in the early '80s, Coors Brewing Company of Golden, Colorado, came up with a new marketing strategy. Their intention was to corner the beer market on Halloween. And why not? Every year Halloween had morphed into more and more of an adult holiday, mainly attributed, I believe, to the gay community, but also in part to Elvira. A quote from the *Wall Street Journal* in 1986 proclaimed, "Halloween, once a romp for kids clad as pirates and princesses, now rivals Saint Patrick's Day and New Year's Eve as a party time for adults. Blame it on Elvira."

Putting a spin on their "Silver Bullet" tagline, Coors introduced the "BeerWolf." Unfortunately, the cheesy-looking hairball didn't quite accomplish what they'd hoped for. In 1986, Coors made one last-ditch effort to bring back the hokey beast, only *this* time he was flanked by the Mistress of the Dark. The brewery saw an enormous rise in sales and took steps to dump the BeerWolf soon after, replacing him with Elvira as their exclusive Halloween "spooksperson." I was now the first female celebrity in commercial history to endorse a beer.

Remember, I'd been raised in Colorado where drinking Coors beer was practically a state law. In Kansas, my dad drank Hamm's beer— "from the land of sky blue waters"—or Pabst Blue Ribbon, but once we moved to Colorado it was Coors all the way. When I was a teenager, Coors 3.2 beer, a lower-alcohol version that tasted like watered-down camel piss, was positively de rigueur (that is, of course, when I wasn't drinking other fine beverages like Ripple).

In addition to the money I was paid, Coors supplied us with all the beer we could drink. I vividly remember the day a huge truck pulled up to our house and unloaded hundreds of cases of Coors into our garage. Party!

So, winding up as the spokesperson for Coors, of all companies, was Kismet. It was also reparation for my dad and other family members who had contributed so much to their bottom line.

The appearance in stores of life-size cardboard stand-ups featuring Elvira holding a six-pack cemented Coors's title as "The Official Beer of Halloween." When the Elvira standees were displayed in markets around the country, they stopped in-store traffic flow faster than a spilled case of Mrs. Butterworth's pancake syrup on aisle thirteen.

In an interview with *Chief Marketer* magazine titled "Trick or Drink," Phil Senes, former manager of Coors promotion, declared, "We couldn't keep the displays up at retail. Consumers, competitors, even the store personnel were taking our Elvira stand-ups out of the stores as fast as they could stock them."

The campaign was so popular that it ran again in 1987 to rave reviews. Yet the company did everything in its power to tone down my sexy image. They requested that whenever shooting promotional photos or commercials, I cover my chest with my hair as much as possible, and they always made sure someone from their marketing team was on hand to make sure I did. What little skin managed to peek through, they were happy to retouch to guarantee that no one who drinks beer would accidentally get a glimpse of cleavage—God forbid! I mean, what was so scandalous? Coors sells booze, not baby formula, right? Check out the Coors commercials and standees online sometime. I could have been a boy for all the cleavage I showed!

During this time, in addition to my other beer-hawking duties, I made extensive tours through the South and Midwest to visit Coors distribution companies in towns like Chillicothe, Ohio, and other out-of-the-way places that took two or three plane changes to get to. The workers at the bottling plants loved me, and I loved them! I think they felt I was an approachable beer-drinkin' gal, an "everyday Joe" they could relate to, instead of a snooty Chardonnay-sipping Hollywood celebrity.

In 1988, something happened that was downright spooky. Rumors circulated that Procter & Gamble's CEO had appeared on several TV talk shows saying that he was giving large amounts of the company's profits to his favorite charity, the Church of Satan. In reality, he not only never said that, but he'd never appeared on any of the talk shows they cited. Apparently, ridiculous conspiracy theories aren't something new. For God's sake, people! How gullible do you have to be to believe a multinational corporation would put *any* god before profits? Even Satan? But why should a silly thing like facts stop people from boycotting P&G? There was also Procter's logo, a picture of the Man in the Moon surrounded by thirteen stars, which had been around since 1851, but suddenly it was the "trademark of the Devil." As proof of the company's being in cahoots with Beelzebub, overly zealous religious nuts even saw horns peeking out from under the Man in the Moon's hair and numerous sixes embellishing the logo. Never a good sign. P&G *claimed* the stars represented the thirteen US colonies. Sheesh, I'm so *sure*! Under the heading of "believe it or not," Procter & Gamble sued their competitor Amway, which was a competing manufacturer of health, beauty, and home care products, for starting the unfounded rumors. Coincidentally, Amway, a multilevel marketing company often referred to as a "pyramid scheme," was cofounded by another famous "religious" family, the DeVoses, as in the oh-so-devout former secretary of education Betsy DeVos and her brother, Erik Prince, former head of Blackwater. I love that story.

Coors heard about P&G's dilemma and, being the good alcohol-pushing Christians they were, feared they, too, might be accused of satanic shenanigans because of a certain spokeswoman known as the Mistress of the Dark.

At this point, my Halloween campaign was one of the few bright spots for a company that was mired in right-wing political backlashes, boycotts, and, consequently, plummeting sales. So, what did Coors president and religious zealot Jeffrey Coors do? He decided to kill the campaign at the very height of its overwhelming success. The PR and marketing guys called us personally to say they couldn't believe what was happening.

Coors marketing scrambled to come up with a fix. They suggested sending a paste-on panel to the retail outlets that carried the 150,000 standees to cover any offending cleavage. They must have been thinking of sending out black turtleneck sweaters because, as I mentioned, there was absolutely *no* cleavage showing. In any case, they soon learned that it wasn't the cleavage that was so offensive to Mr. Coors. According to the book *Citizen Coors: A Grand Family Saga of Business, Politics, and Beer*, "Elvira stirred in Jeffrey [Coors] a deep sense of revulsion and fear. He dubbed Elvira satanic." And so, the decision was made to drop me.

Eric, Mark, and I were completely blindsided. This was the most lucrative source of income we'd had since the character began, and we knew the campaign was a huge success. We were more than a little unhappy to see it disappear through no fault of our own. But even more devastating than losing the income was the loss of visibility that national radio and television exposure brought us. It could have meant the death knell for Elvira.

Not long after, however, Pepsi, a company that obviously had no fear of the dark side, came along and turned our frowns upside down. Pepsi snapped me up at double what Coors was paying, to promote their two newest products, Mandarin Orange Slice and Mug Root Beer. Pepsi developed the brand's largest-ever promotion featuring Elvira and partnered with Universal Studios to exploit it. The director of my commercial was the comedian David Steinberg, who was a joy to work with, and we shot on the Universal Hollywood lot at the original *Psycho* house, an added bonus for me!

In '89 and '90, Elvira was featured in newspaper, radio, and TV commercials promoting the "Go Psycho with Elvira" contest. Consumers who tried Slice or Mug Root Beer received a chance to win a trip to Universal Studios Hollywood for a ginormous party hosted by "Yours Cruelly." The standees Pepsi produced that appeared in grocery stores across the country showed a lot more skin than the Coors version, even though I'm pretty sure Pepsi products are alcohol-free.

When the Pepsi promotion was done, Coors came knocking again, hat in hand. In the interim, their revenue had taken a giant step backward.

They had run a campaign called Rocktoberfest featuring a guy surrounded by young women in tight silver lamé, believing they'd learned the all-important lesson: sex sells. Unfortunately for them, it tanked. When the sex angle didn't work, they tried the comedy approach. They hired actor Leslie Nielsen to play his bumbling detective character as "The Phantom of the Fridge" and brought him back again in 1990 in "The Search for Halloween Headquarters." But even that campaign brought disappointing sales. Now what kind of character could they find that not only combined both sex *and* comedy but was also a Halloween icon? Hmmm.

Amid these campaigns a groundswell was forming among Coors distributors, employees, and the beer-swilling public to bring back Elvira. "As long as we had Elvira, we were the preferred beer supplier for Halloween," said Senes. She once again starred in Coors Halloween commercials, this time representing Coors Light. Elvira remained Coors's reigning Queen of Halloween through 1995.

First, let me say that the reports of Coors and Elvira's amicable parting of the ways were grossly exaggerated. After the 1995 season, even though the Elvira campaign was the most successful they'd had up until that time, they made the nonsensical decision to scale back her presence for Halloween. The Coors execs called to inform us that they were making the move from life-size standees to mini countertop stand-ups, using the excuse that the life-size ones were too expensive to produce and so many had been taken from stores that they couldn't replace them fast enough.

"Oh, and by the way, we won't be doing any more radio or TV ads either." To put the sour cherry on the shit cake, they added, "*and* we'll only be paying you half as much—since you're not doing radio and TV ads anymore."

"Wait, what? Elvira did a hugely successful ad campaign that helped make Halloween the second biggest beer-consumption holiday of the year, they just begged me to come back, and now they're choosing to back off?" It made absolutely no sense. The thought crossed our minds that minimizing Elvira's presence would allow the campaign to die a slow death, thereby letting Coors off the hook and laying the blame for the failure at Elvira's feet.

Could this have had something to do with a bizarre anecdote we'd recently heard from a member of the Coors marketing team? Considering the company we were dealing with, I suppose it's not that far-fetched. Feeling confident and proud of their latest Elvira standee, the marketing team took the prototype to the big honcho, Joseph Coors Sr., for his approval. In his late seventies at the time and semiretired, Joseph leaned back in his cushy office chair and glared at it for a few moments. Then, in an ominous voice, he rasped, "I see demons there."

The marketing guys were caught off guard and assumed he was joking. They chuckled and countered with, "Oh, right! Would that be the little green ones, or the big red kind?"

Mr. Coors was *not* amused. He slammed his fist down on his desk and shouted, "*I see demons there!*" Now how are you supposed to reason with that kind of logic?

Obviously, there was *something* at play behind this sudden change of heart, but we never really got an honest answer from anyone as to what it was. Was it that they really believed my fun, tongue-in-cheek character was one of Satan's little helpers? Or were the rumors true that Mothers Against Drunk Driving (MADD) had set their sights on Halloween and Coors was afraid of the negative press they would garner by promoting beer as a holiday beverage? That was the reason they gave us, anyway, and we had twenty-four hours to consider their crappy offer and get back to them. Mark, Eric, and I made the tactical decision to "save face" and walk away rather than stick it out and allow the seriously slashed campaign to make Elvira, at the peak of her career, look like she was no longer a hot commodity. Reluctantly, we declined their offer and ended our long partnership with Coors.

Since the beginning of *Movie Macabre* in 1981, and years before Coors hired me, I'd referred to my character as the "Queen of Halloween." I'd used the title during several episodes of *Movie Macabre* and in many of the Halloween specials and promotions I'd done before signing with Coors. They apparently liked the moniker as much as I did, because they registered and trademarked it and continued to use it long after I left, adopting it for their Halloween promotions for the next several years. My replacement, their new Queen of Halloween, was actress Pamela Anderson. Now don't get me wrong. I love me some Pam Anderson, especially because she's a champion of animal rights and because she survived being married to Tommy Lee and Kid Rock, but when I think of Halloween, the tan, blonde beach bunny is not the first person who pops into my mind.

Around the same time, I had a lucrative appearance booked in Denver at one of the largest gay discos in the West. Just before I was to leave LA for Colorado, Mark got a call from the club owner telling him that a funny thing had just happened. He'd been in the club right before opening hours when who should walk through the door? None other than Peter Coors, vice chairman and CEO, and son of Joseph Coors.

According to the owner, Pete said, "If you'll forego booking Elvira, we'd be happy to supply you with an appearance by Pamela Anderson, free of charge." The club owner stared back at him slack-jawed and responded, "This is a gay bar. What the fuck would we want with Pamela Anderson?"

Year after year, Coors continued to slap the title "Queen of Halloween" on such spooky icons of horror as Jenny McCarthy, Daisy Fuentes, and Salma Hayek. After that, they dumped the celebs and figured they could just get by with anonymous sexy babes wearing skimpy black outfits and a Queen of Halloween banner plastered across their ample chests.

But, as luck would have it, my ass was rescued once again. In 1996, we were approached by a couple of members of the Coors team: Bob Fox, head of marketing for Coors; and brand manager Mike Wiley. They had been champions of the Elvira campaign and, fed up with the silly decisions being made there, quit. In 1996 the market for craft brewery beer was just heating up. Bob and Mike found investors to pump money into a one-hundred-year-old failing brewery in Minnesota called Cold Springs. Elvira's Brewhouse, Inc., was born, making me the first celebrity to market her own beer, Elvira's Night Brew—a "dark, full-bodied, and robust lager."

To get the new beer off the ground, I flew out to Colorado to promote Elvira's Night Brew at Denver's prestigious Great American Beer Festival, the premiere beer competition in the country. Bob and Mike had a booth set up inside the Colorado Convention Center, with displays that included our newest Elvira stand-up, this time showing plenty of cleavage! After my bad experience with Coors, I was excited to show them what the Elvira name, attached to a beer, could do.

To say Coors held a grudge would be an understatement. When I hadn't accepted their shitty offer and then had the audacity to come out with my own beer, with the help of their two top marketing guys no less, they were *not* amused. There was no room in Coors's world for female entrepreneurial competition, especially a female who was so obviously in cahoots with the devil! Wearing my full Elvira drag, I pulled up in front of the convention center in my limo. Fans and photographers greeted me and cheered as I made my way to the entrance. Just as I began to cross the threshold, two big, burly security guards threw their arms out and stopped me dead in my tracks. "Sorry, Miss, but we can't allow you in here wearing that outfit. You'll need to change clothes." I honestly thought I was being punked.

"You're joking, right?" I asked, incredulous.

Nope. They weren't joking. Since I had begun playing Elvira fifteen years earlier, apart from pulling more hair over my cleavage, I'd never once had to compromise the integrity of the character, or lack thereof, and I wasn't about to start now.

"But, but, but…" I stammered. "We have a booth inside that we've paid for! I'm promoting my new beer and fans are already waiting in line!"

As my PR people and I gave the security guards every reason we could think of to allow me entrance, Old Milwaukee's Swedish bikini team paraded past and into the Convention Center wearing—guess what?—*bikinis*! Compared to them I looked like I was wearing a burka! After several minutes of shouting and arguing, it became obvious that there was no reasoning with these guys. They weren't going to let me in no matter what I said. By this time, we were causing a scene. A crowd had gathered, curious to see what was going down. Everyone seemed to be on my side and several people jumped into the fray, coming to my defense. More security guards were called. We must have created quite a stir, because moments later several members of "Denver's finest" showed up and escorted me and my entourage from the premises. Even though my limo was parked on a public street in front of the convention center, we were told we'd have to move to another location. I was beyond livid! Instructing the driver to pull the car directly across the street, I hollered to my publicist, "Call every newspaper, radio, and television station in town and tell them what's going on here!" Within minutes, dozens of reporters showed up. I stood outside my limo for the next couple of hours, doing interview after interview. I couldn't have *bought* that kind of publicity! I also signed a ton of autographs for fans who'd heard about the *brew*-ha-ha—see what I did there?—and were lining up to give me their condolences. There's no proof, of course, that Coors was behind this absurdity, but c'mon people, I didn't just fall off the tuna truck! I'd made appearances dressed as Elvira at food conventions, video-game conventions, and even the Toy Fair in New York, and had never once been asked to "cover up." But *now* I was being turned down at a convention for *beer*? Beyond ridunculous!

Even though Elvira's Night Brew did amazingly well and was available in forty states, after one year, our deal went *flat*—see? I did it again—when the venture capitalist backing the brewery pulled out and the company's initial public offering failed to go through. This, coupled with the shoddy treatment I'd received at Denver's '96 Great American Beer Festival, spelled the end of Elvira's Night Brew.

There *is* one gratifying postscript, however. During the festival, in a blind taste test of thirty-eight beers, Night Brew placed fourth. Satanic power has its perks.

CHAPTER 21

MISTRESS OF THE DARK

Elvira was at an all-time high—national TV commercials, guest appearances on all the talk shows, and *Movie Macabre* airing from coast to coast—when we were asked to meet with Brandon Tartikoff, president of NBC. Brandon completely "got" the character and wanted to explore the idea of creating a sitcom around her. However, I had this idea up my butt that I wanted to make a movie first. Back then, movie actors could always make the transition from films to TV, but almost no one could make the leap from TV to film. Once you were categorized as a TV actor, you would always be a TV actor. After talking it over with Mark and Eric, we agreed that the best plan would be to do a film first, if at all possible, and turn down the sitcom. At that time, I had enough clout that I could pull that off.

Brandon apparently wanted to utilize the Elvira character so much that he came back to us with a surprising offer. NBC was willing to back a feature film release if we were willing to do it! New World Entertainment (coincidentally founded by Roger Corman and run by former Groundling Steve White) was slated to distribute. From the moment Eric and Mark started pulling the deal together to the last day of filming—with just a few moments of drama thrown in along the way—making *Mistress of the Dark* was one of the best experiences of my life.

John Paragon and I were set to write it, along with network-approved writer/producer Sam Egan, whose credits included *The Incredible Hulk*, *Northern Exposure*, and *The Outer Limits*. I'd met Sam in 1984 when he was the writer on the first of two Halloween episodes of *The Fall Guy* I'd appeared in, and we immediately clicked. I have a feeling he was also hired by NBC to babysit John and me, who had no film experience. *Someone* had to be the adult in the room.

We were the perfect team. We all worked on every aspect, but Sam's strength was the structure while John's forte were the jokes, and I helped with a little of both. NBC set us up in an office in Burbank, where we worked every day from 9:00 a.m. to 5:00 p.m., just like grown-ups. I felt we all contributed to the story equally, but Sam did most of the heavy lifting, actually putting our wacky ideas into script form.

We sat in our office day after day, ordering lots of submarine sandwiches and laughing our friggin' asses off. My initial idea was a story line similar to *The Wizard of Oz*, a movie I'd looked forward to watching on TV every Thanksgiving when I was a kid. Although the story line of the movie changed quite a bit from its inception to what eventually ended up on the screen, a little of the initial *Wizard of Oz* influence stuck: Gonk replaced Toto, the Macabre Mobile replaced the tornado, and the town of Falwell (yes, named after Jerry Falwell, the televangelist) stood in for Oz. Our opening scene, a clip from the '56 movie *It Conquered the World,* is black and white, like Dorothy's Kansas. I even wrote myself a line near the end of the film, when I didn't think my dream of making it in Vegas would pan out, that was a riff on one of Dorothy's famous monologues:

> Dorothy: "Well, I... I think that it... that it wasn't enough to just want to see Uncle Henry and Aunt Em... and it's that, if I ever go looking for my heart's desire again, I won't look any further than my own backyard; because if it isn't there, I never really lost it to begin with."
>
> Elvira: "Y'know, I think I've learned something here today. I've learned that friendship is like cheese. The longer it sits around, the stronger it gets... and that, that... friends are like cheap toupees. You've gotta hang onto 'em when things get stormy. But most of all, I've learned that you can search and search the wide world over, but in the end, your own backyard is right... behind... your house."

I fought like hell to keep it in, but our director, Jim Signorelli, vetoed me and the lines were cut.

Another hitch came when we turned in our first draft and got the word back from the network that "you need to add teenagers to the story line so that teenagers will go see the movie." Until this demand, the whole teens plotline wasn't in the script. I threw out shining examples of blockbusters that had played largely to teen audiences but didn't feature teenagers in the cast, like for example *Jaws, Raiders of the Lost Ark, Return of the Jedi, Alien,* and *Ghostbusters.* But the "powers that be" were not convinced and we were forced to add the teens. While I think we did a pretty good job weaving them into the story line, the subsequent reviews often criticized the film for having too many characters and not enough character development. Thanx, NBC execs, but when I want your opinion, I'll *beat* it outta ya!

Joel Thurm, the former head of NBC casting, was also an executive producer on my film, and John, Sam, and I got to attend all casting sessions and add our two cents. Naturally, being an actor myself, I wanted to hire everyone we interviewed and couldn't stand turning anyone down.

Being in on the casting process was an eye-opening experience. I learned one very important lesson about casting that I'll share with you budding actors: most of the time, the people casting the film know if they want you within ten seconds of you walking in the door and open-ing your mouth. Unless you absolutely *suck*, they'll give you a shot and work with you if you've got the look they want. You can guarantee that everyone on the project has read and reread that script until they've developed a picture in their mind of how the person they're casting should look. When the person walking into the room matches the pic-ture in their head and can also manage to get words out in a coherent way, they got the part, so don't take rejection too personally. There you go. Don't say I never did anything for ya.

During the casting process, I vividly remember one of the actors who read for the role of Randy, the "lead teen." This guy was just about the cut-est thing I'd ever seen in my life and, on top of that, he did an excellent reading. I knew, however, that if he got anywhere within ten feet of Elvira, he was so damned irresistible that she'd throw Bob over for him in a hot second! Because he was supposed to be playing a seventeen-year-old, the whole statutory-rape thing would be ugly, so we reluctantly made the deci-sion not to hire him. I jotted down "Yum Yum" in the comment box on my casting sheet next to his name: Brad Pitt. I've heard rumors that this young fellow went on to make a career for himself in the film industry. Years later, when I met him again, I told him he owed me a big debt of gratitude for personally saving his career by not casting him in my movie.

The first thing we did was ask to see as many Groundlings as pos-sible. Edie McClurg was a no-brainer for Chastity Pariah, which was based on a character she'd made popular at the Groundlings called "Mrs. Marv Mendelsohn." Unfortunately, other than Chastity, there weren't many juicy roles for our age group, just a few quick walk-ons. We hired one of my favorite Groundlings, Lynne Marie Stewart—Miss Yvonne on Pee-wee's Playhouse—to play a bowling-alley waitress:

Elvira: "I'll take a Bloody Mary."
Lynne: "No alcohol on Sunday. Would you like a virgin?"
Elvira: "Maybe. But I'll have a drink first."

Voice-over talent, former Groundling (and, coincidently, voice of Booberella on *The Simpsons*) Tress McNeil played the newswoman at the TV station where Elvira works.

Tress: "Does *anything* embarrass you?"
Elvira (pointing to the newscaster's blouse): Wearing *that* might
    do it.

The only other Groundlings we could squeeze in were John Paragon as the gas-station attendant and Daryl Carroll as Charley, a bowling-alley patron. A few Groundlings were pissed off and friendships damaged during the casting process. Paul and I commiserated because he'd had the same experience when casting *Pee-wee's Big Adventure*. Luckily, he hired me for a part, playing the "Biker Mama," so we're still speaking.

I also populated the cast with actor friends from my past, including my ex-boyfriend from the '70s, Bill Cable (Boo-Boo), as the highway patrolman who pulls me over for speeding:

Bill: "Do you know you were doing fifty in a twenty-five-
    mile-an-hour zone?"
Elvira: "No. But if you hum a few bars I can fake it!"

My friend from New York, Joey Arias, played a hitchhiker:

Elvira (as Joey runs from the car, terrified): "Hey! Ya forgot your
    ax!"

Mario Celario, one of the Argentinian Gouchos from my Vegas days, played Rudy, the stage manager in the opening scene of the film. And my grandfather-in-law's eighty-two-year-old girlfriend, Eve Smith, was the "little old lady" who tries to steal Bob away from me in the picnic scene.

My mom and dad even make a guest appearance in the crowd during one scene. They're standing right over my shoulder when I jab my finger at Chastity Pariah's chest and say, "Yeah, and ya never will with those soup cans on your head." My parents had never been on the set of a big-time Hollywood movie, much less *in* one, and they were nervous but thrilled.

The part of my love interest, Bob Redding (a tribute to Robert), was the hardest person to cast. Elvira, being the female chauvinist pig she is, would definitely go for the male equivalent of a blonde, big-busted bimbo. All the guys we saw were either the perfect hunky type but couldn't act for shit, or they were good actors but looked like Steve Buscemi. After weeks of searching, ex-Florida State football player Daniel Greene came along and nailed the part. Big, handsome, muscular, and with a wonderful naïve quality, he was exactly the "big lug" we'd been looking for.

The shooting process was amazing. I had my own fancy-schmancy "honey wagon"—a big-ass Winnebago motor home with a TV, my very own bathroom, and lighted makeup mirror. Except for a few crew members and the director, I was usually the first one there in the morning and the last one to leave at night. Each day began at 6:00 a.m. with a two-hour hair-and-makeup job while blasting Guns N' Roses' *Appetite for Destruction* album on the stereo. Pamela Westmore, a third-generation member of the famous Westmore Hollywood Makeup family, did my face and various hairdressers fucked up, uh, I mean *styled* my wig. I'm sure my dear friend Robert was rolling over in his grave watching *that* process.

One thing I overlooked while writing was that I unwittingly allowed myself to be written into almost every single scene—no breaks, no half days, no days off *at all* for me. It was a grueling schedule, but despite being exhausted, I had the time of my life.

Luckily, Susan McNabb, a model with a similar build to mine and the then-girlfriend of one not-very-well-known comic, Jerry Seinfeld, was hired to do just about everything that didn't show my face or other distinguishing body parts, like…uh…my eyes. She did close-ups such as her hand turning the key in the Macabre Mobile ignition, her foot stomping on the gas pedal, and a rear-view of Elvira fleeing evil Uncle Vinny through the streets of Falwell. Every minute that allowed me to take a short nap was heaven!

Susan later worked as my "roadie," traveling with me for seventeen years whenever I did live appearances. We became close friends, which we still are to this day. Even though she's much younger than me, I referred to her as "mom" because she basically got me on the plane, dealt with the clients, woke me up every morning, and got me fed and to work on time. She assisted me until she married in 2004 and moved back to her home state of North Carolina. She's become a very talented writer of, among other things, vampire novels, under the pen name Suki McMinn, and a book called *The Opposite of Famous* that covers some of our escapades on the road. So I guess you could say I was a positive influence on her.

All the actors we hired turned out to be perfect for their roles and a delight to work with. Everyone on the set was friendly, easygoing, and happy to be there—no prima donnas or divas (other than me, of course). Even the actor Jeff Conaway of *Taxi* fame, who played one of Uncle Vinny's two henchmen, Travis—named after my ex-boyfriend—kept it together most of the time despite his widely known drug and alcohol abuse issues.

As executive producers it was up to Mark and Eric to deal with day-to-day problems that might arise and to protect me and the project from "the suits" at NBC. Between those duties, Mark diligently documented the behind-the-scenes goings-on with his deluxe new home video camera. Eric sat in his special director's chair on the set, wheeling and dealing nonstop, using the latest in technology that almost no one had yet seen—a portable mobile phone—which was about the size of a shoebox.

Without a doubt, the most difficult scene to shoot was the one where the townspeople attempt to burn me as a witch. It was shot over a period of three long, long nights. We began shooting the moment it got dark and filmed until the sun peeked over the Burbank hills, which really screwed with my sleep pattern. The shoot took place in November, so it was uncomfortably cold at night, especially if you were wearing an Elvira costume. It involved hundreds of extras as well as fire, rain, children, *and* animals—every filmmaker's worst nightmare. Because I was tied to a stake in the center of a blazing pyre, my dress and wig had to be coated in flame-retardant chemicals. Not only did they make my dress as stiff as a board, but it smelled like paint thinner and, to top it off, made me itch like crazy. My hands were tied behind my back for much of the time, so I couldn't get them out to scratch, which almost drove me mad! Much of the time I was freezing, but when the pyre was lit, I was surrounded by flames and the heat was overwhelming. For the better part of three nights, I was drenched in sweat, chemicals, and soot.

Another not-so-fun day of shooting came at the end of the *Flashdance* scene, on what was initially to be the final day of shooting. A stunt double performed the acrobatics (I'm not *that* limber!), but the director wanted to make sure the audience saw it was me that got the bucket of tar dumped in her face. It was a "one-take only" shot—no time or money for a do-over. At the end of the song "Maniac," I flung myself into a chair à la Jennifer Beal, reached up, and yanked a rope. A big bucket full of black tempera paint cascaded from above—way too far above—hitting my upturned face like a punch from Muhammad Ali. My head was thrown back so far I'm lucky my neck wasn't broken. I had black paint coming out of my nose, eyes, and ears for a month!

Shooting the Vegas number became a *big* issue. Because we'd gone a little over budget, NBC decided that the Las Vegas finale scene wasn't necessary. They decreed that the end of the movie would be a scene we'd shot earlier, in which the elderly mechanic returns the Macabre Mobile to me and the townspeople show up to make amends for their bad behavior. John, Sam, and I knew that without the Vegas scene, there was no movie.

After several unreturned calls to Brandon, NBC's president, I marched into his office unannounced.

"I'm sorry, Mr. Tartikoff isn't in." his secretary huffed.

"That's okay, I'll wait." I parked myself on the couch in his outer office and waited. And waited. And waited. Hours passed, but eventually Brandon showed up and I wheedled my way past the secretary and into his office.

"So, let me get this straight," I whined. "Elvira's goal through the whole movie is to achieve her dream of becoming a Vegas star, and now the movie's going to end without her reaching her goal?! What kind of ending is *that*?" I continued begging, cajoling, and tossing out reasons why not having the Vegas ending would ruin the movie, and it worked! "All right, all right," he sighed, standing up from behind his desk to signal the end of the meeting. "Let me see what I can do." Overcome with emotion, I ran to him and flung my arms around his shoulders, blubbering all over his expensive suit. The secretary suddenly knocked and simultaneously burst through the door to find Brandon and me in an embrace that, although it may have appeared suspicious, I guarantee was not.

Tragically, the Hodgkin's lymphoma that had plagued Brandon for years caught up with him a decade later, and he passed away at the age of forty-eight. I'm thankful to have been working with NBC when he was in charge. He was a funny, smart, creative person, and instinctively knew what made programming work. You don't find much of that at the networks these days. I'll always be grateful to him for believing in me and "Elvira" and giving us a chance.

Much to everyone's relief, we resumed shooting a few weeks later at Raleigh Studios. Only one snag: the day of filming, I came down with the flu. But *nothing* was going to stop me from shooting that scene! Despite nausea, chills, and a 103-degree temperature, I slogged through the day, singing, dancing, and tassel-twirling my little black heart out— victorious! I can't imagine *Mistress of the Dark* without that ending. Can you?

Optimistic about the film's release, NBC dropped a load of cash on two star-studded opening parties, one at the Hollywood Roosevelt Hotel in Los Angeles and another at Tavern on the Green in New York City, where guests included '80s stars like Irene Cara from the movie *Fame*, Nicolas Cage, Richard Chamberlain, Cheech Marin, Larraine Newman, and Ricki Lake.

The day the movie opened in LA was both one of the best and worst of my life. My parents had driven their Winnebago out to Hollywood to attend the premiere, and from the time they arrived, my dad complained that his neck was hurting. I called my chiropractor, who came to the house to adjust him, and thank *God* he was savvy enough to know something was very wrong. He immediately sent my dad to get an X-ray. The devastating results came back the morning of the premiere: bone cancer. It was all I could do to get through the premiere party and keep a smile on my face.

Elvira, Mistress of the Dark opened on September 30, 1988, in 637 theaters across the country. It quickly became the number-three-grossing film, right behind *Punchline*, starring Tom Hanks and Sally Field, and *Gorillas in the Mist*, starring Sigourney Weaver in an Academy Award–winning performance. It continued to do well at the box office until the end of week three, when the news broke that Michael Milken, the "junk bond king" who'd been responsible for financing New World's launch three years prior, was being investigated for racketeering and fraud. The share prices of almost all public companies that had used Milken's junk bonds as their primary funding plummeted. New World Pictures was one of them. Even though the movie's gross had actually been increasing as the days went on—a very rare phenomenon—the theater chains worried that New World would no longer be able to provide the millions of dollars in advertising revenue necessary to support the film's release. It was immediately pulled from almost all theaters.

Add to that, with few exceptions, the critics *hated* the movie. Even Elvira fan, critic Roger Ebert, and his partner, Gene Siskel, trashed it on their film-review program *At the Movies*, saying the plot was "corny and dumb" and the film "wasn't the least bit sexy or funny." Gene even said that all Elvira did throughout the movie was "walk around in her beehive hairdo, or whatever it is. Too much hair, if I can say that." (Jealous much, baldy?)

In 1988, I received not only the Saturn Award for best actress from the Academy of Science Fiction, Fantasy and Horror Films, but also the coveted "Razzie" for worst performance by an actress at the ninth Golden Raspberry Awards. Quite an achievement.

The project I'd spent three years of blood, sweat, and tears working on—from pitching, writing, and preproduction to filming, postproduction, and promotion—was DOA. I went into what can only be described as a kind of postpartum depression. An empty work calendar yawned before me. I was sure my career was over and my most important achievement behind me.

Despite the bad reviews and tanking at the box office, it connected with the audience in a way that never ceases to amaze me. Some may describe it as a low-budget, lowbrow piece of fluff, but I can't count the times fans have told me, sometimes between sobs, that *Elvira, Mistress of the Dark* made a huge impact on their lives.

The movie is the story of a misfit who, even though she's mischaracterized by almost everyone she meets, overcomes conflict, accomplishes her dreams, and, in the end, even gets the guy. Elvira breezes into the tiny town of Falwell, empowers the kids, fights against self-righteousness and hypocrisy, and stands up to sexism—all while wearing six-inch stiletto heels. Regardless of her bodacious body, she never allows herself to become a "sex object." She unapologetically flaunts her sexiness, but is also fiercely independent, strong, and self-empowered. If you reduce her to nothing more than a pair of boobs, you might miss that she's intelligent, witty, and altruistic. Throughout the film, Elvira is subjected to sexual harassment, false accusations, and being judged on her appearance alone, but she demands respect without ever having to compromise her (however warped) integrity. She knows she's not perfect, and she's okay with that. Elvira stands up for herself and solves her own problems without waiting for anyone—especially a man—to rescue her. She's tough and flawed, but also exudes a vulnerability that connects with people, making her an odd, yet positive, role model. Time and again I've heard how my movie gave someone hope, strength, courage, or just a laugh when they were going through hard times. Box office success or not, that's made it all worthwhile.

The home video of *Mistress of the Dark* went on to reach number twelve on Billboard's US Top Video charts and, according to industry sources, became one of the sixty best-selling videos of all time. When it premiered on network TV in 1990, it earned NBC the highest rating for the season in its time slot, and over the years has achieved cult-classic status. I'm happy to say that despite showing "too much hair," *Elvira, Mistress of the Dark* is one of my proudest achievements.

CHAPTER 22

SATURDAY NIGHT DEAD

In 1987, in anticipation of our upcoming collaboration with NBC on *Mistress of the Dark*, Brandon Tartikoff prevailed upon Lorne Michaels, the head honcho of *Saturday Night Live*, to let me host the Halloween episode. Unbeknownst to me or my management at the time, and for reasons I may never learn, Lorne flat-out refused. Brandon, being his boss, apparently laid down the law and insisted. *Saturday Night Live* was the hottest show on television at the time and it was an opportunity we obviously couldn't pass up. Eric, Mark, and I flew out to New York City, excited out of our minds that I was doing the show. When I walked into Monday's group meeting, presided over by Michaels, I was happy to see my former Groundlings pals Phil Hartman, Jan Hooks, and Jon Lovitz, and also Kevin Nealon, who I knew from animal-rights events we'd done in the past. After hugs and hellos, we got down to the business of putting on the week's show. I immediately got the vibe that something was off. Lorne Michaels not only didn't introduce himself to me but continued to ignore me throughout the meeting, looking right through me when I spoke to him. From former *SNL* female friends, I had already heard that Lorne was hardly a champion of women comedians, so I did my best to ignore the rude treatment and chalked it up to his infamous mind games. A few minutes into the meeting, I was shocked to find out that I was now going to be sharing the hosting duties on the Halloween show with veteran actor Dabney Coleman. Not exactly a Halloween icon, but okay. This is the first time I was hearing anything about it, but what am I supposed to do?

As the week ground on, while meeting with writers and going over sketches, every time Lorne passed by to see what I was doing, he'd say something like, "Let's give that sketch to Dabney" or "Jan should do that line," even going so far as giving one of my entire bits to that week's musical guest, Ric Ocasek from The Cars. By the end of the week, I was not only no longer a cohost, but I barely had anything to do in the show at all. There were rumblings and grumblings about it from the writers and cast members, but at *SNL* Lorne was king, and there was little any of my friends could do besides apologize to me when he was out of earshot.

To top off a horrible week, Phil called me into his office one day, excited to tell me some news. I was shocked when he produced a little blue velvet box from his desk drawer that held a sparkling diamond ring.

"Who's that for?" I asked, knowing full well.

"Brynn. I'm asking her to marry me tonight," he said. I was in shock. Phil had been married twice before and both times had lost his ass when he'd divorced. I'd met his latest girlfriend several times and honestly couldn't understand what he saw in her.

"Oh my God, Phil! You've gotta be kidding!" I whined, slapping my forehead. "Can't you just live together? Do you have to marry *every* girl you go out with?" That didn't go over too well. Phil returned the ring to its box, opened his office door, and told me to get out. We didn't speak again for almost a year, which was so painful. The lesson I learned: if you want to remain friends with someone, keep your mouth shut when it comes to their choice of spouse, no matter what your opinion.

Saturday night was fast approaching, and so far, the week had been a fiasco. The night before the show was to go live, I ran across the street to a "health food" restaurant to grab an egg salad sandwich and ended up spending Friday night draped over the toilet with food poisoning, barfing my guts out. The next morning, exhausted, shaky, and weak, I showed up to do the final run-through of the show before that night's live airing. There were only two sketches left that I was involved in: the opening with Dana Carvey, doing his take on Robin Leach of *Lifestyles of the Rich and Famous*, and a short segment during "Weekend Update."

As I ran through my lines for the Weekend Update, Lorne marched up to me and shouted, "Would you stop doing that stupid Valley Girl voice and just read it straight?"

"But, but, but..." I stammered, "that's my *character!* That's how Elvira talks!" I was dumbfounded. Can you imagine me, dressed in Elvira drag, delivering my spiel in my normal voice?

"Well not here, she doesn't," Lorne snapped. After a lot of emotional back and forth between Mark, Eric, and myself, we decided the best thing to do was just do it his way in rehearsals and do it my way when we shot the live show. What could he do about it after it was done?

But things proceeded to get even worse. In an earlier run-through we learned that during my segment on Weekend Update, the music that was going to accompany me was "The Star-Spangled Banner." Seriously? While I talked about "the true meaning of Halloween," on Halloween night, the freakin' Star-Spangled Banner was going to be blaring behind me? We were in shock. Luckily, we knew the musical director, Hal Willner. We took our case to him and he agreed one hundred percent that Lorne's choice of music made no sense whatsoever and pulled another, more macabre song to use during my bit. When Lorne heard the new music during the next run-through, he blew a gasket! He charged up to me, jabbed a finger in my face, and shouted, "How *dare* you change that music!" Mark stepped up to defend me and the next thing I knew, he and Lorne were in a vicious shouting and shoving match on the stage floor in front of the entire cast and crew. I remained in character during the Weekend Update, the show aired, and I kissed my chance of ever doing *SNL* again goodbye.

Maybe Lorne hadn't liked being told what to do or maybe he just didn't think I was funny. Whatever the reason, that, as they say, is showbiz.

CHAPTER 23

HEY SWAMI

We promoted *Elvira, Mistress of the Dark* throughout the world in '88 and '89, visiting countries like Spain, Belgium, Italy, and France, where the film won both the Public Award and the Journalist Award at the *Festival International de Paris du Film Fantastique*. At least Europe appreciated me!

During the extensive global press tour, the film was screened at the Cannes Film Festival, where we promoted the hell out of it. The rush of actually being at the festival with all the glitz and glamour that entailed was thrilling beyond belief! There I was, Cassandra Peterson from Kansas, attending screenings and parties and hobnobbing with the rich and famous. I felt like a regular movie star!

One especially memorable evening occurred at a celebrated French restaurant, Le Moulin de Mougins, in the hills above Cannes where my in-laws lived. All the New World and NBC mucky-mucks joined Mark, Eric, and me at one long table, ordering expensive wine and food like it was the Last Supper. We'd come from attending a screening of *Mistress of the Dark* earlier in the evening, so I was still wearing my Elvira drag, which caused quite a stir and permanently endeared me to Roger Vergé, chef and owner of the iconic restaurant.

During dinner, I made a trip to the unisex restroom, accompanied by Eric's wife, Janis, where we were startled to see that the door to the men's urinal was glass. I inadvertently found myself staring at an older, tuxedoed man's pecker, which was in plain sight while he drained his snake. As he left the men's room, he couldn't help checking me out. Dressed in my Elvira garb, I was pretty hard to ignore. At the end of the dinner when the bill arrived, Eric made the polite gesture of offering to pick it up, obviously expecting the New World or NBC execs to grab it—after all, it was a business expense. Instead, they said, "thank you" and we wound up with a dinner tab in the thousands of dollars. When I picked myself up off the floor, the man whose penis I'd seen earlier approached us and introduced himself as Saudi businessman Adnan Khashoggi. You'd think as the world's richest man he might have offered to pay the check, but no. Instead, he invited us back to his house to meet his guru, Chandraswami, which was an offer none of us could refuse. Khashoggi loaded the entire table of guests into a fleet—yes, a fleet—of Rolls Royces and off we sped to one of his posh homes overlooking the Mediterranean. Upon our arrival, Khashoggi disappeared. We were greeted by an elegant Indian man in traditional dress who offered us each a piece of what turned out to be absolutely inedible candy and invited us to sit in a circle to speak with the swami.

The rotund, bearded Indian sat in his kaftan, cross-legged on a sofa, Rolexes up to his elbows and neck adorned with more gold chains than

Kanye West. I'd never met a swami, but this was definitely not what I had in mind. Weren't they supposed to take a vow of poverty or something? He proceeded to pass around an album full of photos of himself posing with the great and formerly great: Ferdinand and Imelda Marcos, Elizabeth Taylor, Margaret Thatcher, the Sultan of Brunei, and Nancy and Ronald Reagan—a veritable who's who of power players. Oohs and ahhs emanated from his captive audience as we admired the photo album. No drinks were served, more disgusting candy was offered, and after an interminable period of awkward silence during which we attempted and failed to make small talk, we all rose to leave. That's when the swami approached me. He asked to take a photo together and invited me to come back the next day for a private "reading."

Always game for an adventure, the next morning I arrived back at Khashoggi's lavish digs with John Paragon as my bodyguard, just in case there was any monkey business. I was led to a small, dimly lit Indian-style pavilion, surrounded by beautiful gardens and set apart from the main house. There was the swami, sitting on an opulent stack of embroidered pillows. While John waited just outside the door, the swami greeted me and offered me a seat on the Oriental carpet–strewn floor opposite him. I got the distinct feeling he was disappointed that I was just a normal person and not the sexy vixen he'd so admired the night before. He handed me a pen and a scrap of paper and asked me to write the name of my favorite flower on it and crumple it into a ball, which I did. "Give me the paper," he commanded. He held it to his forehead, took a deep breath, and closed his eyes. "It is the peony," he murmured in his heavily accented English. He aced it! Pretty impressive, but that was basically it. No insight into my future fame, success, wealth—nothin'! I asked whether he'd mind giving my friend John a reading and, although he didn't seem too excited about it, he agreed. I waited outside the door while John went in. After what seemed like an eternity—really, fucking *forever*—John tiptoed through the door with his finger to his lips, signaling me to be quiet. I followed him to the car, where he told me what had taken place: the swami had asked him to write down his favorite song on a scrap of paper, crumple it up, and pass it to him. Gripping the ball of paper, the swami closed his eyes. The minutes ticked by. John waited expectantly. The minutes continued to tick by. Suddenly, the swami began to snore loudly, which was John's cue to split. We couldn't stop laughing all the way back to our hotel.

Once we were back in the US, our licensing and merchandising business continued to grow, keeping us afloat. In addition to doing brisk sales on Elvira costumes, we now had more records and comic books coming out, along with calendars, Macabre Mobile model cars, collector's porcelain plates, beer steins, dolls, posters, and my own award-winning pinball machine from Bally, which, as a die-hard pinball fanatic, was something akin to winning an Oscar.

Soon, more appearances came my way: a third guest spot on *The Tonight Show*, a presenter at the MTV Awards, host of *Monday Night Football*, a guest-starring spot on *The Magical World of Disney*, and even a cohosting job on TBS's *Halloween Havoc*, where I got to rub elbows with the likes of wrestling legends Rowdy Roddy Piper, Jesse Ventura, and Hulk Hogan. The end of the year found us writing and producing a series called *Thriller Theatre* for Australia's Network 10, which premiered with an astonishing fifty-percent share of the audience "Down Under."

CHAPTER 24

BRIARCLIFF MANOR or WHY *DID* THE CHICKEN CROSS THE ROAD?

This is another chapter in my life that deserves its own...chapter. It might seem strange to devote so much space to a house, but it was more than just a house to me. It was magic. No story of my life would be complete without telling the tale of Briarcliff Manor.

In the spring of 1989, as I was walking my rottweilers, Vlad and Bela, through the Hollywood hills, an odd thing happened. Well, not odd for rural Kentucky, but odd for the middle of Hollywood in the '80s. A chicken ran across the road in front of us. Its loud clucking and flapping wings startled not only me but also the dogs, who began barking like crazy and lunging at the end of their leashes, y'know, on account'a them being "Hollywood" dogs an' all.

The plump, white hen scurried past me into a tall, overgrown bougainvillea hedge and disappeared. I tied the dogs to a nearby telephone pole as fast as I could, got on my hands and knees, and crawled through the thicket after her. There, beyond the prickly undergrowth, loomed a massive, dark craftsman mansion. I stared in disbelief at what obviously had once been a grand home, now fallen into disrepair. What was a huge property like this doing in the middle of Hollywood and how was it possible that I'd walked by it a hundred times before and never noticed it? Even with all the missing wooden side shingles and a pigeon poop–frosted roof, it was still an incredibly beautiful, unusual house. As I gingerly backed my way out of the brambles, I spied a sign, partially concealed by overgrown shrubbery: FOR SALE BY OWNER. I committed the phone number to memory, grabbed the dogs, and ran all the way home.

In the following days, Mark and I went back to the mansion again and again. We crawled under the thorny bushes like the prince drawn to Sleeping Beauty's castle to gaze at the house and surrounding property. I dialed the number many times and left messages, but no one returned my calls. Finally, a week later, a woman called back. In a heavy accent I couldn't quite place, she introduced herself as the owner, confirming the house was for sale—maybe. While she made up her mind, she'd be happy to give us a tour, however. We agreed to meet at the house the next day.

The owner, a diminutive, sexy little Indonesian package in her sixties, sporting a super-short skirt and tons of makeup and jewelry, navigated her way around the property in her sky-high heels as we followed. She led us over what seemed like miles of winding paths past massive trees; two ponds; a stream; a waterfall; an Olympic-size, heart-shaped pool; and a cave made of borax stone. Ducks, turkeys, and chickens roamed freely and a horse lifted his head to snort at us from his large makeshift corral.

The house was magnificent. It was constructed in 1910 by a builder clearly influenced by the early-twentieth-century architects the Greene brothers, and we recognized that the twenty-one-room, 5,600-square-foot, craftsman-style home had been based on the iconic Gamble House in Pasadena, which Mark and I had long admired and visited many times.

Unfortunately, it had once been the home of the Scientology Celebrity Center, so the entire house was painted a very uncraftsmanlike baby blue. We would later hire a woman who worked for almost one year, five days a week, getting it back to its original dark brown color by removing each and every cedar shingle on the sides of the entire house, stripping off the paint, and reattaching them.

The foundation had been dynamited into solid granite at the top of a rocky hill. From the front view, amid towering deodar pines, giant eucalyptus trees, and swaying palms loomed Briarcliff Manor's three somber stories, and in back, a brick cellar with windows and an exterior door constituted a fourth. The interior walls were paneled in solid mahogany and sheets of burnished copper, an enormous brick fireplace graced the living room, and the wood staircase railing was inlaid with ebony. The floors throughout were of quarter-sawn oak—beautiful despite the chicken shit that adorned them. Even though the interior walls of the house were dark, the many wood-framed windows and glass doors offered views of the surrounding foliage and made us feel as if we were in a forest and not in the middle of Hollywood. From a large veranda off one of the five spacious bedrooms was a spectacular view of Hollywood and the Pacific Ocean beyond.

From that day on, Mark and I couldn't stop thinking about Briarcliff Manor. We *had* to have it. Weeks went by while we tried to finagle our finances to come up with the money. When we heard a Japanese developer was interested in buying the property and tearing down the house to build two apartment buildings, we took the plunge and went in way over our heads, taking out a *jumbo* loan to buy it. Dealing directly with the owners and their grown children quickly became a nightmare. All the specifics of the agreement changed daily, depending on their moods, and drove us and our agents out of our minds, but eventually, we got the house.

Briarcliff was a work of art and we were thrilled to be able to preserve and restore it to its former glory, but we weren't prepared for what we'd gotten ourselves into. The Indonesian owners, who would later go to prison for slave trading (yes, I said slave trading), left us a filthy, decrepit mess complete with ancient ball-and-tube wiring, archaic forced-air heating, and antique plumbing. Many rooms had no lighting. There were five bathrooms and not one toilet flushed. Original hardware was missing from cabinets, windows, and doors. The grounds didn't have one pipe that supplied water to the hundreds of trees and shrubs on the property, and the gigantic pool and pond filters seemed timed to break down the day after escrow closed. Flocks of pigeons nested in the rafters and chickens roamed freely, so the place was covered in bird shit, both inside and out. In addition, the former owners kept several large, exotic parrots and cockatoos scattered throughout the house on perches, so their birdseed supplied ample food for the jillions of rats and mice that shared our new home. We couldn't sleep at night because of the sound of rodents scampering across the bedroom floor. Our three cats soon took care of that problem, however, often leaving a bloody rat head on my pillow to make sure I knew what a bang-up job they were doing.

The former owners left us with not only a mountain of repairs, but also ten ducks, two turkeys, another cat, and around twenty chickens. I didn't mind at all, though; in fact, I loved it. I adore animals and thought it would be great to have a little farm in the middle of Hollywood. The chickens were so darned *cute*! They had the run of the property by day, but at night they lined up in a row and marched into their coop to stay safe from the coyotes, possums, and raccoons that roamed the Hollywood hills.

Being a Kansas farm girl hadn't prepared me for the reality of raising fowl, however. The three roosters started to annoy the crap out of us immediately. It would have been one thing if they had only crowed at dawn, but these rat-bastards crowed every time a car snaked its way through the narrow, hilly streets at night and shined its headlights in their direction—which was often. Dozens of times a night, we were awakened to the shrill crowing of first one rooster, then the next, then the next, right beneath our bedroom window. And if that wasn't bad enough, I was afraid to feed the chickens after one of the crazy cocks flew at my face with his spurs bared! Let me give you a little tip in case you ever have any roosters you want to give away: *nobody* wants them! After months of searching, I eventually found a new home for the little fuckers with someone who promised not to eat them.

I loved the turkeys so much because they followed me around all day like fluffy, feathered puppy dogs, begging for treats. Of course, I couldn't turn them down when they gobbled, cocked their heads, and looked at me with those cute little beady eyes. Unfortunately, they both died in separate tragic overeating incidents. How was I supposed to know that turkeys can eat themselves to death when given unlimited access to food?

The ducks laid all their eggs in the larger of the two ponds, ostensibly to keep them safe from predators but in the process clogging up all the drains and destroying the pump. This necessitated draining the entire pond, a very expensive and time-consuming endeavor, and clearing out the dozens of rotten, stinking eggs at the bottom, then buying a brand-spanking-new pump each time. After the third time, the ducks moved to a new, happier home.

And the chickens...don't even ask! What I didn't consider was that because I allowed them to roam free, they laid eggs not only in their coop, but also anywhere else an egg would fit: under shrubs, inside the cave, and more than once, in my shoes. As time went on and the chicken population grew to more than sixty, every morning became a frantic Easter-egg hunt with me running all over the property to gather eggs before they were allowed to hatch and we had even *more* chickens. They were starting to cause problems with our neighbors, too, by escaping over the fence and crapping all over their pool decks. Nobody told me chickens could fly!

One thing that impressed me, however, was that even though we had three big dogs I never had to clean up dog poop because I never saw any—a big relief after scooping tons of poop in our previous small backyard. I figured the property was just so darned big that their poo was seriously spread out. I mentioned it to the gardener one day and I'll never forget her response. "Oh Meesus Cassandra, dee cheekuns eat all dee dog poop." Omelets were off the menu from that day on. Eventually, I got a formal notice from the City of Los Angeles stating that the chickens had to go. If we didn't comply, the former owner, who had brought them onto the property without a permit, would go to jail. Yep, you heard me right. Go. To. Jail. I was still so angry with them for screwing us that after allowing the city to set dozens of Havahart traps throughout the grounds, I snuck out every night and released them. And guess what? The owner's husband actually *did* go to jail! Yay! It was a win-win situation for both me *and* the chickens. (This was before his slave-trading rap, so it was good practice for prison.) Eventually, however, I had to get rid of the little devils. They were adopted by the best free-range farm I could find and we wished them a fond farewell. Other than my organic vegetable garden, my farming days were over.

CHAPTER 25

LIVIN' IN A HAUNTED HOUSE

A nd now for the ghost stories. After all, I *am* Elvira, right? Things got strange the very first day we moved into Briarcliff Manor. Before the movers carted our furniture into the house, I specifically instructed them not to take anything up to the third floor—just one large room circled on all sides by windows—because we had no idea what we were going to do with it. Later in the day, as I was unpacking boxes on the second floor, I stopped dead in my tracks. I distinctly heard a loud clomp-clomp-clomping coming from above my head on the third floor. I stood still and listened. Not only did I hear footsteps, but I could see the ceiling vibrate with each step. Annoyed, I plunked down the carton in my hands and jogged up the narrow, dark stairwell to the third floor.

"'Scuse me, guys!" I called as I made my way up the stairs. "I asked you not to bring anything up…" My voice trailed off as I reached the top step and saw that the room was empty. I ran down to the first floor and told Mark about what had happened, but he wrote it off to a window banging in the wind or a branch hitting the side of the house. I didn't see how that would make the ceiling on the second floor vibrate, but okay.

After we'd settled in and begun work on the house, odd little things continued to happen: strange sounds emanating from behind closed doors, objects relocating themselves from one spot to another, and our dogs standing stock still in the middle of a room, growling into the dark at something that wasn't there. All this became the new normal. I'd never experienced anything like it before.

It was not only the house; the pool was weird, too. We found out from our ninety-year-old neighbors, who lived next door in what used to be Briarcliff's lodge-style ballroom, that the Olympic-size, heart-shaped swimming pool was the first to be built in Hollywood at a private residence. As you know, I'm not a swimmer, but I liked dog-paddling my way across the pool and splashing around when the weather was hot. It was enormous and I rarely went into the deep end, but the few times I did, I couldn't help noticing a dark shadow that appeared to float near the bottom. It didn't seem to matter what time of day it was, because even when I swam at night with the pool lights on, it showed up. It was roughly the shape of my body, but after experimenting, I discovered it didn't move when I moved. It just floated, inches from the bottom in that one general area. I did all kinds of juggling in my mind to make sense of what it could be—a shadow from a tree, a cloud, a reflection from the sun? Not even my husband, "Mr. Logical," understood it.

An incident happened one late summer afternoon that kept me out of the deep end of the pool from then on. My eight-year-old niece, Paige, was staying with us for the summer. She was playing on the side of the pool while I dog-paddled aimlessly around, attempting to stay cool.

We'd recently adopted a wild and crazy German shepherd mix we called Bram, who kept us on our toes with his Houdini-like escape routines. Try as we might to patch any possible escape routes in the thousands of feet of fencing that circled the property, we would still get calls every couple of days from one of the twenty-plus contiguous neighbors asking us to please come get our water-lovin' dog out of their swimming pool.

Still paddling around in the deep end, right near where the infamous "shadow" sometimes appeared, I was suddenly hit from behind with what felt like a ton of bricks. Our seventy-pound dog had taken a flying leap from the side of the pool, about five feet away, and landed directly on top of my head and shoulders. I panicked and went straight to the bottom. When I struggled to come up for air, he stayed right on top of me as if I were his personal pool float. I locked onto the dog, kicking and fighting to stay above the water, but only managed to pull us both under. Every time I clawed my way to the surface for a frantic gulp of air, his long, thick claws dug into my neck, chest, and shoulders. I was quickly getting exhausted and knew I wasn't going to be able to fight him off much longer. Thank *God* Paige was there. At eight years old, she had the presence of mind to grab a water mattress and paddle over to me as fast as she could. I was able to grab a hold of the mat and pull myself out from under the dog. I'd never come so close to drowning. I have no doubt that I owe my life to Paige. If she hadn't been there that day and been as clever and quick as she was, I would no doubt have permanently joined "the shadow" at the bottom of the pool.

Living in a nearly century-old house made entirely of wood, fire was our biggest fear. One night, a faint whiff of smoke jolted me awake. I sniffed, cocking my head, and hoped the smell had only been in my imagination. The door at the end of our bed stood wide open, offering an unobstructed view into the dark expanse of the great room. Allowing my eyes to adjust, I squinted into the shadowy recesses beyond the doorway. A soft breeze whistled through the window casings, making an eerie, high-pitched moan as a hazy wisp of smoke curled into view. I froze. Before I had time to come to my senses and shake Mark awake, the smoke swirled and floated into the doorway, coalescing into what appeared to be a living, breathing human being. A woman, wearing a white 1930s-style nurse's uniform and a short, navy-blue cape, stood in the doorway for a moment before drifting, soundless, toward me. My throat tightened and I could feel the hair on my forearms raise. Bending very close to me, she whispered, "I have to take him." Her gaze lifted, then settled on Mark, still sound asleep. I swallowed hard. Even though it was a warm summer night, an ice-cold chill coursed through my body and tingled across my scalp.

"Take him...where?" I choked out. Mark sighed and shifted in his sleep. The alarm clock on the bedside table gave off an electric glow that illuminated the chiseled cheekbones of the nurse's face from beneath. Her eyebrows were penciled in a sharp, dark arch above her aquiline nose and perfect red lips.

"Into the pool," she said, then disappeared, literally in a puff of smoke. I lay wide awake for the rest of the night, heart pounding, and occasionally reaching over and laying my hand on Mark, just to feel the rise and fall of his chest. I played the scene over and over in my mind, telling myself that it had to be a dream, but I knew it wasn't.

Mark woke up when the morning light finally crept into the room. I didn't want to tell him what had happened. I was afraid of planting the thought of him drowning into his head. Besides, what if this time he'd think I really *was* losing my mind? The very first thing he said was, "I'm going to take a swim," which he *never* did first thing in the morning. I convinced him not to, and for the rest of the day, came up with one excuse after another why he shouldn't go in the pool—the chlorine smelled too strong, it was too cold, we'd be late for dinner. For days I was frightened to death every time I saw him go near the pool.

One night, just before a party at our house, it happened again. I'd been upstairs getting dressed and when I came rushing down the stairway to the main floor, the first thing I saw was a man sitting in our big wingback chair, gazing into the fireplace. The room was growing dark as evening approached and the glow from the fire was the only source of light. Mark and I entertained a lot, so it wasn't all that odd to imagine that one of our friends had shown up early and brought someone who I didn't know along with them, so I wasn't afraid. In the glow of the fire, I could see he wore his short hair swept straight back, not really the style in the '90s, and was definitely overdressed for our casual get-together, wearing a necktie beneath a starched white collar and a vest under his natty suit. But, hey, it was Hollywood where anything goes.

"Hello," I called out, "I'm Cassandra." Staring into the fire, he turned his head to look at me. A cold chill ran up my spine. "Are you here with ...?" I turned away to shout up the stairs. "Mark? Uh, can you come down here for a minute?" When I turned back, the stranger was gone. I stood shivering in the spot until Mark arrived. "There was a man there, in front of the fireplace. He just disappeared!" Mark could tell I was dead serious. We crept around the main floor, from room to room, but saw no sign of anyone. I was shaken and it took everything I had to keep it together for the rest of the evening.

After this incident, Mark and I began doing some research into Briarcliff Manor's history. We learned about Thomas Thorkildsen, the wealthy industrialist who had bought the house in 1916. He apparently discovered his wife in the arms of another man during an intimate dinner party at the house and the troublemaker was later found dead on the property. According to Thorkildsen, he had "accidentally" fallen and hit his head as he was running back to the borax cave to retrieve his clothes. No charges were ever filed.

A workman discovered a newspaper article in the crawl space of the house describing a 1921 star-studded gala at Briarcliff to unveil the new swimming pool. For the occasion, the surface had been covered with flowers. However, the evening's festivities were marred by a scandal. Apparently during the party, one of the Ziegfeld Follies girls, who had been in attendance to keep the gentlemen entertained, fell into the pool and slipped below the surface. Her body wasn't discovered until the following day when the flowers were removed.

One night we invited Mark Hamill, of *Star Wars* fame, over to dinner. My husband had met Mark when they both lived in Malibu years before and had become friendly. When Mark arrived, you could see by the look on his face that he was blown away. "You're not gonna believe this!" he exclaimed. "This was where I lived in the '60s when I was going to LA City College." He went on to tell us that he'd moved out after one of his housemates died by suicide. On a tour of the house, he pointed out where they'd discovered his body. You might know, he'd hung himself in our master bedroom closet. The story was later confirmed by our elderly neighbors, who'd come running when they saw the police and coroner arrive. At this point, I'd had it—living in Briarcliff Manor was just becoming too damn creepy! At the time, however, the housing market was in the dumper, so we wouldn't have been able to sell it for anything close to what we had in it. Not in a position to lose everything, we took another tack. After a little research, we found a Native American shaman *and*, just for good measure, a priest who performed exorcisms. It was something I didn't know much about and I wasn't sure if I even believed in it, but I had to try *something*. I couldn't stand living in that house another day. After much burned sage, incense, holy water, and chanting, the house was deemed "cleared." Whether it was just my mind that was cleared, or the restless spirits of three untimely deaths that were finally released, didn't matter. From that day on, there were no more otherworldly incidents, and a sense of peace and tranquility prevailed at Briarcliff Manor.

CHAPTER 26

THE PIGEON FROM HELL

On a scorching summer's day in 1989, while still living at Briarcliff, I found myself driving my old diesel Mercedes station wagon down Los Feliz Boulevard. It was the middle of July and I was hot, tired, and sweaty after dragging myself around Sunset Nursery and filling my car with plants in the one-hundred-degree heat. I had the air conditioner on and the radio cranking—"Love SHACK, baby, love SHACK, Ooooo, that's where it's at!" All I could think of as I whizzed along down the wide boulevard was getting home as fast as I could and jumping into the pool. Then I saw him—a pigeon, flying straight for my car, coming closer and closer on a kamikaze mission with my windshield.

"Pull up! Pull UP!" I shouted in the split second before he hit the windshield head-on, *thwack*! Right in front of my face.

Now, anyone who knows me knows I love animals. I always have. I've been surrounded by animals ever since I could crawl and have, at one time or another, kept everything from cats, dogs, and horses to—unfortunately, because I didn't know better—a chipmunk, a skunk, assorted snakes, lizards, and turtles. I'd become an animal-rights activist years earlier, volunteering at various events for PETA, Last Chance for Animals, and any other animal-rights organization that would have me. I've spent an inordinate amount of time rescuing homeless dogs and had so many of them neutered that I dubbed myself the Lorena Bobbitt of the animal world.

As I continued on my way home, I pondered the possibility that the bird might still be alive. What if he was only stunned? Naaah. He'd hit the windshield way too hard. But I kept picturing the injured bird, lying by the side of the road, roasting in the hot summer sun. After driving another block, worry and curiosity got the better of me. I took a quick glance in my rearview mirror, hoping to catch some sign of life, but all I saw was a lone In-N-Out Burger wrapper being carried down the boulevard by a sweltering gust of the Santa Ana winds. I pulled over and slammed on the brakes. Cars zoomed around me, honking, as I weighed the options between right and wrong, pigeon or pool. The moment the traffic let up, I whipped a U-ie in the middle of the boulevard and headed back as fast as my tank of a car would go. I pulled over to the scene of the crime, and sure enough, there was the pigeon on the parkway strip, staggering around like a drunken sailor on leave. I could almost see the tiny people circling his head.

His beak had been smashed flat, which head on, made him look like a five-year-old's drawing of a bird. I leaned in to get a closer look, expecting him to flutter away, but he was too loony to realize I was even there. He was a bloody mess. As if his squashed beak wasn't bad enough, there was a big tumor growing over one eye. That explained his poor depth perception.

It was obvious there was no saving him. How's a guy supposed to live with only one eye and no beak? As sad as it was, I knew I needed to put an end to his suffering. He could lie there dying a slow, painful death for hours. I decided to back my car over him. It would be a mercy killing. I corralled the dazed bird with my hands and gently shooed him off the curb, into the gutter behind my rear wheel. I got back in the car, slammed it into reverse, then just sat there. I put the car back into park and stared out the window. I flashed back to our farm in Kansas. I could see my dad stuffing twelve newborn kittens into a gunnysack to toss into the river. Their mother, one of our many farm cats, had abandoned them, and my parents didn't have the time or wherewithal to keep them alive. I pictured myself crying and tugging at my dad's shirttail.

"Please, Daddy, don't! Don't!"

And him telling me, "I have to, Soni. I don't have a choice. Don't you want what's best for the little kitties?"

I got out of the car again, walked around to the other side, and just stared at the bird. I couldn't make myself do it. I decided a better choice was to take him to the vet to be euthanized—time, money, and heat be damned. Then I remembered it was Sunday. All the vets were closed and back then there was no such thing as a twenty-four-hour emergency vet that I knew of. I picked up the pigeon, cradling him in my hands, and tried my best to ignore the frantic flapping and splattering blood. I jumped back into my car and took off for home, one hand gripping the steering wheel, the other holding the pigeon. I had to put this poor bird out of its misery and make it as quick and painless as possible!

I pulled in through the enormous iron spiderweb gates at the end of our driveway, bird in hand, and thank God, my husband's car was there. I got out just as all three of my big dogs came bounding down the hillside to meet me. I hoisted the bird high above my head to keep them from mistaking the pigeon for a treat and ran around the side of the house.

As I've mentioned, the property was big, so it wasn't all that unusual not to be able to find each other even though we might both be home. I burst in through the kitchen door, bleeding pigeon in hand, hollering, "Mark? Are you here?" Silence. I ran upstairs to the second floor. "Mark? Where are you?" Still nothing. I ran up the staircase to the third floor. "MARK!" I yelled at the top of my lungs. No response. I couldn't waste any more time. The pigeon was suffering, and it was up to me alone to help him.

I once read somewhere that the most painless ways to die were (a) suffocation and (b) freezing. I decided on a combo of the two. I took the poor bird back to the kitchen, put him in a plastic bag, and closed it with a twist tie. I opened the freezer door and stuck him inside on the middle shelf. I gave him one last look, cringed, and slammed the door. All I wanted to do was the right thing, the most humane thing: end the pigeon's suffering. Why did I suddenly feel like Jeffrey Dahmer?

I got myself as far away from the kitchen as I could while still staying in the house. A guilty sense of relief washed over me. In my mind I told myself, "That was smart. You're a good person. It was hard, but you did the right thing." I made plans to bury him next to Vlad, my first rottweiler, and Lucy, who was pecked to death by her fellow chickens. I would make him a little cross out of sticks. The pigeon would finally be at peace.

After a short but respectful period, I tiptoed back toward the kitchen to check on his progress. Before I even opened the kitchen door, I could hear the rattling sound. I walked into the room to see the refrigerator shaking back and forth like a washing machine on the spin cycle. My stomach turned inside out and my palms became clammy when I came to the realization that the pigeon was still alive and kicking. Who was this bird, anyway? The fucking Terminator? I jerked open the freezer door. Spatters of blood sparkled among the ice crystals and feathers stuck to last year's leftovers. There he was, standing next to an open bag of Jolly Green Giant peas, staring daggers at me with his one good eye. How the hell did he get out of the plastic bag? With his beak in that condition, there's no way he pecked through it. I briefly imagined him clawing his way out of his icy tomb like Ray Milland in *The Premature Burial*.

I grabbed the pigeon from the freezer and ran outside toward the farthest point of the property, which Mark and I referred to as "the lower forty." I hauled ass down the borax steps, across the hard-packed dirt road that wrapped around the house, and hopped the meandering dry creek bed. All the chickens that had been milling around, ready to head for the safety of their coop for the night, squawked and scattered in every direction. I passed one of our turkeys, who stopped short and looked at me with an accusatory cock of his head, then gave a short, garbled gobble that sounded like "Murderer."

"Thank God! Where have you *been*?" I yelled when I finally spotted Mark down by the vegetable garden. "Help me!"

Caught off guard, Mark squinted at me and then at the pigeon. "What the heck are you doing with that bird?" he asked. I told him the *Reader's Digest* version of the story, omitting the part about the plastic bag and the freezer. Mark took charge, and as he strode away, commanded, "Stay here!" In a moment he was back carrying the ax he used to chop firewood. At Mark's direction, I placed the bird on the chopping block, a thick slab of eucalyptus trunk, and did my best to hold him still and comfort him while Mark raised the ax above his head. I squeezed my eyes shut tight and jerked my hands away in the nick of time as the ax hit the block—*whack*!

The next thing I heard was the fluttering of wings. I opened my eyes and much to my shock and surprise, there was the pigeon, literally flying off into the sunset. What the *hell*? He was still alive!? I stared after him in stunned silence, thinking for a split second that maybe a miracle had occurred and he'd had a spontaneous healing. But when I glanced down, there on the chopping block, in a glistening puddle of blood, were his two little severed feet.

CHAPTER 27

THE ELVIRA SHOW

After three years of fighting bone cancer, Daddy succumbed to it and died in September, a few days before my fortieth birthday. Going to see him in Colorado Springs for what I knew would be the last time nearly destroyed me. His death was much harder for me to deal with than I could have ever imagined. After his funeral, I returned to LA, and a bewildering flood of emotions washed over me. All the love I'd felt for him as a child came rushing back and I missed him so much it physically hurt. But at the same time, I was overcome with feelings of deep anger.

"How could you?" I wanted to scream at him. "What made you feel it was okay to leave me alone with Mother every day?" Why hadn't he protected me? He was an adult and I was just a little girl. He could have stopped her from tormenting me, but for whatever reason, he chose to look the other way. After weeks of anguish, and at the urging of my therapist, I wrote Daddy a long letter, pouring my heart out—all the love, all the rage, all the resentment and betrayal I felt. When I was finished, I sealed it in an envelope, and with a great sense of both loss and relief, knelt on the ground in my backyard and lit the letter on fire. I watched, tears streaming down my face, as the smoke and ash curled their way up into the night sky. I released all the feelings I'd buried inside for so long and I forgave him.

It had been quite a while since I'd had anything on TV or the big screen, so in 1993, when John and I pitched an idea to CBS for an Elvira sitcom,

237

* * *

we were over the moon when they ordered a half-hour pilot, appropriately titled *The Elvira Show*.

The plot centered around Elvira and her aunt, played by the fabulous Katherine Helmond, who are witches on the run, trying to keep their cheesy brand of magic on the down-low, forcing them to move from town to town. Along with their smart-ass talking black cat, Renfield, they end up in the conservative town of Manhattan, Kansas. To keep their creditors at bay, Elvira pawns herself off as a psychic, giving bad advice and "magic" potions to customers willing to cross her palm with "gold." Things get tricky when their long-lost niece, Paige, shows up on the doorstep. They soon discover that the shy, conservative teen, fresh out of Catholic school, is a witch too, but with a much more powerful brand of magic. Paige is reluctant to use her powers, however, because—typical teen—all she wants to do is fit in and not be labeled as some kind of freak. After a spell goes awry and Elvira gets herself into a metaphysical jam with a hunky cop, Paige is forced to use her magic to rescue her aunt and save the day.

During the casting process, we had to decide between two adorable young actresses, Phoebe or Hilary, to play the part of my niece. I loved them both, but it finally came down to Phoebe Augustine. Years later, at Gold's Gym, I ran into the actress we didn't choose.

"Oh my god, Hilary!" I exclaimed, happy to see her all grown up. "I *still* feel bad we didn't hire you for my show. What are you up to these days? Still acting?"

"Oh hi! Um, yes, still acting." she replied.

"Fantastic! Done anything I might have seen?"

"Well . . . I just won the Oscar for best actress."

Oh shit. It was Hilary Swank and she'd just starred in *Boys Don't Cry*. I could have died of embarrassment! Here I was proving once again that when it comes to casting, I sure know how not to pick 'em.

We shot the show before a very enthusiastic live audience. So enthusiastic, in fact, that afterward I was told by the soundman that it was only the second time in his career that he hadn't had to "sweeten" the soundtrack by adding canned laughter—a very good sign. During the writing and shooting process, John and I had an office at 20th Century Fox. Word about our show got around and when I walked from my office to the set, everyone I passed congratulated me. Each day when I turned up for lunch in the commissary, I was always given the best table in the executive dining room—I was the darling of the lot! Everyone seemed to agree that *The Elvira Show* was a slam-dunk for CBS's fall lineup and I couldn't have been happier!

When the show was "in the can" and it came time to decide on the CBS fall lineup, the president of CBS, Jeff Sagansky, who had practically guaranteed the show would be picked up, fell ill and didn't make it in to work that day. His boss, Howard Stringer, happened to be walking down the hall at CBS and heard raucous laughter coming from a screening room. He popped in and stood in the back for a few moments, watching my pilot. "Who ordered *this?*" he roared. "We can't have tits like that on CBS!" The screening screeched to a halt. The room went silent. Several people involved with the production protested, but when they saw he couldn't be swayed, walked out in frustration. One guy actually quit his job on the spot. *The Elvira Show* was cancelled before the pilot even aired.

On my last day at 20th Century Fox, I walked through the studio lot like a ghost, everyone looking right through me. Security guards chased me down to take my office keys, apparently afraid I'd snag some paperclips on my way out the door, and to top it off, I couldn't even get a seat in the commissary! Hollywood can be a fickle mistress.

A year later, CBS had a smash hit with *Sabrina the Teenage Witch*, about a young witch living with her two aunts and a talking black cat, which just poured salt in the wound. I felt like I couldn't catch a break. Here I was again with yet another project that a major network had backed and was enthusiastic about, but then, by some strange twist of fate, it went from a shoo-in to a no-go overnight. But by now, I'd developed a pretty thick skin, and even though I was extremely disappointed, I knew my choices were to either give up and quit or pick myself up and keep plugging away. Once again, I chose the latter and forged ahead.

CHAPTER 28

LITE A FLAME

We went through some crazy times at Briarcliff, like the Rodney King riots in 1992 during which, from our deck, we could see hundreds of fires burning across the city. For three days we cowered below window height with no electricity, while helicopters buzzed overhead and gunfire could be heard whizzing by. Then there was the big Northridge earthquake of 1994, coincidently the night our baby was conceived. Our huge, old house rocked and rolled like a ship in a storm. We lost our three-story chimney, but little did we know what we'd gained.

In the '90s, I continued to devote as much of my time as possible to my two favorite causes, supporting gay rights and raising awareness about HIV and AIDS and working on animal-rights issues. I served as grand marshal for the twentieth annual Gay Pride parade in West Hollywood and, among other LGBTQ events that year, did a fundraiser for AIDS prevention at a local Eastside gay bar, where my friend Lynne Stewart and I got a little tipsy and ended up stripping down to our skivvies to raise money—proving once again (as Elvira would say) that I really *will* do anything for fifty bucks!

Around this time, I was approached by PETA. The organization's charismatic young campaign director, Dan Mathews, had seen *Mistress of the Dark* the week it debuted and thought I was a perfect match for PETA's theatrical approach. Dan flew to LA from DC faster than a chicken fleeing Colonel Sanders!

Coincidentally, our paths had crossed before. In 1982, when I'd hosted a costume contest at Grauman's Chinese Theater for the movie premiere of *The Thing*, I'd chosen seventeen-year-old Mathews out of hundreds of contestants as the winner. The handsome, six-foot-five kid was dressed as Joan Crawford in *Mommie Dearest*. He'd brought along a friend, dressed as Linda Blair's character in *The Exorcist*, and beat her with a wire hanger as she pretended to masturbate with a cross onstage in front of God and everyone. Talk about a dynamic duo!

Dan explained that as a vegan his first step had been to stop eating fish when he was in high school. "Was that around the same time you realized you were gay?" I asked. That cemented our friendship. Dan proceeded to show me horrifying photos and video of the brutal reality of the fur trade and that was it—my eyes were opened.

In 1985, I changed the license plate on our Mercedes station wagon to read BAN FUR. Along with Dan, now a senior VP at PETA, I also led a massive protest at a fur convention in Las Vegas, heralding the breakthrough of the antifur movement. With the help of Belinda Carlisle and Jane Wiedlin of the Go-Go's and Rue McClanahan of *The Golden Girls* fame, we held a news conference in the old Landmark Hotel where I'd worked as an extra in the James Bond film *Diamonds Are Forever* decades before. The demonstration was such a success that to this day, there's never been another fur convention held in Las Vegas.

Later, I joined Dan in another attention-grabbing campaign called "Fur Is a Drag," which was a parody of fur-fashion shows but with drag models sporting mink coats covered in red paint and accessorized with steel traps. We did shows in New York and LA with comedy queens like Lady Bunny and Jackie Beat, and in London with drag legend Leigh Bowery performing while Chrissie Hynde sang and Boy George and the Pet Shop Boys watched from the wings.

When my perfume, Evil, came out that year, it was the first cosmetic product to bear PETA's Cruelty-Free symbol. I was proud and humbled to later receive PETA's humanitarian award for my participation in numerous campaigns, including the antifur ad campaign, "What Disgraces a Legend Most." With his iconic "I'd Rather Go Naked Than Wear Fur" campaign that followed, I became a staunch admirer of Dan's fierce, creative, "take-no-prisoners" approach to making people aware of animal-rights issues.

In 2019 California actually banned fur, most designers have dropped fur from their lines, and Macy's has closed all of its hundreds of fur salons across the US. Even Queen Elizabeth now refuses to wear the stuff!

I'm extremely proud to have played a pioneering role in curtailing the horrible cruelty involved in killing animals solely for their fur—a luxury item that *nobody* needs, not even the Queen of England *or* the Queen of Halloween.

One of my favorite animal rights events was a star-studded vegan Thanksgiving dinner Mark and I hosted at Briarcliff, sponsored by Dan and PETA founder Ingrid Newkirk. The guests included two of my favorite female singers, Melissa Etheridge and k. d. lang, along with radio personality Casey Kasem and actors Katey Sagal and River Phoenix. A live turkey was the guest of honor.

I was so excited to be hosting this special sit-down dinner that I spent days preparing for it. I'd cooked a huge pumpkin stuffed with wild rice, nuts, raisins, and various veggies and a yummy fresh corn and green-chili casserole, among other things. All the guests were seated at the dining room table when River cruised in late, looking extremely disheveled. Although there was only one more seat at the table, he'd brought along four of his young siblings—Rain, Summer, Liberty, and Leaf (who later changed his name to Joaquin)—which caused a mad last-minute scramble to find extra food and seating, throwing me into a bit of a tizzy. When I set my casserole on the table in front of River, he bent over it to take a whiff and his grimy, old stocking cap fell from his stringy hair right into the center of it. I was already pissed about the uninvited extra guests but tried my best not to let this send me over the edge. River snatched his creamed corn–covered cap out of the casserole as I put on my best fake smile and whisked it back to the kitchen, where I spent the next few minutes picking greasy hairs and rainbow-colored yarn fibers out of it. On their way out the door, however, River, along with his brother and sisters, came over to me and gave me the biggest, warmest group hug ever. They thanked me so sweetly and sincerely that all was immediately forgiven.

In 1990, I was offered a guest spot on the popular TV show *Circus of the Stars*. My part entailed riding and training an elephant and my initial reaction was, "Wow—fun! I *love* elephants!" But when I learned that elephants in circuses are trained through beating and electric prods, I wouldn't have been able to live with myself if I'd participated. I turned down the job and (reluctantly) the $10,000 payment that came with it. My refusal to do the show made the cover of *USA Today* and brought a lot of attention to it. It would take another twenty-five years, but PETA eventually closed down the Ringling Bros. and Barnum & Bailey Circus altogether based mainly on the outrage over how elephants are mistreated. If you want to go to the circus, there's always Cirque de Soleil, where you can be sure that all the entertainers are willing participants.

CHAPTER 29

HELLO, GOODBYE

U nfortunately, the cleansing rituals we'd undergone to get rid of the ghosts hadn't done a thing to make our bills disappear. Five years had passed since we'd moved into Briarcliff and the place was still a money pit. We'd made a couple of half-hearted attempts to sell it, but because we'd bought at the top of the market and house sales were now in the dumper, only one person came to see it: record producer Rick Rubin, who took a quick, unappreciative look around and sped off in his Rolls-Royce without saying a word. Despite our real-estate agent's urging, we weren't in a position to drop the price and lose all the money we'd put into it.

Expecting our first child any day, we were determined to stay in Briarcliff and make it our "forever home." Throughout my pregnancy, and despite my bulging belly, I'd been forced to take every job I was offered in order to support our huge mortgage payments. Obviously, doing a live show at Knott's that year wasn't an option, but I did do a photo session in a bathtub with bubbles up to my chin and even shot a Coors commercial—from the chest up.

The house was finally coming together. Little by little, I'd found some beautiful and affordable pieces of original mission-style furniture and bought several plein air paintings by early California artists that played into the home's arts-and-crafts vibe. Our baby's room was almost ready, and the house was starting to feel like a home instead of a construction site. Mark surprised me with a big forty-third birthday party/ baby shower, and life was good.

Almost nine months pregnant, on a sweltering Southern California afternoon in 1994, instead of sitting in my usual spot—on the steps of the pool, submerged up to my nostrils like a water buffalo—I just happened to be in the house (probably peeing for the thirty-fifth time that day) when the front-gate bell rang.

I waddled to the front door and pushed the intercom button. "Who's there?" I asked.

The response came back: "Brad Pitt." I paused for a second, then laughed and said, "Hilarious, John!" sure it had to be Paragon playing a trick on me because he was well aware of my infatuation with the actor.

The manly voice replied, "Uh, really. It's Brad Pitt."

John *was* doing a damn good impression of Brad's voice, I had to admit.

I was pregnant, remember? And I'd been having some crazy, horny dreams about Mr. Pitt almost every night for the previous month after seeing him costar in *Interview with the Vampire.*

"No, really," I said, becoming a little cranky. "Who *is* this?"

"Brad Pitt," the voice came back. "Nick Cage told me about your house, and I was wondering if I could see it."

Now, Nicholas Cage is a whole *other* witchy story. Almost seven years earlier, after seeing him in the film *Moonstruck*, I'd become obsessed with *him*. One evening, while sitting with a girlfriend in a Hollywood nightclub, waxing erotic about the many virtues of Mr. Cage, I suddenly felt a hand on my shoulder. My friend's mouth gaped open and she looked at me like bats had just flown out of my cooch. "Can I interest you ladies in a drink?" came a deep, sexy voice. I turned around and there was Nicolas Cage! Sometimes I scare me.

But back to Brad…

Rather than buzz the gate to let in the ax murderer I knew was lurking behind it, I decided to lumber down the driveway to take a peek. When I reached our spiderweb gates, I found myself staring into the impossibly blue eyes of Brad freakin' Pitt! Seriously, I almost dropped the baby right then and there. (Which would have made a great conversation starter for my kid later in life.)

"Would you mind if I came in and took a look around?" Mind?! I couldn't get the gate open fast enough! I gave Brad the grand tour of the property and the house, all the while trying to act cool and keep myself from staring a hole through him. He was getting ready to shoot his next film, *Legends of the Fall*, and his hair was long and blond, his eyes were bluer than eyes have a right to be, and he was so damned beautiful I could hardly breathe. Top all that off with the fact that he was as sweet and down-to-earth as a person could be, and I thought I'd died and gone to Hollywood heaven! Before leaving, Brad asked if he could come back and take another look sometime, and of *course* I said yes. Duh!

Brad came back a few days later with his girlfriend, a beautiful little ballet dancer named Jitka, who looked like a female version of him. Mark made sure he was home so I wouldn't try anything funny in my hormonally charged state. After another quick run-through of the house, we sat in the living room with the adorable couple yakking about the history of Briarcliff and showing off the old photos we'd collected. Brad seemed genuinely interested and asked lots of questions about the house's history and architecture.

The next day, we got a call from Brad's lawyer saying that he would like to buy Briarcliff and was prepared to make an offer. Brad hadn't mentioned a word about being interested in buying it, so we were completely blindsided and a little bit stunned. Even though we'd wanted to sell a year before, now that all the major work was done, the house furnished, exorcisms performed, and baby on the way, we'd made up our minds to tough it out and stay, no matter what. After spending a sleepless night thinking it over, we called the attorney back the next day and politely declined. She called back the following day and upped the offer. I went into a tailspin. I was about to give birth for the first and last time in my life and was in serious nesting mode! I couldn't imagine selling the house at this point and *moving*. Where would we go? What would we do with our twenty-one rooms of recently purchased furniture? I decided the stress of moving when I was nine months pregnant was just too much, and again, we declined the offer. But when the *third* offer came in, enough to cover what we'd paid for the house plus all the money we'd sunk into it, we caved. The next thing we knew, we were putting a humongous moving van full of furniture into storage and moving into a rental house in Brentwood.

As fate would have it, after I gave birth, we ended up buying a much more manageable house on the same private road, directly next door to Briarcliff. During our time there, I could see Brad's house from our upstairs balcony every morning when I woke up and every night before I went to bed. I missed that house so much I physically ached. Sometimes I'd stand on the deck just staring at it—and, no, I wasn't spying on Brad—mourning its loss. I've never been so attached to any place in my life the way I was to that house.

A wacky footnote: two weeks after we moved into our new home next door to Briarcliff, Brad's attorney called again to say Brad wanted to make an offer on our *new* house. I lost it—I'd just had a baby and moved twice! We turned down the offer without hesitation. I began having dreams about Brad again, only *this* time he was stalking me. I've got to be the only woman in the world who's ever had nightmares about Brad Pitt!

We remained living next door to Brad for the next eight years—through Jitka, Gwyneth, Jennifer, and all the way to Angelina.

CHAPTER 30

BABY LOVE

In October 1994, after thirteen years of marriage, Mark and I finally had the baby we'd been wishing for for so long. I was glad that I didn't have a child until the ripe old age of forty-three because things had calmed down and I had a lot more time to devote to being a mother. Well, not a *lot* more; maybe a *little* more. Actually, maybe not any more at all. Our entire income hinged on me continuing to work.

Until I turned thirty-four, I'd never had the time or desire to have a child, but suddenly the craving struck with a vengeance. I threw away the birth-control pills and we began trying. We didn't have to try too hard. I became pregnant immediately and we were ecstatic! After announcing my pregnancy to the world, decorating the baby's room, and making all the plans that go along with expanding a family, three months later, I miscarried. It was devastating and I went into a long period of mourning.

At the doctor's suggestion, we waited several months and then tried again. Once more, I became pregnant immediately, but after performing one of my shows at Knott's Halloween Haunt, I began cramping and bleeding and miscarried once again. The sadness I felt was only outweighed by the guilt. If only I hadn't continued to work when I was pregnant!

Having a baby became my main focus. Nothing or nobody was going to tell me that I couldn't do something that I set my mind to, even my own body. We went to various specialists to see whether we could pinpoint the problem, but no one could find any reason why I couldn't carry a baby to term. I was healthy and fit, and there was no history of miscarriage in my family or Mark's. During one test, we discovered that my husband's DNA was so similar to mine that there was a chance my body was rejecting the fetus as "foreign tissue." One doctor actually asked if there was a possibility we might be brother and sister! We went through a series of expensive and painful "blood-swapping" processes at the University of California–Los Angeles Medical Center, but to no avail.

After my first miscarriage, Cheech Marin and his wife, Patty, who had adopted a baby through Los Angeles County channels, suggested we give that a try, but years went by without a single response. The adoption agency admitted later that because we were white and older, we were at the bottom of the list. As the years passed and I continued to work and carry on my Elvira duties to pay the bills, I tried and became pregnant four more times, all ending in miscarriages. I quit doing anything strenuous, even staying in bed full-time during one pregnancy, but it didn't help. Every miscarriage was more heart-wrenching than the last. I finally knew I had to come to terms with the possibility of never having the baby I wanted so desperately. I told myself I didn't need to have a child to live a happy life; that there were millions of women who have had fulfilling lives without having children. I thought of my Aunt Lorrayne in particular, who, although childless, managed to have the most positive and loving influence on me and my cousins. I remember the exact moment I gave up my dream of motherhood. It was a gray, windy day, and as I stood on the deck at Briarcliff staring out at the city stretching before me and the dark clouds passing overhead, I let my dream of being a parent go. The clouds momentarily parted and a beam of sunlight shone across my face. A deep sense of well-being came over me and I knew, with every cell in my body, that it would all be okay.

The next day, I discovered I was pregnant again.

I knew the feeling like I knew my own name. After all, I'd been pregnant six times, so it was very familiar. A home pregnancy kit confirmed it. But instead of the elation I'd felt in past pregnancies, I was a wreck. I threw myself face down on the old fake-leather couch in our den and cried, inconsolable. First thing the next morning I called my obstetrician, told her I was pregnant again, and, between sobs, asked whether she could give me something to "get rid of it," so I wouldn't have to go through the emotional and physical pain of another miscarriage and D&C (dilation and curettage). Reluctantly, she agreed to help, and I headed straight to her office. Once there, she literally begged me to let her do just one more ultrasound, just to make sure, before we went any further. I'd had dozens of ultrasounds because of all the past pregnancies and didn't understand the need to have another one. I knew that seeing the tiny fetus would only make me more heartsick and miserable than I already was. But after more pleading on my doctor's part, I finally relented. As the doctor ran the warm metal wand over my abdomen, all I remember was her shouting, "This one's a keeper!" I looked at her like she was speaking a foreign language. It took her saying the same thing over and over for it to finally sink in.

After six miscarriages, I finally had a perfectly normal pregnancy and the next nine months was one of the happiest times of my life. Mark and I couldn't wait for our baby to arrive! I felt healthy and energetic the whole time—so much so that I even participated in a celebrity-mom workout video with Tom Cruise's ex, Mimi Rogers, when I was eight months along.

It had been worth waiting for, worth all the pain and sadness. The child I'd hoped for, for so many years, was finally on the way. After twenty-four hours of labor and ultimately a C-section, I gave birth to my sweet, special baby—lucky pregnancy number seven.

In 1995, not long after I'd given birth, I got an offer from Hugh Hefner himself, asking whether "Elvira" would consider posing for a *Playboy* layout. My initial reaction was "No way." Why would I need to do that at this point in my life? I was a new mom and my career was doing just fine, thank you ever so. But when I was offered the same amount of money they'd paid Farrah Fawcett, a record price at the time, we had to give it some serious consideration. It could get us out of debt and make life a lot easier. While we mulled over the *Playboy* layout, I began working with a trainer, Rich Guzman, at the Hollywood Gold's Gym, training for the first time in my life to get back into my prepregnancy shape, just in case the *Playboy* thing happened.

Often, when I was doing my preworkout warm-up on the treadmill, I couldn't help noticing one particular trainer—tan, tattooed, and muscular—stalking across the gym floor, knit cap pulled so low over his long brown hair that it nearly covered his eyes. Dark and brooding, he gave off such intense energy that when he crossed the enormous gym floor, the waters parted and people stopped in their tracks to stare. A typical sexy bad boy, he was unaware he was so charismatic that he'd garnered his own unofficial fan club. Watching him from the safety of my treadmill made my heart beat faster and the time pass much more quickly. I mean, c'mon, I was married, not dead.

One day, as I was walking into the ladies' room at the gym, *boom!* I ran straight into him on his way out. Wait a minute. What? *He* was a *she?* Wow—that really threw me! Not long afterward, Rich announced he was leaving Gold's, but not to worry, he had someone taking over his clients, who in his opinion was the star trainer of the gym. It turned out to be my former bad-boy crush from the infamous "ladies'-room incident," Teresa Wierson, or T, as she was known at Gold's. A former bodybuilder, track runner, and cyclist, she was an incredibly sweet person, despite her tough exterior. She had the ability to make something even as mundane as working out fun, and we trained together three times a week for the next six years, striking up a close friendship along the way.

I gave up the idea of doing the *Playboy* layout after asking a group of fans what they thought of the idea during a panel at a Comic-Con. Much to my surprise, they overwhelmingly gave it a thumbs-down. It was their consensus that Elvira would lose much of her "mystery" by exposing it all, which made good sense. Thanks to my fans, I passed on the offer, and I've always felt it was the right decision. From that day on, Hef referred to me as "the one who got away."

One day, while sitting at my desk in our home office, I received a call from Florida. "This is the Pinellas County Police Department. Is this Mrs. Pierson?" My blood ran cold. The first thing that came to mind was that something had happened to my sister, Robin.

"Yes," I answered hesitantly. "Is something wrong?"

"Are you Whitney and Paige's aunt?" she asked. When I confirmed that I was, she explained that both of my sister's children had been removed from their home and were about to be transferred into the foster care system unless a relative was willing to take them. Robin had lost custody of them after being declared "unfit" when she had a DUI accident with both kids in the car, and now their father had gone to jail after hitting my thirteen-year-old niece in the head with a metal pipe giving her a concussion and two black eyes. The state of Florida, where they lived, had finally figured out that they should no longer be left alone with either of their parents. "Yes!" I said without a moment's hesitation. "We'll take them!" We arranged for my nephew, Whitney, who was eleven at the time, to stay with my mother in Florida so he could continue attending the school he was in, and we put Paige on a plane to Los Angeles the next day. We immediately filed for legal custody. What we hadn't considered is that Paige came with a lot of baggage because of her extremely dysfunctional upbringing. At the age of thirteen, she was already an alcoholic, a problem that would plague her well into adulthood. Over a period of weeks and several medical and psychological evaluations, it was decided that the best thing for us to do would be to enroll her in a live-in therapeutic school in Oregon, kind of a "kiddie rehab." As heartbreaking as it was to send her away, we knew it was the smartest thing we could do for her at the time. She lived with us off and on until she turned seventeen, then returned to Florida to graduate from high school. Their parents' years of drug abuse and hard drinking had made both her and my nephew's lives a chaotic mess.

On his deathbed, I'd promised my father that I would take care of my sister Robin. As hard as I tried, I wasn't able to do that. Robin was found dead in a motel room in Florida in 2006, after overdosing on a combination of opioids and alcohol. All I could do was try my best to make a positive impact on her two children. I'm blessed that after years of debilitating alcoholism, both Paige and Whitney miraculously got sober and have turned their lives around. It's an enormous gift to see them both, now in their thirties, breaking the chain of substance abuse and living happy, productive lives.

CHAPTER 31

ELVIRA'S HAUNTED HILLS

By this time, Phil Hartman and I had resumed our friendship. After he and his family moved back to LA, they came to our holiday parties, and we went to their house fairly often, but once he was married to Brynn, things between Phil and me were never quite the same. I tried my best to put my feelings about her aside just so I could spend time with Phil, but it was hard. She rubbed me and many of Phil's friends the wrong way.

On a Sunday morning in 1998, Phil called the house to speak to Mark about an upcoming boat trip to Catalina they were planning. Mark was out, so I ended up lying in bed talking to Phil for over an hour, probably the longest phone conversation we'd ever had. We chatted about work, reminisced about the Groundlings, and talked about life in general. His father had recently passed away and he became very introspective, telling me how losing someone so close made him reflect on his own life. "The loss of my dad has really made me appreciate what I have," he said. "Life is short." The last thing he told me before we hung up was much too prescient. "So far, my life has surpassed anything I could've ever dreamed possible. I've achieved all my goals and more," he said, his voice overcome with emotion. "I have the most beautiful wife and the two most wonderful children any man could ever ask for, and if I died tomorrow, I'd die the happiest man in the world." He and Brynn were gone in a tragic murder/suicide just a few days later on May 28, 1998. To this day, whenever I see a crescent moon, which Mark dubbed "a Phil moon" because it reminded us of Phil's ear-to-ear grin, I think of him and all the sad, angry feelings come rushing back. When Phil was taken from us, the world was robbed of a creative genius and one of the kindest, most authentic people I've ever known.

Here it was, almost a decade after *Elvira, Mistress of the Dark* had been released and we hadn't been able to launch another film. Because of the amazing home-video numbers, we knew there was an audience out there, but getting a studio onboard, after *Mistress of the Dark* was perceived as a box-office flop, just wasn't happening. It didn't help that it was a female-driven film, which back then was even harder to get "green-lit" than it is today—surprise, surprise. While at John Paragon's house one day, he and I decided to consult his Magic 8-Ball, which contained a small amount of Phil's ashes. Okay, possibly not the best strategy when considering a financial venture, but John and I never said we were businesspeople. "Should we make another Elvira movie?" we asked the 8-Ball, focusing every ounce of concentration on it. The answer slowly drifted into the shadowy window: "Yes—definitely." I wasn't getting any younger, so I felt like it was now or never. Mark and I decided to finance the movie ourselves. (Bad, bad, not good.) We took out a gigantic loan, and we were off to the races.

John and I hit on the idea of making a gothic-horror comedy romp with the look and feel of the early films of super-low-budget director Roger Corman—films like *The Tomb of Ligeia, House of Usher*, and especially *The Pit and the Pendulum*—which had been some of my favorite films and just happened to star my childhood horror idol, Vincent Price.

Just a quarter of the way into the script, John had to bail on the project when he fell from a horse while riding with a friend and was badly injured. With a deadline looming, I was forced to finish writing the film on my own. Having only written projects in partnership with John for the previous nineteen years, it was a major challenge for me, but by this time we had already committed time and money and there was no going back. With a little help from my friends and former Groundlings, John Moody and Doug Cox, who punched up the finished script with some additional jokes, we had a script for *Elvira's Haunted Hills*.

It just so happened that Mark's stepsister's husband, Robert Dorn-helm, was a film director from Transylvania. I know. Perfect, right? Not only did the Transylvania region have the look we wanted, but American dollars went a lot further in Romania than in Hollywood. While I con-tinued to write, Robert graciously helped us secure Media Pro, a film studio outside of Bucharest, where our very talented Romanian produc-tion designer, Radu Corciova, created beautiful interior sets, perfectly capturing the '60s goth-horror vibe we were after. Robert also found us an outstanding Romanian director of photography, Viorel Sergovici, and his crew, who turned out to be worth their weight in gold.

Our search for a director turned up the creative, ultraprofessional, and *fun* Sam Irvin. I'd met Sam at a party for *SNL* cast member Terry Sweeney in 1991 and discovered he'd directed a little-known film I loved, *Guilty as Charged*, starring Rod Steiger. When he came to my house to interview for the project, I asked, "Are you familiar with the Roger Cor-man films based on Edgar Allan Poe's short stories?" Without a pause, he shouted, "Am I?!" and to prove his point, launched into a word-perfect rendition of Vincent Price's monologue from *The Pit and the Pendu-lum*: "Do you know where you are, Bartolome? You are about to enter hell! *Hell!* The Netherworld. The infernal region. The Abode of the Damned…" etc., etc., etc. I knew I'd found my man!

We began the search for an actor who could bring Vincent's sinister vibe to the production. Our first choice for the role was Count Dracula himself, Christopher Lee. But his agent turned us down flat, saying, "Mr. Lee doesn't do *those* kinds of films anymore. He's put all that behind him." Sheesh, it wasn't like we were asking him to do porn! But whatever. My friend Richard Chamberlain was my next choice, and although he was game, around the same time he was offered a role on a film that actually paid a living wage and naturally couldn't turn it down. Sam and I went through a long list of actors we thought would be good for the role, even going so far as contacting Mick Jagger. When we were almost out of options, our Romanian brother-in-law came to the rescue again. He suggested his friend Richard O'Brien of *The Rocky Horror Show* fame, who we all agreed would be *perfect*! We were elated when Richard agreed to come onboard.

Meanwhile, Robert, Mark, and Sam (who had directed other films in Romania like the sci-fi western *Oblivion*) were busy with the enormous task of pulling a production together in a foreign country. Unfortunately, due to the low budget, the fact that we were spending *our* money, and the nonstop tension that had been building between Mark and myself, the experience turned out to be one of the most difficult and miserable of my life—the exact opposite of my first film.

We rented a drafty, ancient palace in the countryside, far from a major city, where the American and English cast and crew stayed. It had a restaurant, I guess you could call it that anyway, but the menu options in winter were basically cabbage and potatoes, with the occasional piece of "mystery fish" or an egg thrown in. That got old fast.

Richard O'Brien and I butted heads on the first day of the shoot, quibbling over lines in the script. As a writer, he had a lot to say about what I should and shouldn't do when it came to writing, even about scenes he wasn't in. The one argument I remember vividly was over the word "spackle." During one scene, as I'm being escorted up the castle staircase by the late Scott Atkinson, who played Dr. Bradley Bradley, my stiletto heel gets caught in a dangerous, gaping crevice and I struggle not to fall. "Jeez, haven't they ever heard of spackle?" I quip. "Dahling, there was no such thing as spackle back in the 1800s," Richard pointed out when the first take finished. "Yeah, I know. And they didn't have the Village People back then either," I retorted, referring to my favorite line from earlier in the same scene:

Dr. Bradley: "The village people say this castle is haunted."
Elvira: "Aw, who listens to the Village People anymore?"

Fortunately, Richard and I were able to put our differences aside and work as a team. Like Sam and me, Richard was a big Vincent Price fan and understood what we were lovingly spoofing. I couldn't have been happier with his performance and we ended the film as the best of friends.

All I can say is thank God for Sam—he was a lifesaver! Not only was he on set all day directing and setting up the next day's shoot, but he took extra time with me every night for last-minute rewrites caused by our limited time and lack of access to, uh...everything. I soon discovered there were reasons shooting in Romania was so affordable. Simple things, like a black cat—de rigueur in all Edgar Allan Poe movies—were apparently impossible to find in Romania. In Hollywood, you ask for a black cat and, for the right price, voilà! In sweeps an animal trainer with several choices of "trained" black cats. In Romania, after a country-wide search that turned up nothing, we agreed out of desperation that a toy cat would have to do. We ended up with a stuffed brown kangaroo, but in the spirit of innovation, Sam had it sprayed black and showed only its tail peeking out from beneath a curtain. That, along with a little stock footage, did the trick. Another compromise came when I asked for four prancing black stallions to pull Elvira's carriage. All they could come up with were four very old, sway-backed, brown nags, whose top speed was "plodding." Their handlers wanted to use a whip on them to get them to gallop, or at least trot, for one necessary scene, but I refused to allow it. In desperation, we set off a stick of dynamite hundreds of feet behind them, which spooked them just enough to cause them to run a few feet, a one-take shot that accomplished the goal.

In the beginning of the film, there's a shot of Elvira and her maid, Zuzu, played by Groundling Mary Jo Smith, fleeing an ancient inn and running through a picturesque 1800s Transylvanian hamlet, complete with villagers. People often compliment me on the incredible production value in that scene and wonder how we could have afforded such an authentic set, realistic costumes, and convincing "extras" on our miniscule budget. Little did they know, it had nothing to do with production value. It was just the people who lived there and the actual town, which hadn't changed in centuries.

The big climax of the film required Elvira to be bound to a slab while a several-hundred-pound pendulum with a sharp blade on the end swung back and forth above her. A stunt double was hired to take my place because it was so dangerous. Unfortunately, when she arrived on set, we discovered she was flat as a board, which just didn't cut it—so to speak. The last-minute prosthetic breasts the prop master rigged up looked ridiculous, so I was left with no alternative but to jump in and do the scene myself. As I lay on my back on the cold, hard cement slab, the enormous blade swooping back and forth from the tip of my toes toward the top of my wig, all I could do was hold my breath and pray the Romanian crew knew what the hell they were doing. The plan was to have the blade swing close enough to my breasts to sever the rope that bound me to the slab, but *not* close enough to end my career. Or my life. We did take after take, the blade inching closer to my heaving breasts each time. Finally, I arched my back and thrust my chest toward the blade and *whoosh*, the rope was cut—but so was my left breast. The injury had to be carefully covered with makeup for the remainder of the shoot.

The one time not getting what we wanted played to our advantage was when it came to hiring my hunky love interest. I was looking for an old-school "romance novel" hunk, à la Fabio (who we actually offered the part to, but even *he* turned us down). The only actor we could find in Romania who fit the bill perfectly didn't speak a word of English. We came up with the idea of having his voice dubbed, slightly out of sync, to give it that old Steve Reeves/Hercules movie vibe. Brilliant voice-over talent Rob Paulsen dubbed the hunky actor's voice in postproduction and killed it! One of the funniest bits in the movie, in my opinion.

It wasn't all doom and gloom. We had the hilarious actress Mary Scheer, another Groundling alumni and regular cast member of MADtv, playing Richard's wife, Lady Hellsubus; and talented actor Scott Atkinson doing his dead-on George Sanders from *All About Eve* impersonation as Dr. Bradley Bradley. Along with adorable *Troop Beverly Hills* actress Heather Hopper, they lightened the mood considerably.

A scene I loved doing was the musical number "Le Music Hall," composed by my dear friend Jerry Jackson. Yes, the same Jerry Jackson who'd recognized my budding comedic skills in *Vive Les Girls* when I was seventeen. We flew Jerry over to Romania to choreograph the number. While filming it, we all concluded that it needed some kind of "button" on the end to give it some pizazz. The number ended with me in a classic cancan pose: back to camera, bending forward and tossing my skirt up to expose my red panties. Sam came up with the idea of having the word "Applause" slapped across my ass, like the cue lights used to prompt live studio audiences to clap. Gets a big laugh every time.

The film was shot in November and it was already cold. I mean *really* cold. Like Siberia cold. A few scenes required us to shoot outside at night in what felt like the Antarctic. Dressed in my Elvira gown and high-heeled boots with only a velvet cape thrown over my shoulders, there were times when I really thought either my feet or my boobs would have to be amputated due to frostbite.

Early every morning, when it was still dark and long before the other actors or crew were called in, I entered the huge, austere building at Media Pro—a perfect example of postwar Stalinist architecture—to shut myself in a cold, sterile room furnished with nothing but a stool, a table, and a mirror. There, all alone under the blue glow of fluorescent lighting, I plastered on my makeup and played Joni Mitchell's album *Both Sides Now* for the hundredth time—standards ranging from "You're My Thrill" and "Sometimes I'm Happy" to "I Wish I Were in Love Again" and "You've Changed." I thought about Mark and wondered where and how it had all gone so wrong. I was gradually coming to the painful realization that, after twenty-five years together, our marriage was falling apart.

Although as producer, Mark accomplished a Herculean feat by getting an entire production together in a foreign country, the way he went about it eventually alienated everyone, from the actors and crew to the studio heads. Instead of praising people and boosting morale, from where I stood, Mark seemed to become more and more critical, dictatorial, and contrary as the production wore on. In my view, he treated no one with respect and he seemed to get off on belittling me in front of cast and crew members.

I was a mess. I'd been in Romania for a month and I missed my five-year-old terribly, never having been apart for more than a couple of days. I was exhausted because of the long hours and demanding schedule, and to top it off, I came down with walking pneumonia. Bombarded with the stress of filming and having to put up with complaints from cast and crew about Mark, I did my best to stay as far away from him as possible, even sleeping in a separate room.

On our last day, while having a celebratory dinner with Sam and the studio heads, Mark made a negative comment about me in front of everyone, and it quickly erupted into an argument. Embarrassed and humiliated in front of a table full of people, I fled the restaurant. Mark followed, and as we drove back to the hotel down a dark highway, we exploded into a furious fight. He suddenly shouted, "I'm done!," pried the wedding band from his finger, and threw it from the speeding car. And that was that. The love I'd felt and that had kept me in our dysfunctional relationship flew out the window with his ring.

Back in the US, we both realized we had too much riding on *Haunted Hills* not to work together to see it to completion. We finished postproduction on the film and then toured, entering it in film festivals and screening it at conventions and theaters across the country. We donated all the opening-night revenue in each city to various local AIDS charities, ultimately raising close to a half-million dollars for them. Although the film did modest business, we didn't come anywhere near recouping our investment, which only made an already rocky time worse.

CHAPTER 32

THE HARDEST PART

When people ask how long I was with Mark, I tell them we had ten wonderful years of marriage. Unfortunately, we were married for twenty-five.

At twenty-nine years old, I felt I'd finally met the ideal man—loving, intelligent, and attractive—exactly what I'd asked the universe for. But over the years it became more and more apparent that he'd been raised in a similarly dysfunctional family. When we met, something deep in my psyche must have recognized a kindred soul.

Allowing my husband to be my manager was my first mistake. It gave him a sense of power and control over me that I wasn't used to anyone having. I'd always been a free spirit, happy doing things when I wanted, the way I wanted, and it worked for me. I loved Mark more than any man I had ever been with, and although there had been many bad times, they never felt like anything that couldn't be fixed.

However, after the baby came along, our marriage took an even more serious nosedive. I never knew what Mark might say or do. He could be happy and upbeat one moment and dark and angry the next, with seemingly no rhyme or reason for his mood swings. It was like growing up with my mother. Even though I knew it wasn't good, it was comfortable. It felt like home.

Just as with my mother, I spent every moment walking on eggshells for fear of rousing Mark's anger. I'd always considered myself funny and engaging around people. Now I couldn't go to a business meeting or dinner with friends without worrying that I might say or do the wrong thing and incur his wrath. I often felt humiliated in front of people because of his constant corrections or proclamations that I didn't know what I was talking about. I eventually resorted to sitting through gatherings with my mouth shut, trying my best to keep a smile on my face. It became so embarrassing that I didn't want to go anywhere with him for fear of what he might say or do. Slowly, over time, I began to lose my enthusiasm for life.

It seemed like everything I did or said was cause for rebuke. Black was white and white was black. If I said I liked something, he hated it. If I said I didn't like something, he loved it. If I paid him a compliment, he would accuse me of having an ulterior motive. If I tried to explain something, he absolutely refused to understand no matter how hard I tried to describe it or how many details I'd give. Crazy making was the order of the day.

Even my feelings were no longer my own. One time Mark and I took a day off from work and parenting to go to a wine festival in the Santa Ynez valley. It was a pleasant spring day and we spread our blanket out on the ground under a big oak tree, along with a crowd of happy wine-sipping guests, and listened to the sounds of live zydeco music playing in the background. I lay on my back gazing up at the branches gently rustling in the cool spring breeze. Every leaf seemed to shimmer with energy. The green color was vibrant and clear against the brilliant blue of the sky.

"This is so perfect!" I sighed, smiling and closing my eyes.

Without warning, Mark exploded, venting his anger loud enough for everyone to hear. I was taken aback. Oh god, here it comes again. This type of interaction with Mark was happening more and more often.

Sitting up, I tried to calm the situation down by placing my hand on his arm and saying in a low voice, "I was just feeling really good and relaxed, that's all."

He jerked his arm away, looked at me with fake wide-eyed astonishment, and accused me of not caring about other people in the world who were less fortunate.

"What happened? I thought we were having a nice time together and..." Mark jumped to his feet, interrupting me midsentence, and laid into me for always having to have the last word, before storming off to our car. I felt like I'd been punched in the gut. Gathering our things, I hurriedly stuffed them into a bag, while people looked on, clearly embarrassed for me. I recognized the pattern—he just couldn't allow me to feel good if he didn't feel good. I was so confused. I began to doubt myself, replaying the situation over and over in my head and wondering what I'd said or done wrong that had set him off. I struggled to make sense of why we could no longer communicate. Once we were in the car together on our way home, it was clear that he'd released all the tension and now felt good. As far as he was concerned, nothing out of the ordinary had happened. He couldn't understand why I was so quiet and unhappy. This was a pattern that increased more and more as time went on. Whatever I did or said couldn't prevent the next attack.

When a prospective job didn't come through, it was always my fault. Mark would say things like I was too old, or my body was out of shape after giving birth, or nobody cared about Elvira anymore. Because of me, he said, we'd go broke. I'd made the mistake so many women do of allowing my husband to control our finances. I never had "permission" to buy anything without okaying it with him first. One of our biggest fights came when I spent five dollars on a Christmas ornament box without asking him. It seemed that he was perpetually angry with me for "throwing money away," yet whenever he wanted anything, like an expensive surfboard, a new computer, or even a new car, he would go right out and buy it without ever mentioning it to me.

I felt trapped, not only emotionally, but financially. Over time, he convinced me that if I divorced him, I'd live out the rest of my life broke and alone. Time after time he would tell me that if I ever left him, I would end up pushing a shopping cart down Hollywood Boulevard, and after a while, I actually came to believe him.

As the cliché goes, it takes two to tango, and I was no angel. When Mark pushed my buttons, I'd draw on the rage that I had been tamping down inside since I was little and had eventually led to my early departure from my family. My mother had taught me that an argument meant screaming, yelling, hitting, and often saying the cruelest, most hurtful things you could come up with. That's how I learned to fight back when I was attacked. To me, it was normal.

What little self-esteem I had was eventually ground down to a nub. If you've never experienced verbal abuse, it's almost impossible to explain the confusion; the feelings of being devalued, diminished, and disrespected; and the gut-wrenching hurt that goes along with it. When I felt I couldn't make it through another day with Mark, I began seeing a new therapist, Lita Singer, at the urging of my friend, songwriter Holly Knight. Lita was a wise, self-proclaimed "crone" in her seventies. When she handed me the book *The Verbally Abusive Relationship* by Patricia Evans, I brought it home and shoved it into a drawer, afraid to confront the issues that might lead to a divorce—something Mark had convinced me was not an option. But not long afterward, I took a trip to Mougins, in the south of France, to visit Mark's parents so they could get to know their newest grandchild, and I took the book along. It was one of the only times Mark "allowed" us to go somewhere on our own and, relieved to be away from him, I finally picked it up and began reading. I wasn't more than a chapter in before I recognized myself and our relationship on every page. I read it in one sitting, crying so hard I could barely see the words. Up until then, I believed abuse by a husband or partner meant being physically beaten, and I knew from my childhood how destructive that could be. I'd never realized how insidious and damaging verbal and emotional abuse were; you're being beaten, it just doesn't leave marks. Finally, I had a name for the pain and hurt I felt. My first thought was, "This can't be happening to me. I'm a smart, successful woman." But I learned that, often, those are exactly the women abusive men are drawn to. Abusers aren't interested in wimps. They like a challenge. If an abusive man perceives his spouse or girlfriend as having more power than he does, taking her down a notch or two gives his self-esteem, security, and identity a boost. It was hard for me to believe that Cassandra Peterson, the creator of a character who women looked up to as strong-willed and independent, had allowed her husband to turn her into a weak, pathetic victim.

From the moment I finished reading that book, and with Lita's help, I slowly began to regain control over my life. I read more books about verbal abuse and joined a women's group. But the more I regained my sense of self and stopped allowing him to control and manipulate me, the worse the fighting became. We argued more often and more intensely, and the atmosphere in our home began to feel like a pressure cooker ready to blow. My greatest worry was the effect it was having on our child.

At first, I desperately wanted to believe that Mark could change—that with professional help he would go back to being his old self, the Mark I'd fallen in love with. But he was adamant that he didn't need therapy or counseling—it was me who had the problem, not him. When I finally got up the nerve to threaten divorce if he didn't get help, he reluctantly acceded and we went to couples therapy. Mark spent the first and only session ranting and raving about what a horrible person I was, until the therapist stopped him halfway through his tirade to tell him that therapy was not a forum to vent his anger and hatred toward his partner. When he ignored her and continued slinging insults, she stopped the session and asked him to leave.

Although I did my best to figure out what I was doing that made him so angry and vowed to be "better," our relationship did not magically improve. I felt like I was suffocating. I would sometimes fantasize about dyeing my hair, changing my name, or grabbing our child and fleeing the country. I often felt so desolate and hopeless I considered death as a means of escape, mine or his—didn't matter. All that kept me from acting on that impulse was being a mother. For so long, I'd believed I was doing the right thing by sticking out the marriage to keep our family together, but I finally realized that staying in such a dysfunctional relationship was worse than the alternative.

My fiftieth birthday was rapidly approaching. I woke up one morning feeling like my soul had been sucked out of my body like a yolk through a pinhole in an eggshell. I'd lost my hope, my self-confidence, my voice. I asked myself, "Do you want to feel this way when you're sixty? When you're seventy?" I only had so much time ahead of me and hating my life and feeling like an angry, bitter victim wasn't how I wanted to spend it. I knew it was taking a terrible toll on my mental and physical state, and worse yet, on our child. As much as I dreaded pulling our family apart and ending our marriage, the only sane option was to leave. I didn't have a choice. If nothing else, I would set an example for our seven-year-old—women shouldn't be demeaned, disrespected, or treated like subhumans, especially by the man who's supposed to love and cherish them. Getting divorced was the hardest thing I've ever had to do. In retrospect, my only regret is that I didn't do it sooner.

I was now a fifty-year-old single mom playing a sexy vamp to make a living. Mark and Eric had long ago split up as business partners, so I was on my own, with no manager and no idea what I was going to do to pay the bills. In California, fifty percent of everything is divided between spouses, but while Mark got all the cash, I retained only the "assets," like my life-insurance policy and pension plan, things I couldn't touch without paying huge penalties. I was beginning to think Mark's comment about pushing a shopping cart might actually come true.

Soon after the divorce proceedings began and Mark moved out, I got hit with another disaster. Our house was flooded during a three-day rainstorm, when a wall of water, rocks, and mud came crashing down a hillside. It cost me a small fortune in repairs, a fortune I didn't have. To top off an already difficult time, I lost half of what little money I had left when the stock market took a dive in 2008. I actually considered giving up, moving back to Colorado, and getting a normal job to support myself and my child.

CHAPTER 33

JUST LIKE STARTING OVER

I was fully prepared to never get involved in another romantic relationship again. I figured that emotionally and sexually I was "closed for business," and I was okay with that. The relief of getting out of that toxic relationship, however, was tempered by the fear of what lay ahead. I wasn't emotionally strong enough to even *think* about dating or getting involved with anyone after what I'd gone through for so many years. I had no idea what the future held—for Elvira or for me personally.

Late one rainy night, after Mark had finally moved out, the doorbell rang. There on the doorstep stood my trainer, T, holding a trash bag full of her belongings, looking sad and bedraggled. She'd split from her longtime partner, spent some time in rehab, and now had no place to go.

"T, this couldn't be worse timing." I explained. "You know I'm going through this divorce and things are a freaking nightmare." But she looked so pitiful that I finally gave in and offered her a place to stay in our "maid's quarters," a little bedroom and bathroom off the kitchen, until she could find a place of her own.

I soon realized that instead of being a burden, having her around was a huge relief. While I worked in the office, she worked around the house, fixing things that needed fixing, taking care of the garden, and keeping the house in order. T was like a big kid, and she turned out to be the best babysitter anyone could ask for. Evenings were spent with all of us laughing, cooking, singing, and dancing around the kitchen while she helped me prep dinner. The black cloud that had hung over our home for so long felt like it had finally lifted. I began to feel happier than I had in years and I could tell my child was feeling the same way.

Soon, my eight-year-old began splitting time between my place and Mark's apartment, which gave T and me time to breathe, have friends over, or occasionally have a night out. One such evening, after coming home from a movie, I told her goodnight and suddenly felt compelled to kiss her—on the mouth. As shocked as she was, I think I was even more surprised. What the hell was I doing? I'd never been interested in women as anything other than friends. I felt so confused. This just wasn't me! I was stunned that I'd been friends with her for so many years and never noticed our chemistry. How could I have missed it? Was it the male energy she exuded that attracted me? Her intense green eyes? Or just my own loneliness? I soon discovered that we connected sexually in a way I'd never experienced, and after a while it became clear I was falling in love with this beautiful, androgynous creature who'd appeared on my doorstep, like an angel, just when I needed someone most.

I saw you walking, head down,
Black knit cap pulled low over black knit brows and angry eyes.
Tattoos caress and curl over velvet skin.
The mermaid with her Mona Lisa smile must feel like she's swim-
    ming upstream,
Just to keep from drowning in a sea of tears.

Soft skin covers hard muscle
Like a threadbare blanket laid on top of rock.

Knives cut and cigarettes burn to form scars
Deep and jagged as the Oregon coastline,
Painful as the tracks and hurdles you can't get over.

You collect words and phrases like tiny bits of broken glass
And paste them together to form sentences that sound like you.

You walk through the door and one small window of time opens.
We let go of the rope and fall through the unknown
Together.

The heat from your skin burns my fingertips.
Energy radiates from your body like the sun,
too bright and hot for my naked eyes.

Looking in the mirror I see your face.
I recognize you.
You're that part of me I love.
Like a wild bird
You beat your wings against the window.
Trapped in my house.
Trapped in my heart.

T and I have been together over nineteen years now. Even though she quit training and became my "roadie" and assistant, we've always managed to keep our personal relationship private, telling only our closest friends and relatives. It hasn't been easy for either of us to live that way, and I'm happy and relieved to finally allow our secret to see the light of day.

I've always equated my career with my self-worth, so I was deathly afraid of doing anything that might jeopardize it. If I didn't have my career, what did I have?

As Cassandra, it wouldn't have mattered to me that people knew about our relationship, but I felt the need to protect Elvira in order to keep my career alive. Elvira has always had a thing for men, and men have a thing for her, so I worried that if I announced I was no longer living the "straight life," my fans would feel lied to, call me a hypocrite, and abandon me. Would my fans hate me for not being what they expected me to be? I'm very aware that there will be some who will be disappointed and maybe even angry, but I have to live with myself, and at this point in my life, I've got to be truthful about who I am.

Despite all the setbacks and struggles, I've had a remarkably successful career and I'm so thankful with how it's turned out. If something as personal as my private relationship causes some fans to no longer enjoy my work, or if a company chooses not to work with me because of it— well, all I can say is, "Fuck 'em." That's *their* problem.

I've never had a long-term relationship in which my partner has treated me with so much love and respect, is always there for me, loves me for who I am, and doesn't try to change me. For the first time in my life, I'm with someone who makes me feel safe, blessed, and truly loved.

CHAPTER 34

CH-CH-CHANGES

To my surprise, my accountant confronted me with the devastating news that to come up with the money necessary to pay Mark off, I would have to sell my house—the house my family had lived in for eight years, the house my child had grown up in. It was jarring and difficult for us to leave our longtime home and the friends and neighbors we'd grown so close to. Because I was going to have to seriously scale back, I held an estate sale, selling most of my furniture and tons of Elvira memorabilia because I would no longer be able to afford a big house in which to keep it all. Everyone who saw the estate sale ad figured I'd died, which in a way I had. Here I was, getting rid of my possessions, with no place to live, no jobs coming up, and no clear direction.

I tried hard to ignore my feelings for T. I was still having a difficult time coming to terms with having a relationship with a woman. I was so confused. I felt like a teenager decoding all the old societal BS that I'd stored in my brain about gender and sexual orientation. Despite our mutual feelings for each other, I pushed her away, and she went back to her hometown of Portland, Oregon.

With no funds to buy a house, I moved into a small rental in East Hollywood. It was a big adjustment, and I was struggling. I was on my own for the first time in almost thirty years, a newly single mom, with no prospects of work before me. I did my best to act as my own man-ager/agent, but although I've always dabbled in the business end of my career, it certainly wasn't my forte.

It took me time to process my relationship with T. I'd been straight my whole life, but now I'd suddenly turned gay overnight? I was having a hard time wrapping my head around it. I was someone who had spent most of her life hanging around with gay men, and now here I was, ashamed of my feelings for a woman. I felt like such a hypocrite. I eventually gave up my ridiculous preconceived notions about what sexual category I fit into and realized that when you love someone, and they love you back, that's all that matters. Eventually I called T and, after telling her what a difficult time I was having trying to cope with all the duties of work, home, and raising a child on my own, she offered to come back to LA and help out. Once again, she came to my rescue and got us through a very dark period, and I never wanted her to leave again.

I scraped together enough money to put a small down payment on a house in the Silverlake area of LA, and T and I moved in together. Around the same time, Eric Gardner, my former manager, came back into my life. He and I had always talked about finding replacements to play Elvira and possibly installing them in malls around the country at Halloween, like Santa Claus at Christmas. Things would be so much more lucrative if there were more of me, right? We came up with the idea of turning our search into a television show, and with Eric's help, we produced a reality show: *The Search for the Next Elvira*. It had a limited run on the short-lived Fox Reality Channel, only four episodes in October 2007, but it made me some much-needed moolah and got Elvira back into the public eye. In the end, the idea of multiple Elviras didn't pan out because fans still demanded the real thing, but there was a big upside. I met Ted Biaselli, one of the writers on the show. Ted had a wicked sense of humor and was so in tune with Elvira's voice that it was spooky! Since John Paragon had moved on, I'd been desperate for another writer, so discovering Ted was a godsend.

In the meantime, my ex-husband bought a large property just north of LA in the mountains outside the small, picturesque town of Ojai. To share custody without making a three-hour round trip every few days, T and I decided that moving up to Ojai would be a good idea. Getting out of the middle of the big city really sounded good to us, too, and whenever a job came up, I figured, I could always drive down to LA. So one year after my divorce, here I was, selling my house again, renting in Ojai, and moving for the third time. Even though we were only an hour and a half outside of Hollywood, it quickly became apparent that, as far as showbiz was concerned, I might as well have moved back to Kansas. Not being in Hollywood networking and meeting people kept me out of the loop, and my business suffered even more. Over the next three years, I spent endless hours commuting to LA for business, but as far as I was concerned there was no other choice. Spending as much time as possible with my teenager, who would soon be graduating from high school and leaving home, was my priority.

A close friend, Joe Kaminkow, who'd helped keep me afloat since my divorce by licensing my character for various gaming-industry projects, did me another enormous favor by introducing me to the man who would ultimately help put Elvira back on the map. Scott Marcus, an entertainment-industry veteran and former marketing exec at a major studio, came onboard, and little by little my merchandise, licensing, and product-development numbers made a comeback. As the first client of his newly formed management company, he brought his invaluable experience onboard and, over time, helped bring Elvira back from the dead. He became not only my manager, but my best friend, and I'm so grateful to have found him.

Frustrated because I couldn't seem to get a Hollywood production company interested in another Elvira project, I decided to jump-start my career by producing twenty-six new episodes of *Movie Macabre* in May 2011. Apparently, I'd learned nothing from my little venture funding *Haunted Hills*, because I gambled my savings, personally bankrolling the project. Ted came up with some of the most hilarious material I'd ever done, and the show exceeded my wildest expectations, but wouldn't you know it, just as it was released in TV syndication, the bottom dropped out of the market. Déjà vu all over again. We were left with terrible time slots in most areas of the country, and you were lucky if you could even *find* my show on TV because it generally aired at around 4:00 a.m., wedged between infomercials for The Clapper and the Snuggie. Fortunately we were able to release the new *Movie Macabre* on DVD, and once again, it became a project that started out slow but gained popularity over time.

I guess I should have seen the signs that moving to Ojai wasn't a good idea. The night we arrived, while lifting Mina, my ninety-pound rott-weiler, out of the car, she threw her head back and broke my nose. I sustained other injuries over the following three years. I fell while hiking, chipping my front tooth, cracking my ribs, and fracturing a cheekbone. Walking out of a restaurant one night, stressed and overwhelmed about my show, I missed a step and sprained my ankle so badly that it also broke two bones in my foot. The cherry on top of our time in Ojai was getting bitten on my shoulder by a black widow—an insanely painful experience, by the way, that I heartily do *not* recommend. Although I'd been to the hospital only once in my forty-something years in LA, other than to give birth, by the time we left Ojai, the emergency-room attendants and I were on a first-name basis.

In 2012, T and I became empty nesters and moved back to Hollywood where we bought a little house on a tree-lined street, just a few blocks from my original starting point at KHJ-TV.

CHAPTER 35

BOTH SIDES NOW

While we lived in Ojai, I celebrated my sixtieth birthday by throwing a party at a Hollywood restaurant, Osteria Mamma, attended by sixty of our closest friends and family, including fellow showbiz buddies Allee Willis, Pamela Des Barres, Richard Chamberlain, RuPaul, Lynne Marie Stewart, and Paul Reubens. Facing my sixth decade, I took time to examine my life and began considering retirement. When I was in my thirties, I swore I'd retire Elvira when I turned forty. When I was in my forties, I was determined to stop at fifty. Now here I was, closing in on my fourth decade as Elvira. Was I going to keep getting into Elvira drag until I was ninety? I began to give some serious thought to where my career and my life were headed.

I'd languished too long in Ojai, so once we moved back to LA, and with Scott's help, I threw myself into reviving the Elvira brand. I returned to doing my show at Knott's Scary Farm in 2013, after an eleven-year hiatus, but made the bittersweet choice to hang up my dancing shoes and perform my last show four years later.

I'd made so many friends at Knott's over the previous thirty-eight years, both behind the scenes and in the audience, that it was a surprisingly emotional decision for me. I'd actually seen many of my fans grow from children to adults with families of their own. One little boy, Christian Greenia, who'd come backstage with his mom years before to meet me, eventually became my website designer and has taken over my social media. When not doing a truly fabulous job for me, he sometimes performs at clubs doing Elvira drag. We've become so close over the years, I refer to him as my illegitimate son.

The last show at Knotts was a live, pared-down version of my movie *Mistress of the Dark* where, among other things, I entered the stage in the original Macabre Mobile, reprised my *Flashdance* number, got burned at the stake while singing Madonna's "Burning Up," and even twirled tassels in the finale! (Which I'm happy to say is like riding a bike; once learned, never forgotten.) I had a blast doing the show and the crowds loved it. On my last night at the park, I received a standing ovation from a packed house of longtime, hardcore fans that brought me to tears and filled me with gratitude for all the years I'd spent performing there.

On November 30, 2018, I went to visit my mother at her nursing home. She was unusually perky and upbeat that day. She'd gone through her costume jewelry with one of the healthcare workers, trying it all on, deciding on a pretty combination of earrings, bracelets, and necklaces to wear. She'd also made calls to several of her friends and relatives that morning. That wasn't normal. I'd taken her to get her hair and nails done the day before, which was probably the thing she liked most in the world. When I arrived, she was up, dressed, and sitting on the edge of her bed, looking better than I'd seen her look in months. As we chatted, she pulled her glitzy little makeup bag out of her purse and rummaged through it. "Soni, I'm out of lipstick," she said. I watched as she twisted the cap from an old tube of "Cherries in the Snow." Using her pinkie, she dug out what was left and spread it over her lips, pressing them together and releasing with a loud smacking sound. "You need to get me some more." She held the empty tube out to me as proof. "How about you go with me on Monday and choose some for yourself?" I said. "Maybe we could even go to lunch at the Farmers Market afterward." The Original Farmers Market was her favorite Hollywood haunt and she hadn't been up to going in years. Her face lit up. "Oh, really?" she said, raising her sparse eyebrows above the rims of her glasses and giving me a skeptical look. "You're joking, right?" "No, Mother. You're doing so well, there's no reason you can't go."

After our visit, she grabbed her walker and shuffled me to the door. We gave each other a quick, tepid hug. "See you Monday," I called on my way out. She smiled and waved goodbye.

Thirty minutes later, as I walked in the front door of my house, I got a panicked call from one of her caregivers. "You need to come back right away! Something's wrong with your mother." T and I jumped in the car and rushed back. When we arrived, we saw an ambulance parked in front of the home. Two paramedics were standing on the curb—not a good sign. I jumped out of the car and ran up to them. "Are you Mrs. Peterson's daughter?" one of them asked. I nodded. "I'm sorry," he said, placing his hand on my shoulder. "Your mother passed away."

With T and my niece Paige there for support, we entered her darkened room. Mother was lying on her back in bed with her hands folded over her chest and as peaceful an expression on her face as I'd ever seen. I stood over her lifeless body for a long time. All kinds of thoughts and feelings bubbled to the surface. I thought about how, when I was little, she'd always made sure I had the best costumes at Halloween. I took off her earrings, bracelets, and necklaces and placed them on her nightstand. I remembered the special birthday parties she'd thrown for me, with fancy paper decorations from her store. I removed the wedding ring she'd worn for sixty-seven years and placed it on my finger. When I was in third grade, I wrote a Thanksgiving poem called "Turkey, Little Turkey," which was published in the local paper. I overheard Mother bragging to my grandparents about how smart I was. In that moment, I had the mom I'd always wished for. I bent over and kissed her cool, waxy cheek.

While we waited for the coroner to pick up her body, I didn't cry. I felt numb, and did for weeks afterward. We had a difficult relationship, but I wasn't ready to let her go yet. Her death meant that my chance to say or do something that would finally make her love me was gone.

Taking care of my mother as she aged, and supporting her for so many years, was often difficult, frustrating, and challenging, but strangely, it helped heal some of the pain from my childhood. It helped me come to believe I was valuable. It helped me realize that the way my mother treated me was more about her failings than about mine.

Although my sister Melody miraculously survived until 2019, she couldn't seem to shake her addictions, even after being confined to a wheelchair with multiple sclerosis. One month after my mother passed, Melody drank herself to death. Between her and my sister Robin, they left my five nieces and nephews to struggle with the lifelong consequences of their mothers' addictions.

EPILOGUE

It's now 2021. I just closed in on my seventieth birthday, and life continues to surprise me—in ways both good and bad. In these unprecedented times, our country has taken twists and turns that I could never have seen coming. Social-justice issues are finally beginning to show signs of taking center stage, and a deadly pandemic has ravaged the country and the world, claiming millions of lives, including two friends from my past: Hal Willner, the music producer from *Saturday Night Live*; and Danny McElroy, the lighting director for my original TV show, *Movie Macabre*.

As far as my personal life goes, it's taken almost seventy years but I'm finally learning to believe in myself and relax a little. There have been so many "almosts," so many uphill battles, and so many difficult, trying, and heartbreaking moments. But many, many wonderful, magical things have also come my way. I have so much to be amazed by and so much to be grateful for.

I guess I shouldn't be surprised that so many people connected with my first movie, *Elvira, Mistress of the Dark*. Look at the impact movies had on me growing up. They're responsible for planting the seeds of ideas in my head, which sprouted and grew into real-life manifestations. While recently sorting through a box of old memorabilia, I came across a photo collection book of Ann-Margret, which she'd signed for me years ago when we first met. On the page opposite her signature, she had a quote: "To everyone who went to a movie theater and saw an image on the screen that changed their life."

Movies and music are forms of "magic." They're storytelling at its best, and stories can be *powerful*—they've been around since the dawn of humanity, influencing lives and changing outcomes. In my opinion, music and film can channel emotions and feelings better than any other forms of art. My life has been shaped by the music I heard and the movies I saw when I was young. However trivial and irrelevant my choice of films—*House on Haunted Hill, Bye Bye Birdie, Sweet Charity,* and *Viva Las Vegas*—without their influence, I'd be a very different person today.

Elvira has taught me some surprising lessons. She has helped me get through the hard times and get back up when I got knocked down. I've come to realize her personality comes from my teenage self—the self that was young enough to believe I could do anything, be anyone, have everything. When I became a teenager, I mysteriously acquired a certain confidence. I became tough and strong, and I didn't take bullshit from anyone. As I grew older, life burnished the edges, but along came Elvira, who picked up those traits and ran with them. She became everything Cassandra wanted to be.

Despite the crazy, chaotic family dynamic I came from, I can't forget that, from them, I also inherited a strong sense of values, accountability, perseverance, and a never-say-die midwestern work ethic that's gotten me through life. I've worked hard, become successful, and realized—while writing this book—just how much the influence of my parents, grandparents, aunts, uncles, and cousins has made me who I am today. There were ups and downs, but ultimately, they gave me the tools I needed to survive, thrive, and be a better person. I love them all and am so grateful to them.

Not long ago, I had lunch with my longtime friend Pamela Des Barres.

"Look how you still pull your hair around your face to hide your scars," she said, after one of my habitual moves. "You do that when you're Elvira, too. Are you aware of that?"

I paused for a moment, considering, then nodded, yes.

"Oh honey," she said, placing a gentle hand on my shoulder. "No one can see them anymore but you."

Through most of my life, I could never shake the image of the little girl who was ashamed and unlovable because of her scars, both physical and emotional. I was so consumed by self-doubt and insecurity that I refused to believe anyone who told me anything positive about myself. I figured they were either lying to be polite or had ulterior motives. One time, when we were headed out to a party together, my dear friend Richard Chamberlain told me I looked beautiful. I sloughed it off and made excuses, as usual. "Cassandra, m'dear," he said, taking my hands in his, "When someone gives you a compliment, just say thank you and leave it at that." I took his advice, and little by little the negative voices screaming in my head have become a whisper.

I keep discovering how truly important my friends are. They remind me of where I've been and where I came from, and what real love and friendship means. These things are more important to me now, and life doesn't seem like such a day-to-day struggle anymore. I no longer have to look for fame and attention. I now take more time to do the things that make me feel good: drinking a cup of coffee in the morning while I read the newspaper; taking our little rescue dog, Vincent, for walks every day with my neighbors; practicing yoga whenever I can. What is it that makes me happy? A good conversation with my interesting, creative adult child; a glass of wine in the evening with my beautiful, sexy partner; cooking a delicious meal; or traveling the world together.

It feels good to recount my experiences here: the vulnerability, the pain, the happy times, and the adventures. So many of the people in these pages are gone now—friends, lovers, and family members—but each and every one has left their indelible mark on me.

I hope this book has been not only entertaining, but possibly enlightening. Maybe it will give you an idea or a thought that will reverberate, inspire, or influence you in some small, positive way.

Decisions I've made haven't always turned out for the best, but against all odds, they got me to today. With all that's happened during my career—the good, the bad, and the funny—the Elvira brand keeps growing, and you know what? I think she just might outlive me.

Every day of my young life, when I looked in the mirror, all I could see were my scars, and I felt like the ugly little girl my mother said I was. I've truly come to believe that had it not been for my childhood accident, I would never have grown into the woman who embraces the strange, the weird, the bizarre. I would never have become the Queen of Halloween.

We all have our own scars. Let them be a blessing and not a curse.

In loving memory of
John Paragon and Robert Redding.

ACKNOWLEDGMENTS

First off, my very sincere thanx to the talented team at Hachette Book Group, especially my editor, Brant Rumble, for his time, patience, sense of humor, and for making my job a whole lot easier; to copyeditor, Felicity Tucker, and production editor, Cisca Schreefel, who both taught me a thing or two (or 500) about grammar and punctuation; and to the talented team at Hachette: Michelle Aielli, Michael Barrs, Julie Ford, Amanda Kain, Mary Ann Naples, Monica Oluwek, Lauren Rosenthal, and Mollie Weisenfeld. I'm so grateful for all of their help and very proud to be associated with them.

Thanx to my friend, accomplice, and manager, Scott Marcus, for shepherding me through every step of the way and believing in me and this project from the very beginning.

Thanx to my literary agent, Peter McGuigan at Ultra Literary, for giving me a chance and for finding my book the perfect home.

Special thanx to: Pamela Des Barres for introducing me to her agent, Peter, and for her very perceptive comments and invaluable help and guidance throughout the pitching and writing process; Dawna Kaufmann for being so intuitive, persistent, and persuasive; my niece Paige for her love, helpful input, and for being a strong, courageous survivor; Eric Gardner, Sam Irvin, and Dan Mathews for "jogging my mammaries"; Jack Grapes Method Writing class and Josh Grapes and fellow students of "Frankenstein's Lab" for helping me shape my story and put it down on paper; Stephen King for his brilliant book *On Writing*, which has been my Bible and made me believe I could really do this; Shelley Miller for her encouragement and suggestions; Christian Greenia, Keira Kang, Michelle and Ash Ghoulmore, and the rest of "team Elvira," who kept my business up and running so I could finally have time to write this damn thing!; Renée Watt for seeing into my future; and Mark and the staff at Bricks and Scones (my writing haven). And especially to T, for reading my book back to me in bed every night, page by page, and giving me her invaluable ideas, suggestions, and feedback that helped make it a reality. I'm so grateful for her love, support, and patience throughout the long and sometimes grueling process.

Additional thanx to my oldest and dearest friends, Richard Chamberlain, Jerry Jackson, Ellen Mersereau, Allen Perlstein, Martin Rabbett, Paul Reubens, and Vance Van Petten for their love, support, and encouragement. They have created a wholly functional loving family for me and have been my cheerleaders throughout this long journey.

To Lance Alspaugh, Jackie Beat, Mike Becker, Ted Biaselli, Marilyn Brecht, RuPaul Charles, Marc Cohen, Chad Colebank and Rick Unvarsky, Doug Cox, Harriet Cresswell, Jennifer and Terry Doty, Ryan Eisenmann, Michelle and Ash Ghoulmore, Joshua Grannell, Christian Greenia, Gris Grimley, The Groundlings, Tom Hardcastle, Joe Kaminkow, Keira Kang, Holly Knight, Jim Kunz and Melissa Kelly, Brian Mariotti, Victor Martinez, Susan McNabb, John Moody, John Paragon, Rob Perez, Greg Peterson, Mary Pickhardt, Andy and Vicki Pierson, Robert Redding, Jamie Samson, Fred Schneider, Jeff Shadic, Brandon Tartikoff, Larry Thomas, Jeannie Touchard, Jeff Tucker, Kat Von D, Dita Von Teese, Mark Webb, Danny Weik, Jack White, Les and Myrna Wierson, and Rob Zombie. I thank you all for showing me kindness, doing me favors, providing inspiration, and making a difference in my career and in my life. There are so many others that I should thank here, but that might verge on making the Acknowledgments as long as the book itself, so, as the King of Hearts suggested, at the beginning of this book, when you come to the end, stop.

Oh, wait wait wait! One more—

My deepest heartfelt thanx to my many loyal fans. Where would I be without you?